Guide to

American Literature

and its

Backgrounds

since 1890

Guide to American Literature and its Backgrounds since 1890

HOWARD MUMFORD JONES
and RICHARD M. LUDWIG

Third Edition, Revised and Enlarged

HARVARD UNIVERSITY PRESS

Cambridge, Massachusetts

1964

Third Edition, Revised and Enlarged

Distributed in Great Britain by Oxford University Press, London

Library of Congress Catalog Card Number 64–19582

Printed in the United States of America

B Z J

hoc opus, hic labor

PREFATORY NOTE TO THE THIRD EDITION

In revising this manual, we have added new titles, removed obsolescent works, and, wherever possible, have noted new editions of important background books and guides. The reading lists have been increased from the second edition by two new lists on the drama, another on biography, and by new titles from the sixties wherever applicable. In addition, the information on periodicals has been brought up to date, and relevant material from the last five years has been added to the table of events and other historical sections. We remind all readers of this guide that our listings are suggestive, not definitive.

Howard Mumford Jones
Richard M. Ludwig

1964

Contents

The Backgrounds of American Literature Since 1890

CONTENTS

CONTENTS

Reading Lists of American Literature Since 1890

CONTENTS

CONTENTS

GENERAL INTRODUCTION

This guide to American literature since 1890 and its background is an attempt to impose intellectual order upon confusion. There are histories of fiction which cover this period; there are a few histories of poetry; there are excellent studies of this or that element in the history of ideas; but there is no single work that presents to the reader in understandable order the combination of intellectual and sociological (political) event and literary productivity, which is at once the peril and the exhilaration of this enterprise.

Neither the outline nor the selected bibliography here given can be thought of as "definitive" or "complete." Whatever may be meant by either term, both completeness and definitiveness are impossible. The number of book titles appearing annually in twentieth-century America now hovers around sixteen thousand. Even if one assumes that a mere tenth of this yearly product is worth examining, no human being could read so vast an incremental library, much less make up his own mind or the minds of his readers as to who or what is entitled to immortality.

The present guide faces an unanswerable question. What is American literature? Is it composed of the books that critics acclaim; and if so, what critics? Or is it composed of the books that some important part of the population reads? Were we to accept the judgment of one group of critics, only those books which display qualities of style or structure satisfactory to a small and special group of intellectuals, "sophisticates," academic writers, *avant-gardists,* or the like, exhibit the proper qualities of art. The special virtue of the judgment of this group is that it calls attention to values in books, especially poetry, literary criticism, and some kinds of fiction, that the hurly-burly of trade publishing ignores. This judgment often establishes qualities which a larger reading public by and by grows ready to accept. On the other hand, that larger segment of the public—one devoted to "good books," the patrons of circulating libraries, book clubs, reading circles, and, more rarely, book stores—mostly has so little interest in the judgments of the critics just discussed as in fact to ignore them.

This larger group of readers, less moved by esoteric poetry, is by no means opposed to poetry, though it wants poetry that is less "difficult." It is by no means hostile to literary criticism, but it wants literary criticism that makes reading easier rather than more complex. Though it is on the whole suspicious of sentimental and commercialized fiction, it demands of its favorite novelists qualities of narrative art and conceptions of character that seem to critics dangerously close to philistinism. Yet if a publisher can attract the interest of this important group, he will succeed, at least on the "good books" level. Does the taste of this group of readers constitute American literature in fact?

Alas, as Brander Matthews long ago pointed out, there are innumerable publics, and these are but two of them. A third important reading group cannot be ignored—the public for nonfictional prose, for the book of ideas, for history and biography. The *avant-garde* critic does not characteristically interest himself in biography unless it be biographical material within the limited range of his group. Yet books like the biographical studies of Gamaliel Bradford, or Freeman's *Lee,* or Dumas Malone's monumental *Jefferson,* not yet complete, are clearly as important landmarks in American writing as are, let us say, the prose of Henry Miller or the fiction of Truman Capote. How great has been the influence of works like Joseph Wood Krutch's *The Modern Temper* or Walter Lippmann's *Preface to Morals* we cannot tell, but obviously it has been vast. How immense the influence of the Beards' famous history, *The Rise of American Civilization!* Yet we do not think it is harsh to say that most discussions of American literary development during the twentieth century minimize or ignore the place of biography, lay philosophy, the prose of public discourse, and historical writing— always excepting a few favored names like those of William James and Henry Adams. It seems clear, however, if we are to understand American thought in the period, that we cannot thus cavalierly neglect the rich development of our literature of knowledge.

2

Indeed, in any generous or total scheme even subliterary work should have its place. Long ago Professor Arthur M. Schlesinger, Sr., pointed out the desirability of considering dime novels, adventure stories, sentimental fiction, and other types of books below the literary salt. Fascinating recent studies of best sellers in America merely underline his theorem. Indeed, the impartial observer has some right to be either puzzled or amused to find the literary historian cherishing all he can discover about such sentimental trash as *The Power of Sympathy* or *Charlotte Temple,* yet declining to soil his hands with Harold Bell Wright or Gene Stratton Porter.

Considerations like these at first sight complicate what is already complex. There are other considerations as well. What is literary history? Whatever its theory may be, practice has oscillated between two poles. At the one extreme the literary historian, rightly fearful lest literature lose its aesthetic bloom if it be too deeply enmeshed in social history, tries to establish a canon of his own, wherein books produce books, authors succeed authors, and style follows upon style as if by some inner law. The virtue of this approach is that it insists upon the aesthetic value of writing as art; it insists upon the value of thought well expressed for its own sake; it insists that artistic work of the highest import has often been produced with small or no reference to the spirit of the times. And yet weakness is also evident—weakness following upon the failure to understand Emerson's wise injunction when he tells us that every scripture has the right to be read in the light of the times that brought it forth. Many works incontestably lose their meaning unless they are read in the context of the problem which produced them.

The other extreme reduces literature to documents in social history or the history of ideas; it seems to produce writers as it produces changes in the tariff; it satisfies itself with a catalogue of titles and names of men; and it is mostly oblivious of the historical importance of aesthetic appeal. In this point of view, for instance, *Uncle Tom's Cabin* is perpetually an antislavery novel, sentimental in tone, that somehow sold thousands of copies. This is scarcely an adequate concept of *Uncle Tom's Cabin.* The book is an antislavery novel, and it sold its thousands, and these are primary facts. But raw fact is not literary history;

3

and the competent literary historian wants to probe further—to uncover (as he does) a lost fictional library on slavery, and to trace in Mrs. Stowe's masterpiece the incongruous elements that make it up. In American literary history, a branch of learning in which political events have been particularly important in shaping literature, one must perpetually guard oneself against too much sociologizing, while accepting the basic truth that in no modern literature is the connection between literature and national event closer than it is in the United States.

If one shifts the angle of vision, if one asks what books have had most to do with shaping the American mind, the American imagination, the American vision of life since 1890, a kind of guiding principle appears. One cannot claim that this is the only principle, just as one cannot claim that this is the only thread through the immense labyrinth of American publishing. Yet it is a principle one finds more helpful than any other.

Books which have shaped the American mind may be of two sorts: individual books of such power that their influence will be granted by any competent student; and classes of books, which can be represented by examples. To the first type William James's *Varieties of Religious Experience* and Herbert Croly's *Promise of American Life* seem clearly to belong; whereas if one wants to study the kind of historical romance that swamped the country after the Spanish-American War and that long conditioned our general interpretation of history, any or all of a dozen representative titles will do.

There is a third consideration. Trends in writing and publishing—call them intellectual, fashionable, artistic, what you will—are also discernible. Such, for example, is the library of books presenting the social gospel; such also is the proletarian literature of the thirties. And a fourth consideration appears—that vague attribute known as "importance." Waiving all such ticklish problems as "Important for what?" or "Important for whom?" one finds there are always titles of this sort, titles of which it can be said, not so much that importance requires their inclusion, as that inclusion in other lists establishes their importance here. If this is too hair-splitting, let us give an example. At the moment the literary importance of Henry L. Mencken is at a low ebb, both among the literati and among general readers; but you can

4

no more consider the twenties and omit Mr. Mencken than you can consider the Restoration and omit Dryden's verse.

This handbook is put together in the light of these considerations. The first half of the book is an organized compilation of titles designed to enable the student better to understand the social and intellectual setting of American literature in the years under survey. The second half is devoted to fifty-one lists which will guide the reader through American literature itself since 1890. Each reading list has a separate Arabic number for quickness of reference as well as for treating any single unit in the guide independently, should this seem desirable. Both halves of the book are nowhere exhaustive. No doubt we have omitted many an important title. One can only plead with Dr. Johnson, "Ignorance, madam, sheer ignorance," and implore the reader to write in the missing title where he thinks it belongs. So rich and sudden has been the efflorescence of American literary art in the last seventy years, it would be quite possible to construct other groups of excellent titles paralleling ours and scarcely duplicating them. All we are trying to do is to offer to those who are puzzled by the embarrassment of our literary riches a scheme, a clue, an outline, a pattern that will make some sort of sense, even though it may not be at all points the right sense. The decision as to what is of permanent worth in this vast library will not be made for another hundred years, but in the meanwhile one is entitled to understand it if one can. No doubt somebody's special favorite is neglected or squeezed into a corner. Around the work of many leading authors—Henry James, Robert Frost, and William Faulkner, for example—a whole library of comment, interpretation, and biographical knowledge has been published. To attempt to list such studies, or to try to be even more inclusive and list references to magazine articles and magazine publication, would be to swell this guide to inordinate length. We have settled, therefore, on just two major divisions: the social and intellectual backgrounds, followed by the major works of American literature since 1890. All dates given for the publication of any of these titles is the date of original publication, unless a revised edition has appeared.

We are indebted to Professor Frederick Merk of Harvard University, to Professor Daniel Aaron of Smith College, and to

INTRODUCTION

Professor Isaac Asimov of Boston University for graciously re-
viewing the material; and very grateful to Miss Ann B. Hopkins
and Mr. James E. Brogan for tirelessly checking the data and
saving us from many blunders. We are also happy to record the
patient and sympathetic interest of Dr. Thomas J. Wilson of
Harvard University Press in planning the form of this work and
in organizing and simplifying it for the greater happiness of its
users.

ABBREVIATIONS USED FOR
PUBLISHING FIRMS

The following abbreviations are used for the publishing houses cited most frequently; the names of the other firms are given in full. In the bibliographical entries the city of publication precedes the name of the publisher except in the case of Princeton, where the name of the city and the abbreviation for the press are identical.

Beacon	Beacon Press
Bobbs	The Bobbs-Merrill Co., Inc.
Bowker	R. R. Bowker Co.
California	University of California Press
Columbia	Columbia University Press
Cornell	Cornell University Press
Crowell	Thomas Y. Crowell Co.
Doubleday	Doubleday & Co., Inc.
Harcourt	Harcourt, Brace & Co.
Harper	Harper & Brothers
Harvard	Harvard University Press
Holt	Henry Holt & Co., Inc.
Houghton	Houghton Mifflin Co.
Illinois	University of Illinois Press
Johns Hopkins	The Johns Hopkins Press
Knopf	Alfred A. Knopf, Inc.
Lippincott	J. B. Lippincott Co.
Little-B	Little, Brown & Co.
Louisiana	Louisiana State University Press

Macmillan	The Macmillan Co.
McGraw	McGraw-Hill Book Co.
Minnesota	University of Minnesota Press
North Carolina	University of North Carolina Press
Norton	W. W. Norton & Co., Inc.
Oklahoma	University of Oklahoma Press
Oxford	Oxford University Press, Inc.
Prentice-Hall	Prentice-Hall, Inc.
Princeton	Princeton University Press
Random	Random House
Regnery	Henry Regnery Co.
Ronald	The Ronald Press Co.
Rutgers	Rutgers University Press
Scribner	Charles Scribner's Sons
Simon	Simon and Schuster, Inc.
Viking	The Viking Press, Inc.
Yale	Yale University Press

The

Backgrounds of

American Literature

Since 1890

I · GENERAL GUIDES

Roy Prentice Basler and others, *A Guide to the Study of the United States of America: Representative Books Reflecting the Development of American Life and Thought* (Washington, Library of Congress, 1960). Almost 1200 pages of annotated bibliography on literary, scientific, historical, economic, religious, and other aspects of American civilization.

Oscar Handlin and others, *Harvard Guide to American History* (Cambridge, Harvard, 1954).

Writings on American History (Washington, Government Printing Office, 1906—). This invaluable annual bibliography has appeared regularly, except that the years 1941–1947 are not covered. It is a supplement to the *Annual Report* of the American Historical Association.

II · GENERAL REFERENCE WORKS

James Truslow Adams and others, *Album of American History*, 5 vols. (New York, Scribner, 1944–1949). Described as "an attempt to tell the history of America through pictures made at the time history was being made." The 4th volume covers 1890–1920; the 5th volume is index.

James Truslow Adams and others, *Dictionary of American History*, 5 vols., revised edition (New York, Scribner, 1946). *Supplement One*, edited by J. G. E. Hopkins and Wayne Andrews, appeared in 1961. Under the advisory editorship of Thomas C. Cochran, *The Concise Dictionary of American History*, edited by Wayne Andrews, was published in 1962.

Gorton Carruth and associates, *The Encyclopedia of American Facts and Dates*, 3rd edition (New York, Crowell, 1962).

Allen Johnson and others, *Dictionary of American Biography*,

20 vols. (New York, Scribner, 1928–1936). A supplementary unnumbered index volume was published in 1937. In addition, Supplement One (Vol. XXI), covering the lives of important persons inadvertently omitted from the original edition, and, more significantly, the lives of important persons whose deaths occurred between the completion of the first twenty volumes and December 31, 1935, was published under the editorship of Harris E. Starr. This is dated 1944. A second supplement (Vol. XXII) under the editorship of Robert Livingston Schuyler and Edward T. James, covering material to December 31, 1940, was published in 1958. The *Concise Dictionary of American Biography* (Scribner, 1964), was prepared under the direction of Joseph G. E. Hopkins. It is a one-volume abridgment of all 14,780 articles in the original dictionary and supplements.

Henrietta Melia Larson, *Guide to Business History. Harvard Studies in Business History,* XII (Cambridge, Harvard, 1948).

Tremaine McDowell, *American Studies* (Minneapolis, Minnesota, 1948). A survey and analysis of academic programs for the study of American civilization. See Robert Harris Walker, below.

Richard Brandon Morris, *Encyclopedia of American History,* revised and enlarged edition (New York, Harper, 1961).

The United States Quarterly Book List (published for the Library of Congress by Rutgers University Press, 1945–1956). A bibliographical and critical listing of recent books of a "scientific, historical, literary, or artistic nature" of serious import. The best cross-section of serious publishing in the United States, unfortunately discontinued. The title occasionally varies.

Robert Harris Walker, *American Studies in the United States: A Survey of College Programs* (Baton Rouge, Louisiana, 1958). Complements and supplements McDowell, above.

III · GENERAL HISTORIES

Duncan Aikman, *The Turning Stream* (New York, Doubleday, 1948). A confused but interesting historical comment on the American experiment in terms of social idealism.

Frederick Lewis Allen, *The Big Change: America Transforms Itself, 1900–1950* (New York, Harper, 1952).

Thomas Andrew Bailey, *The American Pageant: A History of the Republic* (Boston, D. C. Heath & Co., 1956).

Charles Austin Beard and Mary R. Beard, *The Rise of American Civilization,* 2 vols., revised and enlarged edition (New York, Macmillan, 1947). *America in Mid-Passage* (New York, Macmillan, 1939) by the same authors continues this history into the 1930's. *The American Spirit* (New York, Macmillan, 1942) is "an effort to grasp the intellectual and moral qualities of the United States since 1776." It is the fourth and last volume in the Beards' history.

Ray Allen Billington, Bert James Loewenberg, and Samuel Hugh Brockunier, *The United States: American Democracy in World Perspective* (New York, Rinehart & Co., 1947). Most of Part II and all of Part III deal with the twentieth century.

Harry James Carman, Harold Coffin Syrett, and Bernard W. Wishy, *A History of the American People,* 2 vols., 2nd revised edition (New York, Knopf, 1960). Volume II begins with 1865.

Thomas Dionysius Clark, *The Emerging South* (New York, Oxford, 1961).

Foster Rhea Dulles, *Twentieth Century America* (Boston, Reynal and Hitchcock, 1945).

Dwight Lowell Dumond, *America in Our Time, 1896–1946* (New York, Holt, 1947).

Oscar Handlin, *The American People in the Twentieth Century* (Cambridge, Harvard, 1954). Part of the *Library of Congress Series in American Civilization.*

John Donald Hicks, George Edwin Mowry, and Robert E. Burke, *The American Nation,* 4th edition (Boston, Houghton, 1963). It covers the years 1865–1962.

Richard Hofstadter, William Miller, and Daniel Aaron, *The United States: The History of a Republic* (New York, Prentice-Hall, 1957).

Quincy Howe, *A World History of Our Own Times,* 2 vols. (New York, Simon, 1949–1953). Vol. I covers the period from the turn of the century to the Armistice of 1918; Vol. II covers the period between the Armistice and the Munich agreement.

Walter Consuelo Langsam, *The World Since 1919,* 7th edition (New York, Macmillan, 1954).

Arthur Stanley Link, *American Epoch: A History of the United States Since the 1890's* (New York, Knopf, 1955).

Samuel Eliot Morison and Henry Steele Commager, *The Growth of the American Republic,* 2 vols., 5th edition, revised and enlarged (New York, Oxford, 1962). Volume II covers the period since the Civil War.

Henry Bamford Parkes, *The American Experience: An Interpretation of the History and Civilization of the American People,* 2nd edition (New York, Knopf, 1955).

Arthur Meier Schlesinger (Sr.), *Political and Social Growth of the American People, 1865–1940,* 3rd edition (New York, Macmillan, 1941). In its most recent form the title of this work has been altered to *The Rise of Modern America,* 4th edition (New York, Macmillan, 1951).

Mark Sullivan, *Our Times,* 6 vols. (New York, Scribner, 1926–1935). I. *The Turn of the Century* (to 1900); II. *America Finding Herself* (1900–1905); III. *Pre-War America* (1905–1908); IV. *The War Begins* (1909–1914); V. *Over Here* (1914–1918); VI. *The Twenties* (to 1926).

Harvey Wish, *Contemporary America: The National Scene Since 1900,* 3rd edition (New York, Harper, 1961).

Harvey Wish, *Society and Thought in America,* 2 vols., 2nd edition (New York, David McKay Co., 1962). Volume II discusses America from 1865 to the present.

Comer Vann Woodward, *Origins of the New South, 1877–1913* (Baton Rouge, Louisiana, 1951). This is Volume IX of the *History of the South,* edited by Wendell Holmes Stephenson and E. Merton Coulter, now in progress.

GENERAL HISTORIES

A · THE NINETIES

Frederick Lewis Allen, *The Lords of Creation* (New York, Harper, 1935). A study of business leadership.

Thomas Beer, *The Mauve Decade: American Life at the End of the Nineteenth Century* (New York, Knopf, 1926). A mannered cultural history.

French Ensor Chadwick, *The Relations of the United States and Spain: The Spanish-American War,* 2 vols. (New York, Scribner, 1911).

Herbert David Croly, *Marcus Alonzo Hanna: His Life and Work* (New York, Macmillan, 1912).

Frank Burt Freidel, *The Splendid Little War* (Boston, Little-B, 1958).

Ray Ginger, *Altgeld's America: The Lincoln Ideal Versus Changing Realities* (New York, Funk & Wagnalls Co., 1958).

Paul Wilbur Glad, *The Trumpet Soundeth: William Jennings Bryan and His Democracy, 1896–1912* (Lincoln, University of Nebraska Press, 1960).

John Donald Hicks, *The Populist Revolt: A History of the Farmers' Alliance and the People's Party* (Minneapolis, Minnesota, 1931).

Richard Hofstadter, *The Age of Reform: From Bryan to Franklin Delano Roosevelt* (New York, Knopf, 1955).

Stewart Hall Holbrook, *The Age of the Moguls* (Garden City, Doubleday, 1953). One of the *Mainstream of America* series.

Arthur Mann, *Yankee Reformers in the Urban Age* (Cambridge, Harvard, 1954).

Walter Millis, *The Martial Spirit: A Study of Our War with Spain* (Boston, Houghton, 1931).

Clifford Wheeler Patton, *The Battle for Municipal Reform: Mobilization and Attack, 1875–1900* (Washington, American Council on Public Affairs, 1940).

Julius William Pratt, *America's Colonial Experiment* (New York, Prentice-Hall, 1950).

Julius William Pratt, *Expansionists of 1898: The Acquisition of Hawaii and the Spanish Islands* (Baltimore, Johns Hopkins, 1936). Reprinted in New York, 1951, by Peter Smith.

1 5

BACKGROUNDS

James Ford Rhodes, *The History of the United States from Hayes to McKinley, 1877–1896,* new edition (New York, Macmillan, 1928). This is Vol. VIII of Rhodes' *History of the United States from the Compromise of 1850.*

Arthur Meier Schlesinger (Sr.), *The Rise of the City, 1878–1898* (New York, Macmillan, 1933). This is Volume X of the *History of American Life* series.

Francis Butler Simkins, *Pitchfork Ben Tillman, South Carolinian* (Baton Rouge, Louisiana, 1944).

W. A. Swanberg, *Citizen Hearst: A Biography of William Randolph Hearst* (New York, Scribner, 1961).

Ida Minerva Tarbell, *The Nationalizing of Business, 1878–1898* (New York, Macmillan, 1936). This is Volume IX of the *History of American Life* series.

Morris Robert Werner, *Bryan* (New York, Harcourt, 1929).

Comer Vann Woodward, *Tom Watson: Agrarian Rebel* (New York, Macmillan, 1938).

B · THE "PROGRESSIVE" ERA

Howard Kennedy Beale, *Theodore Roosevelt and the Rise of America to World Power* (Baltimore, Johns Hopkins, 1956).

John Morton Blum, *The Republican Roosevelt* (Cambridge, Harvard, 1954).

Claude Gernade Bowers, *Beveridge and the Progressive Era* (Boston, Houghton, 1932).

John Chamberlain, *Farewell to Reform: The Rise, Life, and Decay of the Progressive Mind in America,* 2nd edition (New York, The John Day Co., 1933).

Tyler Dennett, *John Hay: From Poetry to Politics* (New York, Dodd, Mead & Co., 1933).

Dwight Lowell Dumond, *Roosevelt to Roosevelt: The United States in the Twentieth Century* (New York, Holt, 1937).

Harold Underwood Faulkner, *The Quest for Social Justice, 1898–1914* (New York, Macmillan, 1931). This is Volume XI of the *History of American Life* series.

Charles Forcey, *The Crossroads of Liberalism: Croly, Weyl, Lippmann, and the Progressive Era, 1900–1925* (New York, Oxford, 1961).

16

GENERAL HISTORIES

Eric Frederick Goldman, *Rendezvous with Destiny: A History of American Reform* (New York, Knopf, 1952).

Samuel Gompers, *Seventy Years of Life and Labor: An Autobiography*, 2 vols. (New York, E. P. Dutton & Co., 1925). Reprinted in one volume in 1943.

William Henry Harbaugh, *Power and Responsibility: The Life and Times of Theodore Roosevelt* (New York, Farrar, Straus & Cudahy, 1961).

Richard Hofstadter, ed., *The Progressive Movement, 1900–1915* (Englewood Cliffs, Prentice-Hall, 1963). Excerpts from contemporaneous writing.

Belle Case LaFollette and Fola LaFollette, *Robert M. LaFollette, 1855–1925*, 2 vols. (New York, Macmillan, 1953).

Robert Marion LaFollette, *LaFollette's Autobiography: A Personal Narrative of Political Experiences* (Madison, Wisconsin, The R. M. LaFollette Co., 1919). This was first published in 1913, but there were various revisions and expansions before the author's death in 1925.

Arthur Stanley Link, *Wilson*, (Princeton, 1947—). Vol. I: *The Road to the White House;* Vol. II: *The New Freedom;* Vol. III: *The Struggle for Neutrality, 1914–1915.*

Arthur Stanley Link, *Woodrow Wilson and the Progressive Era, 1910–1917* (New York, Harper, 1954). Part of the *New American Nation* series.

Walter Lord, *The Good Years: From 1900 to the First World War* (New York, Harper, 1960).

Robert Sidney Maxwell, *LaFollette and the Rise of the Progressives in Wisconsin* (Madison, State Historical Society, 1956).

Henry Farnham May, *The End of American Innocence: A Study of the First Years of Our Own Time, 1912–1917* (New York, Knopf, 1959).

Elting Elmore Morison and others, eds., *The Letters of Theodore Roosevelt*, 8 vols. (Cambridge, Harvard, 1951–1954). The volumes run: *The Years of Preparation, 1868–1900*, 2 vols.; *The Square Deal, 1901–1905*, 2 vols.; *The Big Stick, 1905–1909*, 2 vols.; and *The Days of Armageddon, 1909–1919*, 2 vols.

George Edwin Mowry, *The Era of Theodore Roosevelt, 1900–1912* (New York, Harper, 1958). Part of the *New American Nation* series.

Amos Richards Eno Pinchot, *History of the Progressive Party, 1912–1916*, edited with an introduction by Helene Maxwell Hooker (New York, New York University Press, 1958).

Henry Fowles Pringle, *Theodore Roosevelt: A Biography* (New York, Harcourt, 1931).

Cornelius C. Regier, *The Era of the Muckrakers* (Chapel Hill, North Carolina, 1932).

James Ford Rhodes, *The McKinley and Roosevelt Administrations, 1897–1909* (New York, Macmillan, 1922). This is Volume IX of Rhodes' *History of the United States from the Compromise of 1850*.

Lincoln Steffens, *Autobiography* (New York, Harcourt, 1931). An American classic, often reprinted.

James Harfield Timberlake, *Prohibition and the Progressive Movement, 1900–1920* (Cambridge, Harvard, 1963).

Kermit Vanderbilt, *Charles Eliot Norton: Apostle of Culture in a Democracy* (Cambridge, Harvard, 1959).

Edward Charles Wagenknecht, *The Seven Worlds of Theodore Roosevelt* (New York, Longmans, Green & Co., 1958).

Arthur Myron Weinberg and Lila Weinberg, eds., *The Muckrakers: The Era in Journalism That Moved America to Reform—The Most Significant Magazine Articles of 1902–1912* (New York, Simon, 1961).

C · WORLD WAR I

See the useful general bibliography on this topic in the *Encyclopaedia Britannica*, Vol. 23, 14th edition, 1936.

Ray Stannard Baker, *Woodrow Wilson: Life and Letters*, 8 vols. (Garden City, Doubleday, Page and Co., 1927–1939).

Burton Jesse Hendrick, *Life and Letters of Walter H. Page*, 3 vols. (Garden City, Doubleday, Page and Co., 1922–1925). Important in itself and also for the light it throws upon British-American cultural ties.

John Bach McMaster, *The United States in the World War, 1918–1920*, 2 vols. (New York, D. Appleton and Co., 1927).

Walter Millis, *Road to War: America, 1914–1917* (Boston, Houghton, 1935). An excellent instance of the revisionist history of the 1930's.

Robert Keith Murray, *Red Scare: A Study in National Hysteria, 1919–1920* (Minneapolis, Minnesota, 1955).

Frederic Logan Paxson, *American Democracy and the World War*, 3 vols. (Boston, Houghton, 1936–1948). The three volumes, originally published separately, are: *Pre-War Years, 1913–1917; America at War, 1917–1918;* and *Post-War Years: Normalcy, 1918–1933.*

Horace Cornelius Peterson and Gilbert Courtland Fite, *Opponents of War, 1917–1918* (Madison, University of Wisconsin Press, 1957).

Charles Seymour, *American Neutrality, 1914–1917* (New Haven, Yale, 1935).

Charles Seymour, *Woodrow Wilson and the World War* (New Haven, Yale, 1921). Part of the *Chronicles of America* series.

Preston William Slosson, *The Great Crusade and After, 1914–1928* (New York, Macmillan, 1930). This is Volume XII of the *History of American Life* series.

Charles Callan Tansill, *America Goes to War* (Boston, Little-B, 1938).

D · THE TWENTIES

Samuel Hopkins Adams, *Incredible Era: The Life and Times of Warren Gamaliel Harding* (Boston, Houghton, 1939). Popular in tone.

Frederick Lewis Allen, *Only Yesterday: An Informal History of the Nineteen-Twenties* (New York, Harper, 1931). Popular cultural history.

Harold Underwood Faulkner, *From Versailles to the New Deal: A Chronicle of the Harding-Coolidge Era* (New Haven, Yale, 1950). Part of the *Chronicles of America* series.

George Harmon Knoles, *The Jazz Age Revisited: British Criti-*

cism of American Civilization During the 1920's (Stanford, Stanford University Press, 1955).

William Edward Leuchtenburg, *The Perils of Prosperity, 1914–1932* (Chicago, University of Chicago Press, 1958). Part of the Chicago *History of American Civilization* series.

Robert Staughton Lynd and Helen Merrell Lynd, *Middletown: A Study in Contemporary American Culture* (New York, Harcourt, 1929). A sociological analysis of Muncie, Indiana. This was followed in 1937 by *Middletown in Transition: A Study in Cultural Conflicts,* by the same authors.

Eugene Lyons, *Assignment in Utopia* (New York, Harcourt, 1937).

George Edwin Mowry, ed., *The Twenties: Fords, Flappers, and Fanatics* (Englewood Cliffs, Prentice-Hall, 1963). Excerpts from contemporaneous writing.

Peter H. Odegard, *Pressure Politics: The Story of the Anti-Saloon League* (New York, Columbia, 1928). How national prohibition came into being.

Kirby Page, ed., *Recent Gains in American Civilization* (New York, Harcourt, 1928). Estimates of contemporary society by fifteen specialists.

James Warren Prothro, *The Dollar Decade: Business Ideas in the 1920's* (Baton Rouge, Louisiana, 1954).

George Henry Soule, *Prosperity Decade: From War to Depression, 1917–1929* (New York, Rinehart & Co., 1947).

Caroline Farrer Ware, *Greenwich Village, 1920–1930: A Comment on American Civilization in the Post-War Years* (Boston, Houghton, 1935). With this should be read Malcolm Cowley's *Exile's Return,* 1934, revised edition, 1951 (New York, Viking).

E · THE GREAT DEPRESSION AND THE THIRTIES

Frederick Lewis Allen, *Since Yesterday: The Nineteen-Thirties in America* (New York, Harper, 1940).

Francis Beverly Biddle, *In Brief Authority* (Garden City, Doubleday, 1962).

GENERAL HISTORIES

Denis William Brogan, *The Era of Franklin D. Roosevelt: A Chronicle of the New Deal and Global War* (New Haven, Yale, 1950). In the *Chronicles of America* series.

James MacGregor Burns, *Roosevelt: The Lion and the Fox* (New York, Harcourt, 1956).

Malcolm Cowley, *Exile's Return,* revised edition (New York, Viking, 1951). Originally published in 1934.

Milton Crane, ed., *The Roosevelt Era* (New York, Boni and Gaer, 1947). An anthology of political and literary documents.

Frank Burt Freidel, *Franklin D. Roosevelt,* 3 vols. (Boston, Little-B, 1953–1956). Vol. I: *The Apprenticeship;* Vol. II: *The Ordeal;* Vol. III: *The Triumph.*

Leo Gurko, *The Angry Decade* (New York, Dodd, Mead & Co., 1947).

Edwin Palmer Hoyt, *The Tempering Years* (New York, Scribner, 1963).

Harold Le Claire Ickes, *The Secret Diary,* 3 vols. (New York, Simon, 1953–1955). Vol. I: *The First Thousand Days, 1933–1936;* Vol. II: *The Inside Struggle, 1936–1939;* Vol. III: *The Lowering Clouds, 1939–1941.*

William Henry ("Will") Irwin, *Herbert Hoover: A Reminiscent Biography* (New York, The Century Co., 1928).

Dexter Perkins, *The New Age of Franklin Roosevelt, 1932–1945* (Chicago, University of Chicago Press, 1957). Part of the Chicago *History of American Civilization* series.

Arthur Meier Schlesinger, Jr., *The Age of Roosevelt* (Boston, Houghton, 1957—). Vol. I: *The Crisis of the Old Order, 1919–1933;* Vol. II: *The Coming of the New Deal;* Vol. III: *The Politics of Upheaval.*

Rexford Guy Tugwell, *The Democratic Roosevelt: A Biography of Franklin D. Roosevelt* (Garden City, Doubleday, 1957).

Dixon Wecter, *The Age of the Great Depression, 1929–1941* (New York, Macmillan, 1948).

Edmund Wilson, *The American Jitters: A Year of the Slump* (New York, Scribner, 1932). A report of October 1930 to October 1931.

F · THE FORTIES: WORLD WAR II AND ITS AFTERMATH

An excellent short account of World War II will be found in the second volume of the Morison-Commager *Growth of the American Republic,* for which see Section III above (General Histories).

(General) Dwight David Eisenhower, *Crusade in Europe* (New York, Doubleday, 1948).

Herbert Feis, *Churchill, Roosevelt, Stalin: The War They Waged and the Peace They Sought* (Princeton, 1957).

Herbert Feis, *The Road to Pearl Harbor: The Coming of the War Between the United States and Japan* (Princeton, 1950).

(Major-General) John Frederick Charles Fuller, *The Second World War, 1939–1945: A Strategical and Tactical History* (New York, Duell, Sloan & Pearce, 1949). This is an excellent one-volume account.

Eric Frederick Goldman, *The Crucial Decade: America, 1945–1955* (New York, Knopf, 1956).

John Gunther, *Inside USA,* revised edition (New York, Harper, 1951).

Charles Grove Haines and Ross J. S. Hoffman, *The Origins and Background of the Second World War,* 2nd edition (New York, Oxford, 1947).

Walter Lord, *Day of Infamy* (New York, Holt, 1957).

Samuel Eliot Morison, *History of U.S. Naval Operations in World War II,* 15 vols. (Boston, Little-B, 1947–1962). Vol. XV is supplement and general index.

Herbert Charles O'Neill, *A Short History of the Second World War* (New York, Frederick A. Praeger, 1950).

Fletcher Pratt, *War for the World: A Chronicle of Our Fighting Forces in World War II* (New Haven, Yale, 1950). Part of the *Chronicles of America* series.

Eleanor Roosevelt, *This I Remember* (New York, Harper, 1949).

Robert Emmet Sherwood, *Roosevelt and Hopkins: An Intimate History* (New York, Harper, 1950).

Henry Lewis Stimson and McGeorge Bundy, *On Active Service in Peace and War* (New York, Harper, 1948).

GENERAL HISTORIES

Harry S. Truman, *Memoirs,* 2 vols. (Garden City, Doubleday, 1955–1956). Vol. I: *Year of Decisions, 1945–1946;* Vol. II; *Years of Trial and Hope, 1946–1952.*

(Major-General) Courtney Whitney, *MacArthur: His Rendezvous with History* (New York, Knopf, 1956).

G · THE FIFTIES

Sherman Adams, *First-Hand Report: The Story of the Eisenhower Administration* (New York, Harper, 1961).

James MacGregor Burns, *John Kennedy* (New York, Harcourt, 1960).

Robert J. Donovan, *Eisenhower: The Inside Story* (New York, Harper, 1956).

Dwight David Eisenhower, *The White House Years: Mandate for Change, 1953–1956* (New York, Doubleday, 1963). The first of two proposed volumes.

Norman A. Graebner, *The New Isolationism: A Study in Politics and Foreign Policy Since 1950* (New York, Ronald, 1956).

Kenneth Ingram, *History of the Cold War* (New York, Philosophical Library, 1955).

John Fitzgerald Kennedy, *The Strategy of Peace,* ed. Allan Nevins (New York, Harper, 1960). Speeches by the then Senator Kennedy.

Merlo John Pusey, *Eisenhower, the President* (New York, Macmillan, 1956).

Richard Halworth Rovere, *Affairs of State: The Eisenhower Years* (New York, Farrar, Straus & Cudahy), 1956.

Edward Albert Shils, *The Torment of Secrecy: The Background and Consequences of American Security Policies* (Glencoe, Illinois, The Free Press, 1956).

Adlai Ewing Stevenson, *Call to Greatness* (New York, Harper, 1954).

Adlai Ewing Stevenson, *What I Think* (New York, Harper, 1956).

IV · SPECIAL ASPECTS

A · SOCIAL AND ECONOMIC HISTORY AND PROBLEMS

1 · General Social History and Discussion

Jane Addams, *Twenty Years at Hull-House* (New York, Macmillan, 1910). Often reprinted, this classic autobiography of a settlement worker has a sequel, *The Second Twenty Years at Hull-House* (New York, Macmillan, 1930).

Frederick Lewis Allen, *The Big Change: America Transforms Itself, 1900–1950* (New York, Harper, 1952).

John Brooks, ed., *The One and the Many: The Individual in the Modern World* (New York, Harper, 1962). A report on the Second Corning Conference.

David Lewis Cohn, *The Good Old Days: A History of American Morals and Manners as Seen Through the Sears, Roebuck Catalogs, 1905 to the Present* (New York, Simon, 1940).

Frederick Warren Cozens and Florence Stumpf, *Sports in American Life* (Chicago, University of Chicago Press, 1953).

Sebastian de Grazia, *Of Time, Work, and Leisure* (New York, The Twentieth Century Fund, 1962).

Sidney Herbert Ditzion, *Marriage, Morals, and Sex in America: A History of Ideas* (New York, Bookman Associates, 1953).

Foster Rhea Dulles, *America Learns to Play: A History of Popular Recreation, 1607–1940* (New York, D. Appleton-Century Co., 1940).

Harold Underwood Faulkner, *American Political and Social History*, 7th edition (New York, Appleton-Century-Crofts, 1957).

John Kenneth Galbraith, *The Affluent Society* (Boston, Houghton, 1958).

Eli Ginzberg, ed., *Values and Ideals of American Youth* (New York, Columbia, 1961).

Thomas Hoag Greer, *American Social Reform Movements: Their Pattern Since 1865* (New York, Prentice-Hall, 1949).

24

SPECIAL ASPECTS

Louis Kronenberger, *Company Manners: A Cultural Inquiry into American Life* (Indianapolis, Bobbs, 1954).

Eric Larrabee, ed., *American Panorama: Essays by Fifteen American Critics on 350 Books Past and Present Which Portray the U.S. in Its Many Aspects* (New York, New York University Press, 1957).

Max Lerner, *America as a Civilization: Life and Thought in the United States Today* (New York, Simon, 1957).

Carl E. Lindstrom, *The Fading American Newspaper* (Garden City, Doubleday, 1960).

Walter Lippmann, *Drift and Mastery: An Attempt to Diagnose the Current Unrest* (New York, Mitchell Kennerley, 1914).

Russell Lynes, *The Domesticated Americans* (New York, Harper and Row, 1963).

Russell Lynes, *The Tastemakers* (New York, Harper, 1954).

Elton Mayo, *The Social Problems of an Industrial Civilization* (Boston, Harvard Graduate School of Business Administration, 1945).

Lloyd R. Morris, *Postscript to Yesterday: America—The Last Fifty Years* (New York, Random, 1947). Listed here rather than in Section II because of the emphasis upon social and cultural history.

Frank Luther Mott, *American Journalism: A History, 1690–1960,* 3rd edition (New York, Macmillan, 1962).

Lewis Mumford, *In the Name of Sanity* (New York, Harcourt, 1954).

David Morris Potter, *People of Plenty: Economic Abundance and the American Character* (Chicago, University of Chicago Press, 1954).

David Riesman, with Reuel Denney and Nathan Glazer, *The Lonely Crowd: A Study of the Changing American Character* (New Haven, Yale, 1950). An abridged version, by the same authors, appeared as a Doubleday Anchor Book, 1953.

Bradford Smith, assisted by Marion Collins Smith, *Why We Behave Like Americans* (Philadelphia, Lippincott, 1957).

Eugene Staley, ed., *Creating an Industrial Civilization: A Report on the [First] Corning Conference* (New York, Harper, 1952).

Harold Edmund Stearns, ed., *America Now: An Inquiry into Civilization in the United States by 36 Americans* (New York, Scribner, 1938).

Harold Edmund Stearns, ed., *Civilization in the United States: An Inquiry by Thirty Americans* (New York, Harcourt, 1922).

George Rippey Stewart, *American Ways of Life* (Garden City, Doubleday, 1954).

Lillian Symes and Travers Clement, *Rebel America: The Story of Social Revolt in the United States* (New York, Harper, 1934).

Dixon Wecter, *The Hero in America: A Chronicle of Hero-Worship* (New York, Scribner, 1941).

2 · General Economic History and Problems

Ernest Ludlow Bogart and Donald L. Kemmerer, *Economic History of the American People,* revised edition (New York, Longmans, Green & Co., 1947).

Harrison Brown, James Bonner, and John Weir, *The Next Hundred Years: Man's Natural and Technological Resources* (New York, Viking, 1957).

James Frederic Dewhurst and associates, *America's Needs and Resources: A New Survey* (New York, The Twentieth Century Fund, 1955).

Joseph Dorfman, *The Economic Mind in American Civilization,* 5 vols. (New York, Viking, 1946–1959). The last three volumes cover the years 1865–1933.

Joseph Dorfman, *Thorstein Veblen and his America* (New York, Viking, 1934).

Peter Ferdinand Drucker, *America's Next Twenty Years* (New York, Harper, 1957).

Harold Underwood Faulkner, *The Decline of Laissez-Faire, 1897–1917* (New York, Rinehart & Co., 1951). This is Vol. VII of his *Economic History of the United States.*

Sidney Fine, *Laissez Faire and the General-Welfare State: A Study of Conflict in American Thought, 1865–1901* (Ann Arbor, University of Michigan Press, 1956).

SPECIAL ASPECTS

John Kenneth Galbraith, *American Capitalism: The Concept of Countervailing Power*, 2nd edition, revised (Boston, Houghton, 1956).

Allan Garfield Gruchy, *Modern Economic Thought: The American Contribution* (New York, Prentice-Hall, 1947).

Louis Morton Hacker, *The Triumph of American Capitalism: The Development of Forces in American History to the End of the Nineteenth Century* (New York, Columbia, 1946).

Walton Hale Hamilton, *The Politics of Industry* (New York, Knopf, 1957).

Burton Jesse Hendrick, *The Life of Andrew Carnegie*, 2 vols. (Garden City, Doubleday, Doran & Co., 1932).

Matthew Josephson, *The Robber Barons: The Great American Capitalists* (New York, Harcourt, 1934).

Edward Chase Kirkland, *A History of American Economic Life*, 3rd edition (New York, Appleton-Century-Crofts, 1951).

Allan Nevins, *Study in Power: John D. Rockefeller, Industrialist and Philanthropist*, 2 vols. (New York, Scribner, 1953).

Allan Nevins, with the collaboration of Frank Ernest Hill, *Ford: The Times, the Man, the Company* (New York, Scribner, 1954). Nevins and Hill have also written a two-volume history of the Ford Motor Company.

Fred Albert Shannon, *America's Economic Growth*, 3rd edition (New York, Macmillan, 1951).

Chester Whitney Wright, *Economic History of the United States*, 2nd edition (New York, McGraw, 1949).

3 · General Political Problems

Herbert Agar, *The People's Choice, From Washington to Harding: A Study in Democracy* (Boston, Houghton, 1933).

Herbert Asbury, *The Great Illusion: An Informal History of Prohibition* (Garden City, Doubleday, 1950).

Alan Barth, *Government by Investigation* (New York, Viking, 1955).

Daniel Bell, ed., *The Radical Right* (Garden City, Doubleday, 1963). First appeared as *The New American Right* (New York, Criterion Books, 1955).

Eleanor Bontecou, *The Federal Loyalty-Security Program* (Ithaca, Cornell, 1953). One of the *Cornell Studies in Civil Liberty*.

Earl Russell Browder, *Communism in the United States* (New York, International Publishers Co., 1935).

William Buckley, *Up From Liberalism* (New York, McDowell, Obolensky, 1959).

Zechariah Chafee, Jr., *The Blessings of Liberty* (Philadelphia, Lippincott, 1956).

Zechariah Chafee, Jr., *Free Speech in the United States*, revised edition (Cambridge, Harvard, 1941). This great work has become standard; and though based on problems of censorship and suppression of speech in World War I, it has been extended to cover later issues.

William Ludlow Chenery, *Freedom of the Press* (New York, Harcourt, 1955).

Henry Steele Commager, *Freedom, Loyalty, Dissent* (New York, Oxford, 1954).

Edward Samuel Corwin and Louis W. Koenig, *The Presidency Today* (New York, New York University Press, 1956).

Charles Pelham Curtis, *The Oppenheimer Case: The Trial of a Security System* (New York, Simon, 1955).

Elmer Holmes Davis, *But We Were Born Free* (Indianapolis, Bobbs, 1954).

Theodore Draper, *The Roots of American Communism* (New York, Viking, 1957). This is the first volume of a two-volume study. Draper's *American Communism and Soviet Russia: The Formative Period* (New York, Viking, 1960) is an independent and self-contained study.

Donald Drew Egbert and Stow Persons, eds., *Socialism and American Life*, 2 vols. (Princeton, 1952).

Arthur Alphonse Ekirch, *The Civilian and the Military* (New York, Oxford, 1956).

Arthur Alphonse Ekirch, *The Decline of American Liberalism* (New York, Longmans, Green & Co., 1955).

Nathan Fine, *Labor and Farmer Parties in the United States, 1828–1928* (New York, The Rand School of Social Research, 1928).

SPECIAL ASPECTS

Robert Jennings Harris, *The Quest for Equality: The Constitution, Congress, and the Supreme Court* (Baton Rouge, Louisiana, 1960).

Morris Hillquit, *History of Socialism in the United States*, 5th edition, revised and enlarged (New York, Funk & Wagnalls Co., 1910).

Arthur Norman Holcombe, *The Middle Class in American Politics* (Cambridge, Harvard, 1940).

Irving Howe and Lewis Coser, with the assistance of Julius Jacobson, *The American Communist Party: A Critical History, 1919–1957* (Boston, Beacon, 1957).

Stanley Kelley, *Professional Public Relations and Political Power* (Baltimore, Johns Hopkins, 1956).

Vladimir Orlando Key, Jr., *Politics, Parties, and Pressure Groups*, 4th edition (New York, Crowell, 1958).

Ira Kipnis, *The American Socialist Movement, 1897–1912* (New York, Columbia, 1952).

Samuel Joseph Konefsky, *The Legacy of Holmes and Brandeis: A Study in the Influence of Ideas* (New York, Macmillan, 1956).

Milton Ridvas Konvitz, *Civil Rights in Immigration* (Ithaca, Cornell, 1953).

Walter Lippmann, *Essays in the Public Philosophy* (Boston, Little-B, 1955).

Samuel Lubell, *Revolt of the Moderates* (New York, Harper, 1956).

Reinhard Henry Luthin, *American Demagogues: Twentieth Century* (Boston, Beacon, 1954).

Dwight Macdonald, *Memoirs of a Revolutionist: Essays in Political Criticism* (New York, Farrar, Straus & Cudahy, 1957).

Alpheus Thomas Mason, *Brandeis: A Free Man's Life* (New York, Viking, 1946).

Alpheus Thomas Mason, *Harlan Fiske Stone: Pillar of the Law* (New York, Viking, 1956).

Alpheus Thomas Mason, *Security Through Freedom: American Political Thought and Practice* (Ithaca, Cornell, 1955).

Eleanor Roosevelt, *The Moral Basis of Democracy* (New York, John Howell Books, 1940).

Clinton Lawrence Rossiter, *Conservatism in America: The Thankless Persuasion,* 2nd edition (New York, Knopf, 1962).

Clinton Lawrence Rossiter, *Marxism: The View from America* (New York, Harcourt, 1960). Strongly anti-Communist.

Arthur Meier Schlesinger (Sr.), *The American as Reformer* (Cambridge, Harvard, 1950).

Bernard Schwartz, *The Supreme Court: Constitutional Revolution in Retrospect* (New York, Ronald, 1957).

David Allen Shannon, *The Socialist Party of America: A History* (New York, Macmillan, 1955).

Lewis Lichtenstein Strauss, *Men and Decisions* (Garden City, Doubleday, 1962). An autobiographical view of federal politics from 1919 to 1960.

Telford Taylor, *Grand Inquest: The Story of Congressional Investigations* (New York, Simon, 1955).

Theodore Harold White, *The Making of the President, 1960* (New York, Atheneum Publishers, 1961).

Harold Zink, *City Bosses in the United States: A Study of Twenty Municipal Bosses* (Durham, Duke University Press, 1930).

4 · *Some Special Themes*

a · *Population Elements*

Charles Abrams, *Forbidden Neighbors: A Study of Prejudice in Housing* (New York, Harper, 1955).

Louis Adamic, *Dynamite: The Story of Class Violence in America,* revised edition (New York, Viking, 1934). Covers a hundred years, beginning in 1830.

Morroe Berger, *Equality by Statute: Legal Controls over Group Discrimination* (New York, Columbia, 1952).

Robert Hamlett Bremner, *From the Depths: The Discovery of Poverty in the United States* (New York, New York University Press, 1956).

Margaret Just Butcher, *The Negro in American Culture: Based on Materials Left by Alain Locke* (New York, Knopf, 1956).

Stewart Grant Cole and Mildred Wiese Cole, *Minorities and the American Promise* (New York, Harper, 1954).

SPECIAL ASPECTS

St. Clair Drake and Horace R. Clayton, *Black Metropolis: A Study of Negro Life in a Northern City*, revised edition (New York, Harper, 1962).

Samuel H. Dresner, *The Jew in American Life* (New York, Crown Publishers, 1963).

Essien Udosen Essien-Udom, *Black Nationalism: A Search for an Identity in America* (Chicago, University of Chicago Press, 1962).

John Hope Franklin, *From Slavery to Freedom: A History of American Negroes,* 2nd edition (New York, Knopf, 1956).

Edward Franklin Frazier, *Black Bourgeoisie* (Glencoe, Illinois, The Free Press, 1957).

Nathan Glazer and Daniel Patrick Moynihan, *Beyond the Melting Pot: The Negroes, Puerto Ricans, Jews, Italians, and Irish of New York City* (Cambridge, The M.I.T. Press and Harvard, 1963).

Oscar Handlin, *Immigration as a Factor in American History* (Englewood Cliffs, Prentice-Hall, 1959).

Oscar Handlin, *The Uprooted: The Epic Story of the Great Migrations That Made the American People* (Boston, Little-B, 1951).

John Higham, *Strangers in the Land: Patterns of American Nativism, 1860–1925* (New Brunswick, Rutgers, 1955).

Jacob Koppell Javits, *Discrimination—U.S.A.* (New York, Harcourt, 1960).

Maldwyn Allen Jones, *American Immigrations* (Chicago, University of Chicago Press, 1960).

Donald Peterson Kent, *The Refugee Intellectual: The Americanization of the Immigrant of 1933–1941* (New York, Columbia, 1953).

Charles Frederick Marden, *Minorities in American Society* (New York, American Book Co., 1952).

Carey McWilliams, *A Mask for Privilege: Anti-Semitism in America* (Boston, Little-B, 1948).

Charles Wright Mills, *White Collar: The American Middle Classes* (New York, Oxford, 1951).

Gunnar Myrdal, *An American Dilemma: The Negro Problem and Modern Democracy*, 2 vols. (New York, Harper, 1944).

Lee Nichols, *Breakthrough on the Color Front* (New York, Random, 1954). A dispassionate study of desegregation in the Armed forces.

Barbara Miller Solomon, *Ancestors and Immigrants: A Changing New England Tradition* (Cambridge, Harvard, 1956).

Dixon Wecter, *The Saga of American Society: A Record of Social Aspiration, 1607–1937* (New York, Scribner, 1937).

Nathaniel Weyl, *The Negro in American Civilization* (Washington, Public Affairs Press, 1960).

Walter Francis White, *How Far the Promised Land?* (New York, Viking, 1955).

Comer Vann Woodward, *The Strange Career of Jim Crow*, revised edition (New York, Oxford, 1957).

b · *Regionalism*

Lewis Eldon Atherton, *Main Street on the Middle Border* (Bloomington, Indiana University Press, 1954).

William Terry Couch, ed., *Culture in the South* (Chapel Hill, North Carolina, 1934).

Edward Everett Dale, *The Range Cattle Industry* (Norman, Oklahoma, 1930).

Donald Davidson, *The Attack on Leviathan: Regionalism and Nationalism in the United States* (Chapel Hill, North Carolina, 1938).

Dorothy Anne Dondore, *The Prairie and the Making of Middle America: Four Centuries of Description* (Cedar Rapids, Iowa, The Torch Press, 1926).

Robert Moore Fisher, *The Metropolis in Modern Life* (Garden City, Doubleday, 1955).

Joe Bertram Frantz and Julian Ernest Choate, Jr., *The American Cowboy: The Myth and the Reality* (Norman, Oklahoma, 1955).

Jean Gottmann, *Megalopolis: The Urbanized Northeastern Seaboard of the United States* (New York, Twentieth Century Fund, 1961).

32

Constance McLaughlin Green, *American Cities in the Growth of the Nation* (New York, John de Graff, 1957). Sixteen sketches of urban experience in America, directed to an English audience.

Seymour Edwin Harris, *The Economics of New England: Case Study of an Older Area* (Cambridge, Harvard, 1952).

Donald Hough, *The Cocktail Hour in Jackson Hole* (New York, Norton, 1956). Life in the Wyoming resort during the off-season.

Emerson Hough, *The Story of the Cowboy* (New York, D. Appleton and Co., 1897).

Emerson Hough, *The Story of the Outlaw: A Study of the Western Desperado* (New York, A. L. Burt Co., 1907).

Jane Jacobs, *The Death and Life of Great American Cities* (New York, Random, 1961).

Merrill Jensen, ed., *Regionalism in America* (Madison, University of Wisconsin Press, 1951).

David Sievert Lavender, *Land of Giants: The Settlement and Development of the Pacific Northwest, 1750–1950* (Garden City, Doubleday, 1958). Part of the *Mainstream of America* series.

Joseph Leach, *The Typical Texan: Biography of an American Myth* (Dallas, Southern Methodist University Press, 1952).

Ralph Emerson McGill, *The South and the Southerner* (Boston, Little-B, 1963).

Lowry Nelson, *American Farm Life* (Cambridge, Harvard, 1954). Part of the *Library of Congress Series in American Civilization*.

William Hord Nicholls, *Southern Tradition and Regional Progress* (Chapel Hill, North Carolina, 1960).

E. Louise Peffer, *The Closing of the Public Domain: Disposal and Reservation Policies, 1900–1950* (Stanford, Stanford University Press, 1951).

John Boynton Priestley and Jacquetta Hawkes, *Journey Down a Rainbow* (New York, Harper, 1955). Priestley describes his visit to Texas, a marked contrast to his wife's visit to the Indian communities of New Mexico.

Theodore Saloutos and John Donald Hicks, *Agricultural Discontent in the Middle West, 1900–1939* (Madison, University of Wisconsin Press, 1951).

Wallace Earle Stegner, *Wolf Willow: A History, A Story, and a Memory of the Last Plains Frontier* (New York, Viking, 1962).

Walter Prescott Webb, *The Great Plains* (Boston, Ginn & Co., 1931).

c · *Business and Industry*

Thomas Childs Cochran and William Miller, *The Age of Enterprise: A Social History of Industrial America* (New York, Macmillan, 1942).

Thomas Childs Cochran, *The American Business System: A Historical Perspective, 1900–1955* (Cambridge, Harvard, 1957). Part of the *Library of Congress Series in American Civilization.*

Sigmund Diamond, *The Reputation of the American Businessman* (Cambridge, Harvard, 1955).

Herrymon Maurer, *Great Enterprise: Growth and Behavior of the Big Corporation* (New York, Macmillan, 1955).

John Anderson Miller, *Fares, Please!* (New York, D. Appleton-Century Co., 1941). A popular history of public transportation.

Charles Wright Mills, *The Power Elite* (New York, Oxford, 1956). See also in this connection Mills' *White Collar*, 1951, and *Power, Politics, and People*, 1963.

Gustavus Myers, *History of the Great American Fortunes*, 3 vols. (Chicago, C. H. Kerr & Co., 1910). More easily available in the Modern Library edition of 1936.

Mabel Newcomer, *The Big Business Executive: The Factors That Made Him, 1900–1950* (New York, Columbia, 1955).

Michael Idvorsky Pupin, *From Immigrant to Inventor* (New York, Scribner, 1923).

Auguste C. Spectorsky, *The Exurbanites* (Philadelphia, Lippincott, 1955).

Francis Xavier Sutton and others, *The American Business Creed* (Cambridge, Harvard, 1956).

34

SPECIAL ASPECTS

Thorstein Veblen, *The Theory of Business Enterprise,* revised edition (New York, Scribner, 1935).

William Lloyd Warner and James C. Abegglen, *Big Business Leaders in America* (New York, Harper, 1955).

William Hollingsworth Whyte, *The Organization Man* (New York, Simon, 1956).

Irvin Gordon Wyllie, *The Self-Made Man in America: The Myth of Rags to Riches* (New Brunswick, Rutgers, 1954).

d · *Labor*

Neil W. Chamberlain and Jane Metzger Schilling, *The Impact of Strikes, Their Social and Economic Costs* (New York, Harper, 1954).

John Rogers Commons and others, *History of Labour in the United States,* 4 vols. (New York, Macmillan, 1935–1936). Volumes III and IV cover the years from 1896 to 1932.

Foster Rhea Dulles, *Labor in America: A History,* 2nd edition (New York, Crowell, 1960).

Philip Sheldon Foner, *History of the Labor Movement in the United States,* 2 vols. (New York, International Publishers Co., 1947–1955).

Marguerite Green, *The National Civic Federation and the American Labor Movement, 1900–1925* (Washington, The Catholic University of America Press, 1956). A study mainly of industrial relations which shows the development of labor attitudes toward nationalism and conservatism.

Matthew Josephson, *Sidney Hillman, Statesman of American Labor* (Garden City, Doubleday, 1952).

Lewis Levitski Lorwin, with the assistance of Jean Atherton Flexner, *The American Federation of Labor: History, Policies, and Prospects* (Washington, The Brookings Institution, 1933).

Carey McWilliams, *Ill Fares the Land: Migrants and Migratory Labor in the United States* (Boston, Little-B, 1942).

Selig Perlman, *A History of Trade Unionism in the United States* (New York, Macmillan, 1922).

Sylvester Petro, *The Labor Policy of the Free Society* (New York, Ronald, 1957).

Philip Taft, *The Structure and Government of Labor Unions* (Cambridge, Harvard, 1954).

Lloyd Ulman, *The Rise of the National Trade Union: The Development and Significance of Its Structure, Governing Institutions, and Economic Policies* (Cambridge, Harvard, 1955).

William Lloyd Warner, *American Life: Dream and Reality* (Chicago, University of Chicago Press, 1953). This is a revised form of his *Structure of American Life* (Edinburgh, 1952).

Mary Nelson Winslow, *Woman at Work: The Autobiography of Mary Anderson* (Minneapolis, Minnesota, 1951).

Leo Wolman, *The Growth of American Trade Unions, 1880–1923* (New York, National Bureau of Economic Research, 1924).

B · THE UNITED STATES IN INTERNATIONAL AFFAIRS

Gabriel Abraham Almond, *The American People and Foreign Policy* (New York, Harcourt, 1950).

Thomas Andrew Bailey, *The Man in the Street: The Impact of American Public Opinion on Foreign Policy* (New York, Macmillan, 1948).

Thomas Andrew Bailey, *A Diplomatic History of the American People,* 6th edition (New York, Appleton-Century-Crofts, 1958).

Samuel Flagg Bemis, *A Diplomatic History of the United States,* 4th edition (New York, Holt, 1955).

Samuel Flagg Bemis, *The United States as a World Power: A Diplomatic History, 1900–1955,* revised edition (New York, Holt, 1955).

Adolf Augustus Berle, *Tides of Crisis: A Primer of Foreign Relations* (New York, Reynal and Hitchcock, 1957).

Chester Bowles, *Africa's Challenge to America* (Berkeley, California, 1956).

Chester Bowles, *Ambassador's Report* (New York, Harper, 1954). On India.

SPECIAL ASPECTS

Chester Bowles, *American Politics in a Revolutionary World* (Cambridge, Harvard, 1956). The Godkin Lectures.

Elmer Holmes Davis, *Two Minutes Till Midnight* (Indianapolis, Bobbs, 1955).

Foster Rhea Dulles, *America's Rise to World Power, 1898–1954* (New York, Harper, 1955). Part of the *New American Nation* series.

William Yandell Elliott and others, *The Political Economy of American Foreign Policy: Its Concepts, Strategy, and Limits* (New York, Holt, 1955). A report to the Woodrow Wilson Foundation.

Louis Fischer, *This is Our World* (New York, Harper, 1956).

William W. Kaufmann and others, *Military Policy and National Security* (Princeton, 1956).

George Frost Kennan, *American Diplomacy, 1900–1950* (Chicago, University of Chicago Press, 1951).

George Frost Kennan, *Russia, the Atom, and the West* (New York, Harper, 1958).

George Frost Kennan, *Soviet-American Relations, 1917–1920* (Princeton, 1956—). Vol. I: *Russia Leaves the War;* Vol. II: *The Decision to Intervene.*

Hans Kohn, *American Nationalism: An Interpretative Essay* (New York, Macmillan, 1957).

William Leonard Langer and S. Everett Gleason, *The Challenge to Isolation, 1937–1940* (New York, published for the Council on Foreign Relations by Harper, 1952).

Samuel Lubell, *The Revolution in World Trade and American Economic Policy* (New York, Harper, 1955).

Julius William Pratt, *A History of United States Foreign Policy* (New York, Prentice-Hall, 1955).

Harry Bayard Price, *The Marshall Plan and Its Meaning* (Ithaca, Cornell, 1955).

Edwin Oldfather Reischauer, *Wanted: An Asian Policy* (New York, Knopf, 1955).

Frank Tannenbaum, *The American Tradition in Foreign Policy* (Norman, Oklahoma, 1955).

James Paul Warburg, *The United States in a Changing World: An Historical Analysis of American Foreign Policy* (New York, G. P. Putnam's Sons, 1954).

Holt Bradford Westerfield, *Foreign Policy and Party Politics, Pearl Harbor to Korea* (New Haven, Yale, 1955).

Sumner Welles and Donald Cope McKay, eds., *American Foreign Policy Library* (Cambridge, Harvard). The following volumes have appeared:

Crane Brinton, *The United States and Britain,* revised edition, 1948.

William Norman Brown, *The United States and India and Pakistan,* revised edition, 1963.

Howard Francis Cline, *The United States and Mexico,* revised edition, 1963.

Vera Micheles Dean, *The United States and Russia,* 1947.

John King Fairbank, *The United States and China,* revised edition, 1958.

Henry Stuart Hughes, *The United States and Italy,* 1953.

Donald Cope McKay, *The United States and France,* 1951.

Dexter Perkins, *The United States and the Caribbean,* 1947.

Edwin Oldfather Reischauer, *The United States and Japan,* revised edition, 1957.

Franklin Daniel Scott, *The United States and Scandinavia,* 1950.

Ephraim Avigdor Speiser, *The United States and the Near East,* revised edition, 1950.

Lewis Victor Thomas and Richard Nelson Frye, *The United States and Turkey and Iran,* 1951.

Arthur Preston Whitaker, *The United States and Argentina,* 1954.

Arthur Preston Whitaker, *The United States and South America: The Northern Republics,* 1948.

Robert Lee Wolff, *The Balkans in Our Time,* 1956.

In 1961, Crane Brinton became general editor of this series. New titles are:

SPECIAL ASPECTS

Charles Frederick Gallagher, *The United States and North Africa,* 1963.

Clinton Hartley Grattan, *The United States and the Southwest Pacific,* 1961.

Nadav Safran, *The United States and Israel,* 1963.

C · EDUCATION IN THE UNITED STATES

Harry Scott Ashmore, *The Negro and the Schools* (Chapel Hill, North Carolina, 1954).

Bernard Berelson, *Graduate Education in the United States* (New York, McGraw, 1960).

Albert Paul Blaustein and Clarence Clyde Ferguson, Jr., *Desegregation and the Law* (New Brunswick, Rutgers, 1957).

Rollo Walter Brown, *Harvard Yard in the Golden Age* (New York, A. A. Wyn, 1948).

James Bryant Conant, *The American High School Today* (New York, McGraw, 1959).

James Bryant Conant, *The Child, the Parent, and the State* (Cambridge, Harvard, 1959).

James Bryant Conant, *The Education of American Teachers* (New York, McGraw, 1963).

James Bryant Conant, *Education in a Divided World: The Function of the Public Schools in Our Unique Society* (Cambridge, Harvard, 1948).

James Bryant Conant, *Education and Liberty: The Role of the Schools in a Modern Democracy* (Cambridge, Harvard, 1953).

Lawrence Arthur Cremin, *The Transformation of the School: Progressivism in American Education, 1876–1957* (New York, Knopf, 1961).

Merle Eugene Curti, *The Social Ideas of American Educators* (New York, Scribner, 1935).

Ernest Earnest, *Academic Procession: An Informal History of the American College, 1636–1953* (Indianapolis, Bobbs, 1953).

Raymond Blaine Fosdick, *The Story of the Rockefeller Foundation* (New York, Harper, 1952).

Paul Goodman, *The Community of Scholars* (New York, Random, 1962).

Seymour Edwin Harris, *Higher Education: Resources and Finance* (New York, McGraw, 1962).

Richard Hofstadter and Walter Paul Metzger, *The Development of Academic Freedom in the United States* (New York, Columbia, 1955).

Richard Hofstadter and Wilson Smith, eds., *American Higher Education: A Documentary History,* 2 vols. (Chicago, University of Chicago Press, 1961). Described as "an anthology of discussion about American higher education throughout our history." The second volume concerns the years 1850 to the present.

Sidney Hook, *Education for Modern Man* (New York, The Dial Press, 1946).

Robert Maynard Hutchins, *Conflicts in Education in a Democratic Society* (New York, Harper, 1953).

Howard Mumford Jones, *One Great Society: Humane Learning in the United States* (New York, Harcourt, 1959).

Clark Kerr, *The Uses of the University* (Cambridge, Harvard, 1963).

Edgar Wallace Knight, *Fifty Years of American Education: A Historical Review and Critical Appraisal* (New York, Ronald, 1952).

James D. Koerner, *The Miseducation of American Teachers* (Boston, Houghton, 1963).

Robert Morrison MacIver, *Academic Freedom in Our Time* (New York, Columbia, 1955).

Allan Nevins, *The State Universities and Democracy* (Urbana, Illinois, 1962). An historical approach.

Mabel Newcomer, *A Century of Higher Education for American Women* (New York, Harper, 1959).

Albert Jay Nock, *The Theory of Education in the United States,* 2nd edition (Chicago, Regnery, 1949).

William Kenneth Richmond, *Education in the U.S.A.: A Comparative Study* (New York, Philosophical Library, 1956).

SPECIAL ASPECTS

Frederick Rudolph, *The American College and University: A History* (New York, Knopf, 1962).

Don Shoemaker, ed., *With All Deliberate Speed: Segregation-Desegregation in Southern Schools* (New York, Harper, 1957).

Mortimer Brewster Smith, *The Diminished Mind: A Study of Planned Mediocrity in Our Public Schools* (Chicago, Regnery, 1954).

Russell Brown Thomas, *The Search for a Common Learning: General Education, 1800–1960* (New York, McGraw, 1962).

Thorstein Veblen, *The Higher Learning in America* (New York, Sagamore Press, 1957). Originally published by B. W. Huebsch in 1918.

D · SCIENCE AND TECHNOLOGY

James Phinney Baxter, 3rd, *Scientists Against Time* (Boston, Little-B, 1946).

Roger Burlingame, *Engines of Democracy: Invention and Society in Mature America* (New York, Scribner, 1940).

Roger Burlingame, *Machines That Built America* (New York, Harcourt, 1953).

Vannevar Bush, *Modern Arms and Free Men: A Discussion of the Role of Science in Preserving Democracy* (New York, Simon, 1949).

Vannevar Bush, *Science, the Endless Frontier: A Report to the President* . . . (Washington, Government Printing Office, 1945).

Walter Bradford Cannon, *The Way of an Investigator: A Scientist's Experiences in Medical Research* (New York, Norton, 1945).

I. Bernard Cohen, *Science, Servant of Man: A Layman's Primer for the Age of Science* (Boston, Little-B, 1948).

Arthur Holly Compton, *Atomic Quest: A Personal Narrative* (New York, Oxford, 1956).

Alexander Richard Crabb, *The Hybrid-Corn Makers: Prophets of Plenty* (New Brunswick, Rutgers, 1947).

Anderson Hunter Dupree, *Science in the Federal Government: A History of Policies and Activities to 1940* (Cambridge, Harvard, 1957).

Morris Fishbein, *A History of the American Medical Association, 1847–1947* (Philadelphia, W. B. Saunders Co., 1947).

Donald Harnish Fleming, *William H. Welch and the Rise of Modern Medicine* (Boston, Little-B, 1954).

John Farquhar Fulton, *Harvey Cushing: A Biography* (Springfield, Charles C Thomas, 1946). Historical Library, Yale Medical Library, Publication No. 13.

Sigfried Giedion, *Mechanization Takes Command: A Contribution to Anonymous History* (New York, Oxford, 1948). A study of technology in industry, with special emphasis upon mass production, moving belt lines, interchangeable parts, and so on.

Courtney Robert Hall, *History of American Industrial Science* (New York, Library Publishers, 1954).

Bernard Jaffe, *Men of Science in America: The Role of Science in the Growth of Our Country,* revised edition (New York, Simon, 1958). This account runs from Thomas Hariot of Virginia fame to the astronomer Hubble.

Waldemar Bernhard Kaempffert, ed., *A Popular History of American Invention,* 2 vols. (New York, Scribner, 1924).

Fred Charters Kelly, *The Wright Brothers: A Biography Authorized by Orville Wright* (New York, Harcourt, 1943).

Richard Gordon Lillard, *The Great Forest* (New York, Knopf, 1947). On the utilization of timber resources.

Stephen Finney Mason, *Main Currents of Scientific Thought: A History of the Sciences* (New York, Henry Schuman, 1953). Revised as *A History of the Sciences* (New York, Collier Books, 1962).

McGraw-Hill Encyclopedia of Science and Technology, 15 vols. (New York, McGraw-Hill, 1960). Annual supplements will be found under *McGraw-Hill Yearbook of Science and Technology.*

William Claire Menninger, *Psychiatry in a Troubled World:*

SPECIAL ASPECTS

Yesterday's Wars and Today's Challenge (New York, Macmillan, 1948).

Robert Andrews Millikan, *Autobiography* (New York, Prentice-Hall, 1950). Nobel Prize physicist, Millikan was executive head of the California Institute of Technology from 1921 until 1945. His autobiography discusses the impact of the physical sciences on modern life.

Gardner Murphy, *Historical Introduction to Modern Psychology*, revised edition (New York, Harcourt, 1949).

Paul Henry Oehser, *Sons of Science: The Story of the Smithsonian Institution and Its Leaders* (New York, Henry Schuman, 1949).

John William Oliver, *History of American Technology* (New York, Ronald, 1956).

Don Krasher Price, *Government and Science: Their Dynamic Relation in American Democracy* (New York, New York University Press, 1954).

Henry Goslee Prout, *A Life of George Westinghouse* (New York, Scribner, 1922).

Abraham Aaron Roback, *History of American Psychology* (New York, Library Publishers, 1952).

Henry De Wolf Smyth, *Atomic Energy for Military Purposes* (Princeton, 1946). The official report on the development of the atomic bomb under the auspices of the United States government, 1940–1945.

John William Navin Sullivan, *The Limitations of Science* (New York, New American Library of World Literature, 1949). Originally published in England in 1933.

Holland Thompson, *The Age of Invention: A Chronicle of Mechanical Conquest* (New Haven, Yale, 1921). In the *Chronicles of America* series.

Abbott Payson Usher, *A History of Mechanical Inventions*, revised edition (Cambridge, Harvard, 1954).

Mitchell A. Wilson, *American Science and Invention: A Pictorial History* (New York, Simon, 1954).

Edna Yost, *Modern American Engineers*, revised edition (Philadelphia, Lippincott, 1958).

BACKGROUNDS

Daniel Aaron, ed., *America in Crisis: Fourteen Crucial Episodes in American History* (New York, Knopf, 1952).

Paul Blanshard, *The Right to Read: The Battle Against Censorship* (Boston, Beacon, 1955).

Herbert Brucker, *Freedom of Information* (New York, Macmillan, 1949).

Roger Burlingame, *The American Conscience* (New York, Knopf, 1957).

Oscar Cargill, *Intellectual America: Ideas on the March* (New York, Macmillan, 1941).

Morris Raphael Cohen, *American Thought: A Critical Sketch,* edited by Felix S. Cohen (Glencoe, Illinois, The Free Press, 1954).

Henry Steele Commager, *The American Mind: An Interpretation of American Thought and Character Since the 1880's* (New Haven, Yale, 1950).

(Commission on the Freedom of the Press), *A Free and Responsible Press* (Chicago, University of Chicago Press, 1947).

Kent Cooper, *The Right to Know: An Exposition of the Evils of News Suppression and Propaganda* (New York, Farrar, Straus & Cudahy, 1956).

Harold L. Cross, *The People's Right to Know: Legal Access to Public Records and Proceedings* (New York, Columbia, 1953).

Merle Eugene Curti, *The Growth of American Thought,* 2nd edition (New York, Harper, 1951).

Merle Eugene Curti and others, *American Scholarship in the Twentieth Century* (Cambridge, Harvard, 1953). Part of the *Library of Congress Series in American Civilization.*

Charles Frankel, *The Case for Modern Man* (New York, Harper, 1956).

Ralph Henry Gabriel, *The Course of American Democratic Thought: An Intellectual History Since 1815,* 2nd edition (New York, Ronald, 1956).

Richard David Mosier, *The American Temper: Patterns of Our Intellectual Heritage* (Berkeley, California, 1952).

44

SPECIAL ASPECTS

Reinhold Niebuhr, *The Irony of American History* (New York, Scribner, 1952).

Vernon Louis Parrington, *Main Currents in American Thought: The Beginnings of Critical Realism* (New York, Harcourt, 1930). This is Volume III of the whole work. It is incomplete, being posthumously published.

Stow Persons, ed., *Evolutionary Thought in America* (New Haven, Yale, 1950).

Harry Lionel Shapiro, *Aspects of Culture* (New Brunswick, Rutgers, 1957).

Lionel Trilling, *Freud and the Crisis of Our Culture* (Boston, Beacon, 1955).

1 · *Theories of Politics, History, and Political Trends*

Daniel Aaron, *Men of Good Hope: A Story of American Progressives* (New York, Oxford, 1951).

Alan Barth, *The Loyalty of Free Men* (New York, Viking, 1951).

Daniel Bell, *The End of Ideology: On the Exhaustion of Political Ideas in the Fifties* (Glencoe, Illinois, The Free Press, 1960).

Robert Kenneth Carr, *The House Committee on Un-American Activities, 1945–1950* (Ithaca, Cornell, 1952). One of the *Cornell Studies in Civil Liberty.*

Francis William Coker, *Recent Political Thought* (New York, D. Appleton-Century Co., 1934).

Merle Eugene Curti, *The Roots of American Loyalty* (New York, Columbia, 1946).

Chester McArthur Destler, *American Radicalism, 1865–1901* (New London, Connecticut College, 1946).

Louis Filler, *Crusaders for American Liberalism,* new edition (Yellow Springs, Antioch Press, 1961).

Louis Hartz, *The Liberal Tradition in America: An Interpretation of American Political Thought Since the Revolution* (New York, Harcourt, 1955).

Richard Hofstadter, *The American Political Tradition and the Men Who Made It* (New York, Knopf, 1948).

Michael Kraus, *A History of American History* (New York, Farrar & Rinehart, 1937).

Charles Allan Madison, *Critics and Crusaders: A Century of American Protest*, 2nd edition (New York, Frederick Ungar Publishing Co., 1959).

Robert Green McCloskey, *American Conservatism in the Age of Enterprise: A Study of William Graham Sumner, Stephen Field, and Andrew Carnegie* (Cambridge, Harvard, 1951).

Russel Blaine Nye, *Midwestern Progressive Politics: A Historical Study of Its Origins and Development, 1870–1958*, revised edition (East Lansing, Michigan State University Press, 1959).

John Homer Schaar, *Loyalty in America* (Berkeley, California, 1957).

Mulford Quickert Sibley and Philip E. Jacob, *Conscription of Conscience: The American State and the Conscientious Objector, 1940–1947* (Ithaca, Cornell, 1952). One of the *Cornell Studies in Civil Liberty.*

Samuel Andrew Stouffer, *Communism, Conformity and Civil Liberties: A Cross-Section of the Nation Speaks Its Mind* (New York, Doubleday, 1955).

Benjamin Fletcher Wright, *American Interpretations of Natural Law: A Study in the History of Political Thought* (Cambridge, Harvard, 1931).

2 · *Philosophy*

George Plimpton Adams and William Pepperell Montague, eds., *Contemporary American Philosophy: Personal Statements,* 2 vols. (New York, Macmillan, 1930). Statements of creeds by 34 philosophers.

Robert Nelson Beck, *The Meaning of Americanism: An Essay on the Religious and Philosophical Basis of the American Mind* (New York, Philosophical Library, 1956).

Joseph Leon Blau, *Men and Movements in American Philosophy* (New York, Prentice-Hall, 1952).

Justus Buchler, *The Philosophy of Peirce: Selected Writings* (New York, Harcourt, 1940).

Frederick William Conner, *Cosmic Optimism: A Study of the Interpretation of Evolution by American Poets from Emerson to Robinson* (Gainesville, University of Florida Press, 1949).

SPECIAL ASPECTS

Merle Eugene Curti, *American Paradox: The Conflict of Thought and Action* (New Brunswick, Rutgers, 1956).

Stanley Matthew Daugert, *The Philosophy of Thorstein Veblen* (New York, Columbia, 1950).

Walter B. Gallie, *Peirce and Pragmatism* (Baltimore, Penguin Books, 1952).

Richard Hofstadter, *Social Darwinism in American Thought, 1860–1915* (Philadelphia, University of Pennsylvania Press, 1944).

Karen Horney, *The Neurotic Personality of Our Time* (New York, Norton, 1937).

Howard Mumford Jones, *The Pursuit of Happiness* (Cambridge, Harvard, 1953). An examination of the history and development of an unalienable right.

Horace Meyer Kallen and Sidney Hook, eds., *American Philosophy Today and Tomorrow* (New York, Lee Furman, 1935). Statements by 25 philosophers.

Ralph Barton Perry, *Philosophy of the Recent Past: An Outline of European and American Philosophy Since 1860* (New York, Scribner, 1926).

David Riesman, *Thorstein Veblen: A Critical Interpretation* (New York, Scribner, 1953).

Isaac Woodbridge Riley, *American Thought from Puritanism to Pragmatism and Beyond,* 2nd edition (New York, Holt, 1923).

Herbert Wallace Schneider, *A History of American Philosophy,* 2nd edition (New York, Columbia, 1963). Valuable both as a history and as an anthology of source materials.

John Edwin Smith, *The Spirit of American Philosophy* (New York, Oxford, 1963).

William Henry Werkmeister, *A History of Philosophical Ideas in America* (New York, Ronald, 1949).

Morton Gabriel White, *Social Thought in America: The Revolt Against Formalism* (New York, Viking, 1949). Studies of Beard, Dewey, Holmes, Robinson, Veblen.

Philip Paul Wiener, *Evolution and the Founders of Pragmatism* (Cambridge, Harvard, 1949).

47

Ralph Bubrich Winn, ed., *American Philosophy* (New York, Philosophical Library, 1955).

Albert Benedict Wolfe, *Conservatism, Radicalism and Scientific Method: An Essay on Social Attitudes* (New York, Macmillan, 1923).

3 · Religious History

Aaron Ignatius Abell, *American Catholicism and Social Action: A Search for Social Justice, 1865–1950* (Garden City, Doubleday, 1960).

Aaron Ignatius Abell, *The Urban Impact on American Protestantism, 1865–1900* (Cambridge, Harvard, 1943).

Mathew Ahmann, ed., *Race: Challenge to Religion* (Chicago, Regnery, 1963). Papers delivered at a national conference on race and religion.

Paul Blanshard, *American Freedom and Catholic Power,* 2nd edition (Boston, Beacon, 1958). First published in 1949. See O'Neill, below.

(Bureau of the Census), *Religious Bodies: 1936,* 2 vols. (Washington, Government Printing Office, 1941). The second volume is in two separately bound parts. This publication gives succinct accounts of the history, creeds, activities, and other affairs of all sects and denominations furnishing information, together with supporting statistics. The accounts of creeds are the best brief statements of American religious beliefs anywhere to be found.

For a good working bibliography of the histories of individual religious denominations see Vol. IV of Smith and Jamison, eds., *Religion in American Life,* below.

Elmer Talmadge Clark, *The Small Sects in America,* revised edition (New York, Abingdon-Cokesbury Press, 1949).

Robert Dougherty Cross, *The Emergence of Liberal Catholicism in America* (Cambridge, Harvard, 1958).

John Tracy Ellis, *American Catholicism* (Chicago, University of Chicago Press, 1956).

John Tracy Ellis, *American Catholics and the Intellectual Life* (Chicago, The Heritage Foundation, 1956).

SPECIAL ASPECTS

John Tracy Ellis, *The Life of James Cardinal Gibbons, Archbishop of Baltimore, 1834–1921* (Milwaukee, The Bruce Publishing Co., 1952).

Vergilius Ture Anselm Ferm, ed., *The American Church of the Protestant Heritage* (New York, Philosophical Library, 1953). A series of essays by various authorities, each on a separate denomination.

Frank Hugh Foster, *The Modern Movement in American Theology: Sketches in the History of American Protestant Thought from the Civil War to the World War* (New York, Fleming H. Revell Co., 1939).

Norman F. Furniss, *The Fundamentalist Controversy, 1918–1931* (New Haven, Yale, 1954).

Evarts Boutell Greene, *Religion and the State: The Making and Testing of an American Tradition* (New York, New York University Press, 1941).

Clyde Amos Holbrook, *Religion, A Humanistic Field* (Englewood Cliffs, Prentice-Hall, 1963). Argues the case for religion as a liberal arts study, reappraising the entire field of religious instruction and scholarship.

Charles Howard Hopkins, *History of the Y.M.C.A. in North America* (New York, Association Press, 1951).

Charles Howard Hopkins, *The Rise of the Social Gospel in American Protestantism, 1865–1915* (New Haven, Yale, 1940).

Mark DeWolfe Howe, *Cases on Church and State in the United States* (Cambridge, Harvard, 1952).

Winthrop Still Hudson, *The Great Tradition of the American Churches* (New York, Harper, 1953).

Winthrop Still Hudson, *American Protestantism* (Chicago, University of Chicago Press, 1961).

Gail Kennedy, ed., *Evolution and Religion: The Conflict Between Science and Theology in Modern America* (Boston D. C. Heath & Co., 1957).

Robert Lee, *The Social Sources of Church Unity: An Interpretation of Unitive Movements in American Protestantism* (New York, Abingdon Press, 1960).

Gerhard Emmanuel Lenski, *The Religious Factor: A Sociological*

Study of Religion's Impact on Politics, Economics, and Family Life (New York, Doubleday, 1961).

Martin E. Marty, *The New Shape of American Religion* (New York, Harper, 1959). Described as "a call for a culture ethic for American Protestantism."

Henry Farnham May, *Protestant Churches and Industrial America* (New York, Harper, 1949).

Frederick Emanuel Mayer, *Religious Bodies of America,* revised edition by A. C. Piepkorn (St. Louis, Concordia Publishing House, 1961).

Thomas Timothy McAvoy, *The Great Crisis in American Catholic History, 1895–1900* (Chicago, Regnery, 1957).

William Gerald McLoughlin, *Billy Sunday Was His Real Name* (Chicago, University of Chicago Press, 1955).

William Gerald McLoughlin, *Modern Revivalism* (New York, Ronald, 1959).

Frank Spencer Mead, *Handbook of Denominations in the United States,* 2nd revised edition (New York, Abingdon-Cokesbury Press, 1961).

Ralph Luther Moellering, *Modern War and the American Churches: A Factual Study of the Christian Conscience on Trial from 1939 to the Cold War Crisis of Today* (New York, American Book Co., 1956).

Roy Franklin Nichols, *Religion and American Democracy* (Baton Rouge, Louisiana, 1959).

James Milton O'Neill, *Catholicism and American Freedom* (New York, Harper, 1952). A reply to Blanshard, above.

Walter J. Ong, S.J., *Frontiers in American Catholicism: Essays on Ideology and Culture* (New York, Macmillan, 1957).

Ralph Lord Roy, *Apostles of Discord: A Study of Organized Bigotry and Disruption on the Fringes of Protestantism* (Boston, Beacon, 1953).

Herbert Wallace Schneider, *Religion in 20th Century America* (Cambridge, Harvard, 1952). Part of the *Library of Congress Series in American Civilization.*

James Ward Smith and A. Leland Jamison, eds., *Religion in American Life,* 4 vols. (Princeton, 1961—). An ambitious survey by more than twenty scholars. Vol. II (*Religious*

SPECIAL ASPECTS

Thought and Economic Society, by Jacob Viner) is now (1964) in preparation; Vol. IV (in two parts) is a critical bibliography, prepared by Nelson R. Burr.

Willard Learoyd Sperry, *Religion in America* (New York, Macmillan, 1946). Written for a British public, this book gives an excellent brief account of American churches and American church life.

Anson Phelps Stokes, *Church and State in the United States,* 3 vols. (New York, Harper, 1950).

William Warren Sweet, *The American Churches: An Interpretation* (New York, Abingdon-Cokesbury Press, 1948).

William Warren Sweet, *American Culture and Religion: Six Essays* (Dallas, Southern Methodist University Press, 1951). On religious traditions in the United States.

William Warren Sweet, *The Story of Religion in America,* 2nd revised edition (New York, Harper, 1950).

Kenneth Wilson Underwood, *Protestant and Catholic: Religious and Social Interaction in an Industrial Community* (Boston, Beacon, 1957).

Elizabeth Gray Vining, *Friend of Life: The Biography of Rufus M. Jones* (Philadelphia, Lippincott, 1958). Concerns the Quakers.

Edward Arthur White, *Science and Religion in American Thought: The Impact of Naturalism* (Stanford, Stanford University Press, 1952). In the Stanford University series in *History, Economics and Political Science,* Vol. VIII.

Amos Niven Wilder, *Theology and Modern Literature* (Cambridge, Harvard, 1958).

F · THE FINE ARTS

John Ireland Howe Baur, *Revolution and Tradition in Modern American Art* (Cambridge, Harvard, 1951). Part of the *Library of Congress Series in American Civilization.*

Sheldon Cheney, *A Primer of Modern Art,* 13th edition, revised and enlarged (New York, Liveright Publishing Corp., 1958).

Erwin Ottomar Christensen, *The Index of American Design* (New York, Macmillan, 1950).

Marshall Bowman Davidson, *Life in America*, 2 vols. (Boston, Houghton, 1951).

Sigfried Giedion, *Space, Time and Architecture: The Growth of a New Tradition*, 4th edition, enlarged (Cambridge, Harvard, 1962).

Henry James, *The Painter's Eye: Notes and Essays on the Pictorial Arts* (Cambridge, Harvard, 1956). A collection of thirty pieces, 1868–1897, edited by John L. Sweeney.

John Atlee Kouwenhoven, *Made in America: The Arts in Modern Civilization* (Garden City, Doubleday, 1948).

Suzanne LaFollette, *Art in America from Colonial Times to the Present Day* (New York, Norton, 1929).

Oliver Waterman Larkin, *Art and Life in America*, revised and enlarged edition (New York, Rinehart & Co., 1960). Valuable among other matters for its bibliography.

Lewis Mumford, *The Brown Decades: A Study of the Arts in America, 1865–1895* (New York, Harcourt, 1931). Revised in 1955.

Lewis Mumford, *Sticks and Stones: A Study of American Architecture and Civilization* (New York, Boni and Liveright, 1924). On the interrelation of the arts, particularly architecture and culture. Revised in 1955.

Ralph Purcell, *Government and Art: A Study of American Experience* (Washington, Public Affairs Press, 1956).

Ben Shahn, *The Shape of Content* (Cambridge, Harvard, 1957). The Charles Eliot Norton Lectures.

1 · *Architecture*

Wayne Andrews, *Architecture, Ambition and Americans: A History of American Architecture* (New York, Harper, 1955).

Wayne Andrews, *Architecture in America: A Photographic History from the Colonial Period to the Present* (New York, Atheneum Publishers, 1960). A brief but impressive survey.

Kenneth John Conant, *Tres Conferencias sobra Arquitectura Moderna en los Estados Unidos* (Buenos Aires, Universidad de Buenos Aires, 1949).

SPECIAL ASPECTS

Carl Wilbur Condit, *The Rise of the Skyscraper* (Chicago, University of Chicago Press, 1952).

Carl Wilbur Condit, *American Building Art: The Nineteenth Century* (New York, Oxford, 1960). A comprehensive history of structural forms and techniques, followed the next year by a companion volume, *American Building Art: The Twentieth Century.*

Ralph Adams Cram, *My Life in Architecture* (Boston, Little-B, 1936).

Thomas Hawk Creighton, ed., *Building for Modern Man* (Princeton, 1949). A symposium on planning man's physical environment.

Finis Farr, *Frank Lloyd Wright: A Biography* (New York, Scribner, 1961).

James Marston Fitch, *American Building: The Forces That Shape It* (Boston, Houghton, 1948).

James Marston Fitch, *Architecture and the Esthetics of Plenty* (New York, Columbia, 1961).

Talbot Faulkner Hamlin, *The American Spirit in Architecture* (New Haven, Yale, 1926). In the *Pageant of America* series.

Talbot Faulkner Hamlin, *Forms and Functions of Twentieth-Century Architecture,* 4 vols. (New York, Columbia, 1952).

Sidney Fiske Kimball, *American Architecture* (Indianapolis, Bobbs, 1928).

Ian McCallum, *Architecture U.S.A.* (New York, Reinhold Publishing Corp., 1959). An excellent survey of contemporary architects.

Richard Joseph Neutra, *Survival Through Design* (New York, Oxford, 1954).

Sherman Paul, *Louis Sullivan: An Architect in American Thought* (Englewood Cliffs, Prentice-Hall, 1962).

Montgomery Schuyler, *American Architecture and Other Writings,* 2 vols., edited by William H. Jordy and Ralph Coe (Cambridge, Harvard, 1961).

Louis Henry Sullivan, *The Autobiography of an Idea* (New York, Press of the American Institute of Architects, 1924). Republished in 1949 in New York by Peter Smith, in 1956 by Dover Publications.

John Szarkowski, *The Idea of Louis Sullivan* (Minneapolis, Minnesota, 1956).

Thomas Eddy Tallmadge, *The Story of Architecture in America,* new enlarged and revised edition (New York, Norton, 1936).

Christopher Tunnard and Henry Hope Reed, *American Skyline: The Growth and Form of Our Cities and Towns* (Boston, Houghton, 1955).

Frank Lloyd Wright, *An American Architecture* (New York, Horizon Press, 1955).

Frank Lloyd Wright, *An Autobiography,* revised edition (New York, Duell, Sloan & Pearce, 1943).

2 · Sculpture

Charles Henry Caffin, *American Masters of Sculpture* (New York, Doubleday, Page and Co., 1903).

Chandler Rathfon Post, *A History of European and American Sculpture: From the Early Christian Period to the Present Day,* 2 vols. (Cambridge, Harvard, 1921).

Jacques Preston Schnier, *Sculpture in Modern America* (Berkeley, California, 1948).

Lorado Taft, *The History of American Sculpture,* new edition with supplementary chapter by Adeline Adams (New York, Macmillan, 1930).

3 · Painting

Virgil Barker, *American Painting: History and Interpretation* (New York, Macmillan, 1950).

Wolfgang Born, *Still-Life Painting in America: An Interpretation* (New York, Oxford, 1947).

Wolfgang Born, *American Landscape Painting* (New Haven, Yale, 1948).

Alan Burroughs, *Limners and Likenesses: Three Centuries of American Painting* (Cambridge, Harvard, 1936).

54

SPECIAL ASPECTS

Holger Cahill and Alfred Hamilton Barr, Jr., eds., *Art in America, A Complete Survey* (New York, Reynal and Hitchcock, 1935).

Oskar Frank Leonard Hagen, *The Birth of the American Tradition in Art* (New York, Scribner, 1940). Although principally confined to Colonial painting, some of the ideas analyzed have present meaning.

Sadakichi Hartmann, *A History of American Art*, 2 vols., revised edition (Boston, L. C. Page and Co., 1932).

Daniel Marcus Mendelowitz, *A History of American Art* (New York, Holt, Rinehart & Winston, 1960).

4 · Music

Whitney Balliett, *Dinosaurs in the Morning: 41 Pieces on Jazz* (Philadelphia, Lippincott, 1962).

Jacques Barzun, *Music in American Life* (New York, Doubleday, 1956).

Rudi Blesh and Harriet Janis (Grossman), *They All Played Ragtime: The True Story of an American Music* (New York, Knopf, 1950).

Rudi Blesh, *Shining Trumpets: A History of Jazz*, 2nd edition, revised and enlarged (New York, Knopf, 1958).

Samuel Barclay Charters and Leonard Kunstadt, *Jazz: A History of the New York Scene* (Garden City, Doubleday, 1962).

Gilbert Chase, *America's Music: From the Pilgrims to the Present* (New York, McGraw, 1955).

Henry and Sidney Cowell, *Charles Ives and His Music* (New York, Oxford, 1955).

Louis Charles Elson, *The History of American Music,* revised by Arthur Elson (New York, Macmillan, 1925).

John Tasker Howard and Arthur Mendel, *Our Contemporary Composers: American Music in the Twentieth Century* (New York, Crowell, 1941).

John Tasker Howard and George Kent Bellows, *A Short History of Music in America* (New York, Crowell, 1957).

Paul Henry Lang, *Music in Western Civilization* (New York, Norton, 1941).

Neil Leonard, *Jazz and the White Americans: The Acceptance of a New Art Form* (Chicago, University of Chicago Press, 1962).

Joseph Machlis, *An Introduction to Contemporary Music* (New York, Norton, 1961). About one-third of the book is devoted to American composers.

Edward Bennett Marks, *They All Sang: From Tony Pastor to Rudy Vallée* (New York, Viking, 1934).

John Henry Mueller, *The American Symphony Orchestra: A Social History of Musical Taste* (Bloomington, Indiana University Press, 1951).

Nat Shapiro and Nat Hentoff, eds., *The Jazz Makers* (New York, Rinehart & Co., 1957).

Nicolas Slonimsky, *Music Since 1900*, 3rd edition, revised and enlarged (New York, Coleman-Ross Co., 1949).

Marshall Winslow Stearns, *The Story of Jazz* (New York, Oxford, 1956).

Oscar Thompson, *The American Singer: A Hundred Years of Success in Opera* (New York, The Dial Press, 1937).

Oscar Thompson, ed., *The International Cyclopedia of Music and Musicians*, 7th edition, revised by Nicolas Slonimsky (New York, Dodd, Mead & Co., 1956). Note the bibliography in the appendix.

Barry Ulanov, *A History of Jazz in America* (New York, Viking, 1952).

Barry Ulanov, *A Handbook of Jazz* (New York, Viking, 1957).

5 · *The Modern Spirit (Exclusive of Literary Criticism)*

John Ireland Howe Baur, ed., *New Art in America: Fifty Painters of the 20th Century* (New York, Frederick A. Praeger, 1957).

George Biddle, *The Yes and No of Contemporary Art: An Artist's Evaluation* (Cambridge, Harvard, 1957).

Rudi Blesh, *Modern Art USA: Men, Rebellion, Conquest, 1900–1956* (New York, Knopf, 1956).

Milton Wolf Brown, *American Painting: From the Armory Show to the Depression* (Princeton, 1955).

SPECIAL ASPECTS

C. Ludwig Brumme, *Contemporary American Sculpture* (New York, Crown Publishers, 1948).

Martha Candler Cheney, *Modern Art in America* (New York, McGraw, 1939).

Sheldon Cheney, *Expressionism in Art,* revised edition (New York, Tudor Publishing Co., 1948).

Sheldon Cheney, *A Primer of Modern Art,* 11th edition, revised and enlarged (New York, Tudor Publishing Co., 1945).

Solomon Fishman, *The Disinherited of Art: Writer and Background* (Berkeley, California, 1953).

Carola Giedion-Welcker, *Contemporary Sculpture: An Evolution in Volume and Space,* revised and enlarged edition (New York, George Wittenborn, 1960). Contains a selective bibliography by Bernard Karpel.

Lloyd Goodrich and John Ireland Howe Baur, *American Art of Our Century* (New York, Frederick A. Praeger, 1961).

Henry Russell Hitchcock, *Modern Architecture: Romanticism and Reintegration* (New York, Payson & Clarke, 1929).

Sam Hunter, *Modern American Painting and Sculpture* (New York, Dell Publishing Co., 1959). A brief survey, paperbound.

Samuel Melvin Kootz, *Modern American Painters* (New York, Brewer & Warren, 1930).

Lewis Mumford, *From the Ground Up: Observations on Contemporary Architecture, Housing, Highway Building and Civic Design* (New York, Harcourt, 1956).

Walter Pach, *The Masters of Modern Art* (New York, B. W. Huebsch, 1924).

John Peter, *Masters of Modern Architecture* (New York, George Braziller, 1958).

Nathaniel Poussette-Dart, ed., *American Painting Today* (New York, Hastings House, 1956).

Mary Chalmers Rathbun and Bartlett H. Hayes, Jr., *Layman's Guide to Modern Art: Painting for a Scientific Age* (New York, Oxford, 1949).

Andrew Carnduff Ritchie, *Abstract Painting and Sculpture in America* (New York, Museum of Modern Art, 1951).

James Thrall Soby, *Modern Art and the New Past* (Norman, Oklahoma, 1957).

Allen S. Weller, *Contemporary American Painting and Sculpture* (Urbana, Illinois, 1963).

G · THE POPULAR ARTS

Erik Barnouw, *Mass Communication: Television, Radio, Film, Press: The Media and Their Practice in the United States of America* (New York, Rinehart & Co., 1956).

Reuel Denney, *The Astonished Muse* (Chicago, University of Chicago Press, 1957).

John Kouwenhoven, *Made in America: The Arts in Modern Civilization* (New York, Doubleday, 1962).

Jean Herzberg Lipman, *American Folk Art in Wood, Metal and Stone* (New York, Pantheon Books, 1948).

Jean Herzberg Lipman, *American Primitive Painting* (New York, Oxford, 1942).

Harry Allen Overstreet, *The Mature Mind* (New York, Norton, 1949). A study of the relation between mass media and adult infantilism.

Posters in Miniature: With an Introduction by Edward Penfield (New York, R. H. Russell, 1897).

Bernard Rosenberg and David Manning White, eds., *Mass Culture: The Popular Arts in America* (Glencoe, Illinois, The Free Press, 1957). Contains excellent bibliographies.

Gilbert Vivian Seldes, *The Great Audience* (New York, Viking, 1950).

Gilbert Vivian Seldes, *The Public Arts* (New York, Simon, 1956).

Gilbert Vivian Seldes, *The Seven Lively Arts* (New York, Harper, 1924). Reprinted in 1957 by Thomas Yoseloff.

Geoffrey Wagner, *Parade of Pleasure: A Study of Popular Iconography in the U.S.A.* (New York, Library Publishers, 1955).

Robert Warshow, *The Immediate Experience: Movies, Comics, Theatre, and Other Aspects of Popular Culture* (Garden City, Doubleday, 1962). At the time of his death at the age of 38,

Warshow was a highly respected critic writing for *Commentary*.

Frank Weitenkampf, *American Graphic Art*, new edition, revised and enlarged (New York, Macmillan, 1924).

1 · Photography and the Movies

Andreas Feininger, *Feininger on Photography* (Chicago, Ziff-Davis Publishing Co., 1949).

Waldo Frank and others, eds., *America and Alfred Stieglitz: A Collective Portrait* (New York, The Literary Guild, 1934).

Nancy Newhall, *The Photographs of Edward Weston* (New York, The Museum of Modern Art, 1946).

Edward Steichen, *A Life in Photography* (Garden City, Doubleday, 1963).

John Szarkowski, ed., *The Photographer and the American Landscape* (New York, The Museum of Modern Art, 1963).

Edward Weston, *My Camera on Point Lobos: 30 Photographs and Excerpts from Edward Weston's Daybook* (Boston, Houghton, 1950).

James Agee, *Agee on Film: Reviews and Comments* (New York, McDowell, Obolensky, 1958). Considered to be the most perceptive critic of his time, Agee wrote for *The Nation* (1942–1948) and *Time* (1941–1948). He died in 1955.

Maurice Bardèche and Robert Brasillach, *The History of Motion Pictures*, translated by Iris Barry (New York, Norton, 1938).

Bosley Crowther, *The Lion's Share: The Story of an Entertainment Empire* (New York, E. P. Dutton & Co., 1957). A history of M-G-M.

Bosley Crowther, *Hollywood Rajah: The Life and Times of Louis B. Mayer* (New York, Holt, 1960).

George N. Fenin and William K. Everson, *The Western: From Silents to Cinerama* (New York, Orion Press, 1962).

Albert Rondthaler Fulton, *Motion Pictures: The Development of an Art from Silent Films to the Age of Television* (Norman, Oklahoma, 1960).

Richard Griffith and Arthur Mayer, *The Movies: The Sixty-Year*

Story of the World of Hollywood and Its Effect on America (New York, Simon, 1957). Generously illustrated.

Ruth A. Inglis, *Freedom of the Movies* (Chicago, University of Chicago Press, 1947). A publication of the Commission on the Freedom of the Press.

Lewis Jacobs, *The Rise of the American Film: A Critical History* (New York, Harcourt, 1939).

Arthur Knight, *The Liveliest Art: A Panoramic History of the Movies* (New York, Macmillan, 1957). A good brief survey, with a useful bibliography appended.

Ben Jehudah Lubschez, *The Story of the Motion Picture, 65. B.C. to 1920 A.D.* (New York, Reeland Publishing Co., 1920).

John Montgomery, *Comedy Films* (London, George Allen and Unwin, 1954). European as well as American comedy.

Hortense Powdermaker, *Hollywood, the Dream Factory: An Anthropologist Looks at the Movie-Makers* (Boston, Little-B, 1950).

Margaret Farrand Thorp, *America at the Movies* (New Haven, Yale, 1939).

Parker Tyler, *The Hollywood Hallucination* (New York, Creative Age Press, 1944).

Parker Tyler, *Magic and Myth of the Movies* (New York, Holt, 1947). Highly personal criticism.

Parker Tyler, *The Three Faces of the Film* (New York, Thomas Yoseloff, 1960).

Martha Wolfenstein and Nathan Leites, *Movies: A Psychological Study* (Glencoe, Illinois, The Free Press, 1950).

2 · *Radio, Television, Records*

The American Radio: A Report on the Broadcasting Industry in the United States, from the Commission on Freedom of the Press (Chicago, University of Chicago Press, 1947).

Gleason Leonard Archer, *Big Business and Radio* (New York, The American Historical Company, 1939).

Leo Bogart, *The Age of Television: A Study of Viewing Habits and the Impact of Television on American Life* (New York, Frederick Ungar Publishing Co., 1956).

Hadley Cantril, *The Invasion from Mars: A Study in the Psychology of Panic* (Princeton, 1940). The sociological and psychological repercussions resulting from Orson Welles' broadcast of an imaginary invasion from Mars.

Francis Seabury Chase, *Sound and Fury: An Informal History of Broadcasting* (New York, Harper, 1942).

Giraud Chester and Garnet R. Garrison, *Television and Radio: An Introduction*, 2nd edition (New York, D. Appleton and Co., 1956). First published as *Radio and Television*.

John Crosby, *Out of the Blue: A Book About Radio and Television* (New York, Simon, 1952). By a former newspaper critic.

Roland Gelatt, *The Fabulous Phonograph: From Tin Foil to High Fidelity* (Philadelphia, Lippincott, 1955).

Paul Lazarsfeld, *The People Look at Radio: Report on a Survey Conducted by the National Opinion Research Center . . . and Interpreted . . .* (Chapel Hill, North Carolina, 1946).

Paul Lazarsfeld, *Radio and the Printed Page: An Introduction to the Study of Radio and Its Role in the Communication of Ideas* (New York, Duell, Sloan & Pearce, 1940).

William F. Lynch, S.J., *The Image Industries* (New York, Sheed & Ward, 1959).

Herbert L. Marx, ed., *Television and Radio in American Life* (New York, H. W. Wilson Co., 1953).

Robert Lewis Shayon, *Television and Our Children* (New York, Longmans, Green & Co., 1951).

Charles Arthur Siepmann, *Radio's Second Chance* (Boston, Little-B, 1946). The second chance is FM.

Judith Cary Waller, *Radio, the Fifth Estate* (Boston, Houghton, 1946).

Max Wylie, *Clear Channels: Television and the American People* (New York, Funk & Wagnalls Co., 1955).

3 · Cartoons and Comic Strips

Stephen Becker, *Comic Art in America: A Social History of the Funnies, the Political Cartoons, Magazine Humor, Sporting Cartoons, and Animated Cartoons* (New York, Simon, 1959).

The Best of Art Young. With an Introduction by Heywood Broun (New York, Vanguard Press, 1936).

Herbert Block, *Herblock's Here and Now* (New York, Simon, 1955). One of America's best political cartoonists, Block followed this collection with *Herblock's Special for Today* (New York, Simon, 1958).

Jules Feiffer, *Feiffer's Album* (New York, Random, 1963). Social satire.

Walt Kelly, *Ten Ever-Lovin' Blue-Eyed Years with Pogo* (New York, Simon, 1959). Social satire.

Bill Mauldin, *Up Front* (New York, Holt, 1945). Mauldin made his reputation in *Stars and Stripes* during World War II. *Back Home* (New York, William Sloane Associates, 1947), was followed by *A Sort of a Saga* (New York, William Sloane Associates, 1949). He now draws political and social satire, collected in *What's Got Your Back Up?* (New York, Harper, 1961).

William Murrell, *A History of American Graphic Humor*, 2 vols. (New York, Whitney Museum of American Art, 1933–1938).

Martin Sheridan, *Comics and Their Creators* (Boston, Hale, Cushman & Flint, 1942).

Coulton Waugh, *The Comics* (New York, Macmillan, 1947).

Frederic Wertham, *Seduction of the Innocent* (New York, Rinehart & Co., 1954).

David Manning White and Robert H. Abel, eds., *The Funnies: An American Idiom* (Glencoe, Illinois, The Free Press, 1963).

Gluyas Williams, *The Gluyas Williams Gallery* (New York, Harper, 1957).

6 2

V · LITERARY HISTORY

A · GENERAL WORKS

Victor Francis Calverton, *The Liberation of American Literature* (New York, Scribner, 1932). Marxist in approach.

Marcus Cunliffe, *The Literature of the United States* (Baltimore, Penguin Books, 1954). A survey by an English historian.

James David Hart, *The Popular Book: A History of America's Literary Taste* (New York, Oxford, 1950).

Granville Hicks, *The Great Tradition: An Interpretation of American Literature Since the Civil War,* revised edition (New York, Macmillan, 1935). A Marxist approach.

Rod William Horton and Herbert W. Edwards, *Backgrounds of American Literature* (New York, Appleton-Century-Crofts, 1952).

Frank Luther Mott, *Golden Multitudes* (New York, Macmillan, 1947). A history of best-sellers.

Fred Lewis Pattee, *A History of American Literature Since 1870* (New York, The Century Co., 1915). A pioneer volume. Concludes with 1910.

Fred Lewis Pattee, *The New American Literature, 1890–1930* (New York, The Century Co., 1930). Overlaps and continues its predecessor.

Arthur Hobson Quinn, with Kenneth B. Murdock, Clarence Gohdes, and George F. Whicher, *The Literature of the American People: An Historical and Critical Survey* (New York, Appleton-Century-Crofts, 1951).

Robert Ernest Spiller, Willard Thorp, Thomas H. Johnson, Henry Seidel Canby, and Richard M. Ludwig, eds., *Literary History of the United States,* 2 vols., 3rd edition revised (New York, Macmillan, 1963). This composite work was originally published in three volumes in 1948, followed by a bibliographical supplement in 1959. The four volumes have been republished in two.

Heinrich Straumann, *American Literature in the Twentieth Century* (London, Hutchinson House, 1951). This work by a Swiss scholar is an excellent one-volume survey of American literature in the first half of the twentieth century.

Walter Fuller Taylor, *The Story of American Letters*, revised edition (Chicago, Regnery, 1956). Originally published as *A History of American Letters*, 1936, with a valuable bibliography.

Willard Thorp, *American Writing in the Twentieth Century* (Cambridge, Harvard, 1960). Part of the *Library of Congress Series in American Civilization*.

William Peterfield Trent, John Erskine, Stuart Pratt Sherman, and Carl Van Doren, eds., *The Cambridge History of American Literature*, 3 vols. in 4 (New York, G. P. Putnam's Sons, 1917–1921). Though superseded by the *Literary History of the United States*, the work has value, especially in its orderly bibliographies. A *Short History of American Literature* in one volume, based on the larger work, was published in 1922.

B · GENERAL REFERENCE WORKS

1 · *"Closed" Bibliographies*

Janet Margaret Agnew, *A Southern Bibliography: Fiction, Historical Fiction, Poetry, Biography* (Baton Rouge, University Bulletin of the Louisiana State University, Vol. 31, n.s., no. 7; Vol. 32, n.s., no. 8 and no. 11; Vol. 34, n.s., no. 7, 1939–1942).

Jacob Nathaniel Blanck, *Bibliography of American Literature*, Vol. I, Adams to Byrne, 1955; Vol. II, Cable to Dwight, 1957; Vol. III, Eggleston to Harte, 1959; Vol. IV, Hawthorne to Ingraham, 1963 (New Haven, Yale, 1955—).

A. T. Dickinson, Jr., *American Historical Fiction*, 2nd edition (New York, Scarecrow Press, 1963). Almost 2,000 titles classified into periods of American history from Colonial times to 1962.

Clarence Gohdes, *Bibliographical Guide to the Study of the Literature of the U.S.A.*, 2nd edition (Durham, Duke University Press, 1963). Provides "lists of books which will aid the professional student of the literature of the United States in the acquiring of information and in the techniques of research."

James David Hart, *The Oxford Companion to American Literature,* 3rd edition, revised and enlarged (New York, Oxford, 1956).

Max John Herzberg, ed., *The Reader's Encyclopedia of American Literature* (New York, Crowell, 1962).

Merle Johnson, *American First Editions,* 4th edition, revised and enlarged by Jacob Nathaniel Blanck (New York, Bowker, 1942).

Stanley Jasspon Kunitz and Howard Haycraft, *American Authors, 1600–1900: A Biographical Dictionary of American Literature* (New York, H. W. Wilson Co., 1938).

Stanley Jasspon Kunitz and Howard Haycraft, *Twentieth Century Authors: A Biographical Dictionary of Modern Literature* (New York, H. W. Wilson Co., 1942). Supersedes *Living Authors* (1931) and *Authors Today and Yesterday* (1933). In 1955 a *First Supplement* was issued under the editorial charge of Vineta Colby.

Lewis Leary, *Articles on American Literature, 1900–1950* (Durham, Duke University Press, 1954). This replaces an earlier edition (1947) covering the years 1920–1945. Supplemented by *Index to Articles on American Literature, 1951–1959, Prepared in the Reference Department of the University of Pennsylvania Library* (Boston, G. K. Hall, 1960). This volume may contain errors and omissions since it was merely assembled from the quarterly bibliographies appearing in *American Literature* and has not been checked.

Lewis Leary, ed., *Contemporary Literary Scholarship: A Critical Review* (New York, Appleton-Century-Crofts, 1958). Chapter 11 and parts of Chapters 12–15 concern modern American literature.

Richard Gordon Lillard, *American Life in Autobiography: A Descriptive Guide* (Stanford, Stanford University Press, 1956).

Fred Benjamin Millett, *Contemporary American Authors: A Critical Survey and 219 Bio-bibliographies* (New York, Harcourt, 1940).

Union List of Little Magazines (Chicago, Mid-West Inter-Library Center, 1956). This is an index of holdings in certain Midwestern libraries only.

James Leslie Woodress, *Dissertations in American Literature, 1891–1955, with Supplement, 1956–1961* (Durham, Duke University Press, 1962).

The following titles, originally "open" or continuing bibliographies, have become "closed" through cessation of publication:

The American Catalogue of Books (New York, 1880–1911). This may be found in various forms of binding and volume. In general it runs to 21 vols., bound as 15, and is the "national trade bibliography" of books for the years covered. In 1941 it was reissued. Today its place is taken by *The United States Catalog: Books in Print,* for which see below.

The American Year Book (New York, 1911–1919, 1925–1951). Contained among other matter an annual survey of American literature.

The Annual Library Index (New York, The Publishers' Weekly, 1906–1911). Covers the years 1905–1910.

The Annual Literary Index (New York, The Publishers' Weekly, 1893–1905). Covers the years 1892–1904.

Appleton's Annual Cyclopaedia and Register of Important Events (New York, D. Appleton and Co., 1876–1903). Vols. 1–15 cover the years 1861–1875; vols. 16–35 (also known as n.s. vols. 1–20) cover the years 1876–1895; vols. 36–42 (also known as 3rd s. vols. 1–7) cover the years 1896–1902. There are various indexes, e.g., the index for the years 1876–1893 is in the 1893 volume.

2 · *"Open" or Continuing Guides*

The Americana Annual: An Encyclopedia of Current Events (New York, 1923—). Useful for its annual survey of American literature.

The Book Review Digest (Minneapolis, H. W. Wilson Co., 1905—). The publishing address was later New York. This began as *The Cumulative Book Review Digest.*

Books in Print (New York, Bowker, 1948—). Issued annually.

Britannica Book of the Year (Chicago, 1938—). Contains among other matter an annual survey of American literature.

66

(U.S. Copyright Office), *Catalogue of Copyright Entries* (Washington, Government Printing Office, July 1, 1891—). Issued monthly or quarterly.

Cumulative Book Index (Minneapolis, H. W. Wilson Co., 1898—). Later issued from New York. This lists all books by American publishers. It appears monthly and is cumulated quarterly, semiannually, and annually, and finally becomes *The United States Catalog: Books in Print,* for which see below.

Literary Market Place (New York, Bowker, 1940—). An annual business directory of American book publishing.

New International Yearbook (New York, 1908—). This is a successor to *International Yearbook 1899–1903,* published by Dodd, Mead & Co., in New York and covering the years 1898–1902. Each number contains a survey of American literature for the year. This annual should not be confused with the *International Year Book and Statesmen's Who's Who,* published in London beginning in 1955.

Paperbound Books in Print (New York, Bowker, 1955—).

PMLA, Supplement (New York, 1923—). This contains an annual bibliography of scholarly investigation in American literature, beginning with 1922. See also *American Literature* in this guide under VI. Critical List of Magazines, below.

Publishers' Weekly (New York, 1872—). Weekly. Each issue lists books just published, and the last issue in January gives the statistics of book production for the previous year. There are also quarterly "Announcement Numbers."

Readers' Guide to Periodical Literature (New York, 1900—). Continues and supplements *Poole's Index to Periodical Literature* (New York), founded in 1848, which with various supplements and revisions lasted until 1908.

Union List of Serials in Libraries of the United States and Canada, 2nd edition (New York, 1943). There were supplements in 1945, 1949, and 1953. In 1956 was issued *New Serial Titles: A Union List of Serials Commencing Publication after December 31, 1949* (Washington, Library of Congress, 1956). A ten-year gathering, *New Serial Titles, 1950–1960,* 2 vols., was published in 1961.

The United States Catalog: Books in Print (New York, 1899—).

Variously bound. This series should be distinguished from *Books in Print,* listed above, which is compounded from publishers' catalogues.

C · LITERARY HISTORIES OF SPECIALIZED SCOPE

Henry Mills Alden, *Magazine Writing and the New Literature* (New York, Harper, 1908).

John Watson Aldridge, *After the Lost Generation: A Critical Study of the Writers of Two Wars* (New York, McGraw, 1951).

John Watson Aldridge, *In Search of Heresy: American Literature in an Age of Conformity* (New York, McGraw, 1956).

Allan Angoff, ed., *American Writing Today: Its Independence and Vigor* (New York, New York University Press, 1957). Essays which made up the special number of the *Times Literary Supplement* (London) published September 17, 1954.

Walter Blair, *Horse Sense in American Humor, from Benjamin Franklin to Ogden Nash* (Chicago, University of Chicago Press, 1942).

John Mason Bradbury, *Renaissance in the South: A Critical History of the Literature, 1920–1960* (Chapel Hill, North Carolina, 1963).

Van Wyck Brooks, *America's Coming of Age* (New York, B. W. Huebsch, 1915). A study of the movement of revolt leading into the 1920's.

Van Wyck Brooks, *The Confident Years: 1885–1915* (New York, E. P. Dutton & Co., 1952). Volume V in Brooks' personalized survey of American literature.

Irene and Allen Cleaton, *Books and Battles: American Literature 1920–1930* (Boston, Houghton, 1937).

Malcolm Cowley, ed., *After the Genteel Tradition: American Writers Since 1910* (New York, Norton, 1937). A group of interpretative essays.

Malcolm Cowley, *The Literary Situation* (New York, Viking, 1954). Conceived of as "a social history of literature in our times."

68

James Frank Dobie, *Guide to Life and Literature of the South-west*, revised edition (Dallas, Southern Methodist University Press, 1952).

Bernard Ingersoll Duffey, *The Chicago Renaissance in American Letters: A Critical History* (East Lansing, Michigan State University Press, 1954).

Joseph Freeman, *An American Testament: A Narrative of Rebels and Romantics* (New York, Farrar & Rinehart, 1936).

Frederick John Hoffman, *The Twenties: American Writing in the Post-War Decade* (New York, Viking, 1955).

Jay Broadus Hubbell, *The South in American Literature, 1607–1900* (Durham, Duke University Press, 1954).

Howard Mumford Jones, *The Bright Medusa* (Urbana, Illinois, 1952). A study of the movements leading into the 1920's.

Howard Mumford Jones, *The Theory of American Literature* (Ithaca, Cornell, 1948).

Sten Bodvar Liljegren, *The Revolt Against Romanticism in American Literature as Evidenced in the Work of Samuel Langhorne Clemens. Essays and Studies in American Language and Literature*, I (Upsala, Sweden, The American Institute in the University of Upsala, 1945). The scope of this study transcends Mark Twain.

Halford Edward Luccock, *American Mirror: Social, Ethical, and Religious Aspects of American Literature, 1930–1940* (New York, Macmillan, 1940).

John Albert Macy, *The Spirit of American Literature* (New York, Boni and Liveright, 1918). This pioneer work was later available for some time in The Modern Library.

Percival Pollard, *Their Day in Court* (Washington, The Neale Publishing Co., 1909). An early example of "revolt."

Louis Decimus Rubin and Robert Durene Jacobs, eds., *Southern Renascence: The Literature of the Modern South* (Baltimore, Johns Hopkins, 1953).

Louis Decimus Rubin and Robert Durene Jacobs, eds., *South: Modern Southern Literature in Its Cultural Settings* (Garden City, Doubleday, 1961).

Franklin Walker, *A Literary History of Southern California* (Berkeley, California, 1950).

Edmund Wilson, *Classics and Commercials: A Literary Chronicle of the Forties* (New York, Farrar & Straus, 1950).

Edmund Wilson, *The Shores of Light: A Literary Chronicle of the Twenties and Thirties* (New York, Farrar, Straus & Young, 1952). This interpretative work considers more than the decades enumerated.

D · SPECIAL THEMES

John Mason Bradbury, *The Fugitives: A Critical Account* (Chapel Hill, North Carolina, 1958).

Benjamin Griffith Brawley, *The Negro in Literature and Art in the United States* (New York, Duffield & Co., 1929).

Edwin Harrison Cady, *The Gentleman in America: A Literary Study in American Culture* (Syracuse, Syracuse University Press, 1949).

Frederic Ives Carpenter, *American Literature and the Dream* (New York, Philosophical Library, 1955).

Frank Pierce Donovan, Jr., *The Railroad in Literature: A Brief Survey of Railroad Fiction . . . Particularly Emphasizing Its Place in American Literature* (Boston, Baker Library, Harvard Business School, 1940). Published for The Railway and Locomotive Society.

Richard Allen Foster, *The School in American Literature* (Baltimore, Warwick and York, 1930).

Marjorie Latta Barstow Greenbie, *American Saga: The History and Literature of the American Dream of a Better Life* (New York, McGraw, 1939).

Harry Hansen, *Midwest Portraits: A Book of Memories and Friendships* (New York, Harcourt, 1923).

Ima Honaker Herron, *The Small Town in American Literature* (Durham, Duke University Press, 1939).

Howard William Hintz, *The Quaker Influence in American Literature* (New York, Fleming H. Revell Co., 1940).

Frederick John Hoffman, *Freudianism and the Literary Mind*, 2nd edition (Baton Rouge, Louisiana, 1957).

Vernon Loggins, *The Negro Author: His Development in America* (New York, Columbia, 1931).

Halford Edward Luccock, *Contemporary American Literature and Religion* (Chicago, Willet, Clark and Co., 1934).

Joseph Mersand, *Traditions in American Literature: A Study of Jewish Characters and Authors* (Brooklyn, The Modern Chapbooks, 1939).

Albert Parry, *Garrets and Pretenders: A History of Bohemianism in America* (New York, Dover Publications, 1960). First published in 1933. Revised with a new chapter, "Enter Beatniks," by Harry T. Moore.

E · THE ENGLISH LANGUAGE IN AMERICA

Lester V. Berrey and Melvin Van den Bark, *The American Thesaurus of Slang: With Supplement* (New York, Crowell, 1947).

Sir William Alexander Craigie and James Root Hulbert, eds., *A Dictionary of American English on Historical Principles*, 4 vols. (Chicago, University of Chicago Press, 1938–1944). See also Joseph Abraham Weingarten, *Supplementary Notes to the Dictionary of American English* (New York, 1948).

Bergen Evans and Cornelia Evans, *A Dictionary of Contemporary American Usage* (New York, Random, 1957).

George Philip Krapp, *The English Language in America*, 2 vols. (New York, Frederick Ungar Publishing Co., 1960). First published in 1925.

Albert Henry Marckwardt, *American English* (New York, Oxford, 1958).

Mitford McLeod Mathews, ed., *A Dictionary of Americanisms on Historical Principles*, 2 vols. (Chicago, University of Chicago Press, 1951).

Henry Louis Mencken, *The American Language*, 4th edition, corrected, enlarged, rewritten (New York, Knopf, 1936). Originally published in 1919. There were supplements in 1945 and 1948. A one-volume edition, abridged by Raven I. McDavid, Jr., appeared in 1963.

Margaret Nicholson, *A Dictionary of American-English Usage, Based on Fowler's Modern English Usage* (New York, Oxford, 1957).

George Rippey Stewart, *Names on the Land,* revised and enlarged edition (Boston, Houghton, 1958). A study of American place names.

Harold Wentworth and Stuart Berg Flexner, *Dictionary of American Slang* (New York, Crowell, 1960).

F · FICTION

1 · *The Novel*

a · *General Books*

John Watson Aldridge, ed., *Critiques and Essays on Modern Fiction, 1920–1951* (New York, Ronald, 1952).

Joseph Warren Beach, *American Fiction, 1920–1940* (New York, Macmillan, 1941).

Richard Volney Chase, *The American Novel and Its Tradition* (Garden City, Doubleday, 1957).

Otis Welton Coan and Richard Gordon Lillard, *America in Fiction: An Annotated List of Novels That Interpret Aspects of Life in the United States,* 4th edition (Stanford, Stanford University Press, 1956).

Alexander Cowie, *The Rise of the American Novel* (New York, American Book Co., 1948). Virtually ends with Henry James.

Chester Emanuel Eisinger, *Fiction of the Forties* (Chicago, University of Chicago Press, 1963).

Harold Charles Gardiner, S.J., ed., *Fifty Years of the American Novel: A Christian Appraisal* (New York, Scribner, 1951). An anthology of essays.

Maxwell David Geismar, *Rebels and Ancestors: The American Novel, 1890–1915* (Boston, Houghton, 1953).

Maxwell David Geismar, *The Last of the Provincials: The American Novel, 1915–1925* (Boston, Houghton, 1947).

Maxwell David Geismar, *Writers in Crisis: The American Novel Between Two Wars* (Boston, Houghton, 1942). Covers the years 1925–1940.

Maxwell David Geismar, *American Moderns: From Rebellion to Conformity* (New York, Hill & Wang, 1958). A midcentury view of the American novel.

LITERARY HISTORY

Harry Hartwick, *The Foreground of American Fiction* (New York, American Book Co., 1934).

Ihab Hassan, *Radical Innocence: Studies in the Contemporary American Novel* (Princeton, 1962).

Frederick John Hoffman, *The Modern Novel in America, 1900–1950* (Chicago, Regnery, 1951). A brief survey.

Claude Edmond Magny,*L'Age du roman américain* (Paris, Editions du Seuil, 1948).

Desmond Ernest Stewart Maxwell, *American Fiction: The Intellectual Background* (New York, Columbia, 1963).

Hermann Mohrmann, *Kultur- und Gesellschaftsprobleme des amerikanischen Romanes der Nachkriegszeit, 1920–1927* (Giessen, Nolte, 1934).

Sean O'Faolain, *The Vanishing Hero: Studies in Novelists of the Twenties* (Boston, Little-B, 1957).

Arthur Hobson Quinn, *American Fiction: An Historical and Critical Survey* (New York, D. Appleton-Century Co., 1936). Conservative in treatment.

Louis Decimus Rubin and John Rees Moore, eds., *The Idea of an American Novel* (New York, Crowell, 1961). Selected documents "that bear on our intense and long-standing self-consciousness about the American novel."

Jean Simon, *Le Roman américain au XXᵉ siècle* (Paris, Boivin, 1950).

Carl Clinton Van Doren, *The American Novel, 1789–1939*, revised and enlarged edition (New York, Macmillan, 1940).

Edward Charles Wagenknecht, *Cavalcade of the American Novel, from the Birth of the Nation to the Middle of the Twentieth Century* (New York, Holt, 1952). Contains an excellent bibliography.

b · *Special Topics*

Lars Åhnebrink (Aahnebrink), *The Beginnings of Naturalism in American Fiction: A Study of the Works of Hamlin Garland, Stephen Crane, and Frank Norris with Special Reference to Some European Influences, 1891–1903. Essays and Studies on American Language and Literature,* IX (Upsala, Sweden, The

73

American Institute in the University of Upsala, 1950; and Cambridge, Harvard, 1950).

James Osler Bailey, *Pilgrims Through Space and Time: Trends and Patterns in Scientific and Utopian Fiction* (New York, Argus Books, 1947). A reliable study.

James Harwood Barnett, *Divorce and the American Divorce Novel, 1858–1937: A Study in Literary Reflections of Social Influences* (Philadelphia, privately printed, 1939). A doctoral dissertation.

Harry Bernard, *Le Roman régionaliste aux Etats-Unis, 1913–1940* (Montreal, Editions Fides, 1949).

Joseph Lee Blotner, *The Political Novel* (Garden City, Doubleday, 1955).

George Bluestone, *Novels into Film* (Baltimore, John Hopkins, 1957).

Robert A. Bone, *The Negro Novel in America* (New Haven, Yale, 1958).

Dorothy Yost Deegan, *The Stereotype of the Single Woman in American Novels: A Social Study with Implications for the Education of Women* (New York, Columbia, 1951).

Leon Edel, *The Psychological Novel, 1900–1950* (New York, Lippincott, 1955).

Leslie Aaron Fiedler, *Love and Death in the American Novel* (New York, Criterion Books, 1960).

Horace Spencer Fiske, *Provincial Types in American Fiction* (Chautauqua, New York, The Chautauqua Press, 1903).

Nick Aaron Ford, *The Contemporary Negro Novel: A Study in Race Relations* (Boston, Meador Publishing Co., 1936).

Wilbur Merrill Frohock, *The Novel of Violence in America*, revised and enlarged edition (Dallas, Southern Methodist University Press, 1957).

Blanche Housman Gelfant, *The American City Novel* (Norman, Oklahoma, 1954).

Hugh Morris Gloster, *Negro Voices in American Fiction* (Chapel Hill, North Carolina, 1948).

Granville Hicks, ed., *The Living Novel: A Symposium* (New York, Macmillan, 1957). Essays by young American novelists.

LITERARY HISTORY

Robert Humphrey, *Stream of Consciousness in the Modern Novel* (Berkeley, California, 1954).

Josephine Lurie Jessup, *The Faith of Our Feminists: A Study in the Novels of Edith Wharton, Ellen Glasgow, Willa Cather* (New York, Richard R. Smith Publisher, 1950).

Howard Mumford Jones, *The Frontier in American Fiction* (Jerusalem, The Magnes Press of the Hebrew University, 1956). Considers Cooper, Mark Twain, Willa Cather.

Ernest Erwin Leisy, *The American Historical Novel* (Norman, Oklahoma, 1950).

Robert Alexander Lively, *Fiction Fights the Civil War: An Unfinished Chapter in the Literary History of the American People* (Chapel Hill, North Carolina, 1957).

Wolfgang Alexander Luchting, *Das Erlebnis des Krieges im amerikanischen Roman ueber den zweiten Weltkrieg* (Munich, 1956).

Kenneth Schuyler Lynn, *The Dream of Success: A Study of the Modern American Imagination* (Boston, Little-B, 1955). Treats Dreiser, London, Norris, Herrick, and Phillips.

John Ormsby Lyons, *The College Novel in America* (Carbondale, Southern Illinois University Press, 1962).

Wright Morris, *The Territory Ahead* (New York, Harcourt, 1958).

Samuel Moskowitz, *The Immortal Storm: A History of Science Fiction Fandom* (Atlanta, The Atlanta Science Fiction Organization Press, 1954).

Walter Bates Rideout, *The Radical Novel in the United States, 1900–1954: Some Interrelations of Literature and Society* (Cambridge, Harvard, 1956).

Mark Schorer, ed., *Society and Self in the Novel. English Institute Essays, 1955* (New York, Columbia, 1956). Includes Schorer's own essay on Sinclair Lewis.

Morris Edmund Speare, *The Political Novel: Its Development in England and America* (New York, Oxford, 1924).

Walter Fuller Taylor, *The Economic Novel in America* (Chapel Hill, North Carolina, 1942).

Charles Child Walcutt, *American Literary Naturalism: A Divided Stream* (Minneapolis, Minnesota, 1956).

2 · *The Short Story*

There are innumerable collections of American short stories of various types, the purpose, scope, or kind of the anthology usually being indicated in the title. The best way to find such volumes is to go to a large, or even a medium-size, library, public or academic. There are also innumerable books on how to write short stories.

a · *"Continuing" Collections*

The Best American Short Stories (New York, 1915—). This annual compilation was begun by Edward J. O'Brien, partly as a protest against the "mechanical" or "commercial" magazine story, and is currently edited by Martha Foley and David Burnett. The introductory matter in each volume is valuable as an appraisal of tendencies in this literary form for the year covered. Since 1952 it has been published by Houghton Mifflin, in Boston. In 1952 Miss Foley edited *The Best of the Best American Short Stories, 1915–1950.*

O. Henry Memorial Award Prize Stories (New York, 1921—). Originally founded as a counter-collection to the above and originally edited by Blanche Colton Williams, this series has since the beginning been published in Garden City by Doubleday. The title has varied, the 1963 volume being: *Prize Stories 1963. The O. Henry Awards.* Recent volumes have been edited by Paul Engle (1954–1959), Mary Stegner (1960), and Richard Poirier (since 1961).

b · *General Books*

Edward Joseph Harrington O'Brien, *The Advance of the American Short Story,* revised edition (New York, Dodd, Mead & Co., 1931).

Fred Lewis Pattee, *The Development of the American Short Story: An Historical Survey* (New York, Harper, 1923).

Ray Benedict West, *The Short Story in America* (Chicago, Regnery, 1956). Supersedes his *The Short Story in America, 1900–1950,* published in 1953.

Blanche Colton Williams, *Our Short Story Writers* (New York, Moffat, Yard & Co., 1920).

LITERARY HISTORY

G · POETRY

Despite the large number of titles having to do with modern poetry, it is difficult to assemble a select list of books principally concerned with the history and development of the art in the United States since 1890. Possibly as good a way as any to trace the history of the poetic movement since 1912 is to consult the files of the magazine expressly founded to champion the new movement: *Poetry: A Magazine of Verse* (Chicago, 1912—), founded by Harriet Monroe (1860–1936) and now edited by Henry Rago.

Gay Wilson Allen, *American Prosody* (New York, American Book Co., 1935).

Alfred Alvarez, *The Shaping Spirit: Studies in Modern English and American Poets* (London, Chatto & Windus, 1958). Published in the United States by Scribner in 1958 under the title *Stewards of Excellence.*

Joseph Warren Beach, *Obsessive Images: Symbolism in Poetry of the 1930's and 1940's,* edited by William Van O'Connor (Minneapolis, Minnesota, 1960).

Richard Palmer Blackmur, *Language as Gesture: Essays in Poetry* (New York, Harcourt, 1952). Treats Pound, Eliot, Stevens, Cummings, Moore, among others.

Louise Bogan, *Achievement in American Poetry, 1900–1950* (Chicago, Regnery, 1951).

John Mason Bradbury, *The Fugitives: A Critical Account* (Chapel Hill, North Carolina, 1958).

William Stanley Beaumont Braithwaite, ed., *Anthology of Magazine Verse . . . and Yearbook of American Poetry* (New York, G. Sully and Co., 1913–1929).

Cleanth Brooks and Robert Penn Warren, *Understanding Poetry,* 3rd edition (New York, Holt, Rinehart & Winston, 1960). Although a textbook and anthology with commentary, it is included here because it has been, since it was first published in 1938, the most widely used introductory book explicating the reading and study of poetry.

John Ciardi, *How Does a Poem Mean?* (Boston, Houghton, 1959).

Stanley Knight Coffman, *Imagism: A Chapter for the History of Modern Poetry* (Norman, Oklahoma, 1951).

Babette Deutsch, *Poetry in Our Time* (New York, Columbia, 1956). Originally published by Holt in 1952 and somewhat expanded over the original text.

Elizabeth A. Drew, in collaboration with John L. Sweeney, *Directions in Modern Poetry* (New York, Norton, 1940).

Lloyd Frankenberg, *Pleasure Dome: On Reading Modern Poetry* (Boston, Houghton, 1949).

Horace Gregory and Marya Zaturenska, *A History of American Poetry, 1900–1940* (New York, Harcourt, 1946). Covers the 1890's in part.

Glenn Hughes, *Imagism and the Imagists: A Study in Modern Poetry* (Stanford, Stanford University Press, 1931).

Edward Buell Hungerford, ed., *Poets in Progress: Critical Prefaces to Ten Contemporary Americans* (Evanston, Northwestern University Press, 1962). Limited to poets whose reputations are chiefly post–World War II.

Randall Jarrell, *Poetry and the Age* (New York, Knopf, 1953).

Carlin T. Kindilien, *American Poetry in the Eighteen Nineties . . . Brown University Studies*, XX (Providence, Brown University Press, 1956). Based on the rich collections in the Brown University libraries.

Joseph Marshall Kuntz, ed., *Poetry Explication,* revised edition (Denver, Alan Swallow, Publisher, 1962). A checklist of interpretations since 1925 of British and American poems past and present.

Amy Lowell, *Tendencies in Modern American Poetry* (New York, Macmillan, 1917). Reissued by Houghton Mifflin in 1921.

Archibald MacLeish, *Poetry and Experience* (Boston, Houghton, 1961).

Josephine Miles, *The Primary Language of Poetry in the 1940's* (Berkeley, California, 1951).

Roy Harvey Pearce, *The Continuity of American Poetry* (Princeton, 1961). The introduction to both the theory and the history of American poetry.

Sister Mary Bernetta Quinn, *The Metamorphic Tradition in Modern Poetry* (New Brunswick, Rutgers, 1955). Discusses Pound, Eliot, Williams, Crane, Stevens, and Jeffers.

Karl Jay Shapiro, *A Bibliography of Modern Prosody* (Baltimore, Johns Hopkins, 1948).

Karl Jay Shapiro, *In Defense of Ignorance* (New York, Random, 1960). Highly personal interpretation of American poetry since World War I.

Donald Alfred Stauffer, *The Nature of Poetry* (New York, Norton, 1946).

Allen Tate, *Sixty American Poets, 1896–1944* (Washington, Library of Congress, 1945). A revised edition of the bibliography was prepared by Kenton Kilmer in 1954.

Leonard Unger, *The Man in the Name: Essays on the Experience of Poetry* (Minneapolis, Minnesota, 1956).

Louis Untermeyer, *The New Era in American Poetry* (New York, Holt, 1919).

Hyatt Howe Waggoner, *The Heel of Elohim: Science and Values in Modern American Poetry* (Norman, Oklahoma, 1950).

Amos Niven Wilder, *The Spiritual Aspects of the New Poetry* (New York, Harper, 1940).

Michael Yatron, *America's Literary Revolt* (New York, Philosophical Library, 1959). Devoted exclusively to Masters, Lindsay, Sandburg, and Populism.

H · THE DRAMA

Eric Russell Bentley, *The Dramatic Event: An American Chronicle* (New York, Horizon Press, 1954). This deals with the Broadway theater in 1952–1954.

Archie Binns and Olive Kooken, *Mrs. Fiske and the American Theatre* (New York, Crown Publishers, 1955). This not only is a biography of Mrs. Fiske but chronicles a struggle against the so-called "theatrical trust."

Harold Clurman, *The Fervent Years: The Story of the Group Theatre and the Thirties* (New York, Hill & Wang, 1957). Originally published by Knopf in 1945.

John Gassner, *Form and Idea in Modern Theatre* (New York, The Dryden Press, 1956).

Philip Graham, *Showboats: The History of an American Institution* (Austin, University of Texas Press, 1951).

Abel Green and Joe Laurie, Jr., *Show Biz from Vaude to Video* (New York, Holt, 1951).

Barnard Wolcott Hewitt, *Theatre, U.S.A., 1668–1957* (New York, McGraw, 1959). A general survey.

Morgan Yale Himelstein, *Drama Was a Weapon: The Left-Wing Theatre in New York, 1929–1941* (New Brunswick, Rutgers, 1962).

Glenn Hughes, *A History of the American Theatre, 1700–1950* (New York, Samuel French, 1951).

Walter Kerr, *How Not to Write a Play* (New York, Simon, 1955).

Wisner Payne Kinne, *George Pierce Baker and the American Theatre* (Cambridge, Harvard, 1954). This concerns the famous "47 Workshop."

Joseph Wood Krutch, *The American Drama Since 1918: An Informal History,* revised edition (New York, George Braziller, 1957).

Mary Therese McCarthy, *Sights and Spectacles, 1937–1962* (New York, Farrar & Straus, 1963). A highly personal view of the drama during these years.

Richard Moody, *America Takes the Stage: Romanticism in American Drama and Theatre, 1750–1900* (Bloomington, Indiana University Press, 1955).

Lloyd R. Morris, *Curtain Time: The Story of the American Theatre* (New York, Random, 1953).

Montrose Jonas Moses and John Mason Brown, *The American Theatre as Seen by Its Critics, 1752–1934* (New York, Norton, 1934). Chiefly concerns the later theater.

George Jean Nathan, *Art of the Night* (New York, Knopf, 1928).

George Jean Nathan, *Materia Critica* (New York, Knopf, 1924).

George Jean Nathan, *Mr. George Jean Nathan Presents* (New York, Knopf, 1917).

George Jean Nathan, *Passing Judgments* (New York, Knopf, 1935).

George Jean Nathan, *The Popular Theatre* (New York, Knopf, 1918).

George Jean Nathan, *The Theatre in the Fifties* (New York, Knopf, 1953).

LITERARY HISTORY

Arthur Hobson Quinn, *A History of the American Drama from the Civil War to the Present Day*, revised edition (New York, F. S. Crofts & Co., 1936).

Elmer Rice, *The Living Theatre* (New York, Harper, 1959).

Wieder David Sievers, *Freud on Broadway: A History of Psychoanalysis and the American Drama* (New York, Hermitage House, 1955).

A. Nicholas Vardac, *Stage to Screen* (Cambridge, Harvard, 1949). A study of pictorial staging from Garrick to Griffith, particularly in American theaters.

Gerald Weales, *American Drama Since World War II* (New York, Harcourt, 1962).

The annals of the Broadway theater during the period can be followed by consulting the *Best Plays* series, published by Dodd, Mead & Co. The bibliography is mildly complicated. *The Best Plays of 1849–1899*, a retrospective collection, was published in 1955; *The Best Plays of 1899–1909*, again retrospective, was published in 1944; and *The Best Plays of 1909–1919*, also retrospective, appeared in 1933. The annual volume, edited by Burns Mantle, first appeared in 1920 (Boston, Small, Maynard & Co.) for the season of 1919–20. Since then, the *Best Plays* has appeared each year. Mantle died in 1948. John Chapman continued the annual series through 1952, Louis Kronenberger through 1961; Henry Hewes has been the editor since 1962.

I · GENERAL PROSE AND CRITICISM

For a useful survey of twentieth-century critical movements, with bibliography, see *Literary History of the United States*, 3rd edition, chapter 80.

Conrad Aiken, *Collected Criticism from 1916 to the Present: A Reviewer's ABC*, edited by Rufus A. Blanchard (New York, Meridian Books, 1958).

Joseph Warren Beach, *The Outlook for American Prose* (Chicago, University of Chicago Press, 1926).

Clarence Arthur Brown, compiler, *The Achievement of American Criticism: Representative Selections from Three Hundred*

Years of American Criticism. Foreword by Harry Hayden Clark (New York, Ronald, 1954).

Robert M. Browne, *Theories of Convention in Contemporary American Criticism* (Washington, The Catholic University of America Press, 1956).

Donald Davidson, *Southern Writers in the Modern World* (Athens, University of Georgia Press, 1958).

Bernard De Voto, *The Easy Chair* (Boston, Houghton, 1955). Essays reprinted from *Harper's Magazine.*

Max Eastman, *The Literary Mind: Its Place in an Age of Science* (New York, Scribner, 1931).

William Elton, *A Guide to the New Criticism,* revised edition (Chicago, Modern Poetry Association, 1953). First published under the title *A Glossary of the New Criticism,* 1949.

James Thomas Farrell, *Literature and Morality* (New York, Vanguard Press, 1947).

Richard Foster, *The New Romantics: A Reappraisal of the New Criticism* (Bloomington, Indiana University Press, 1962).

Charles Irving Glicksberg, *American Literary Criticism, 1900–1950* (New York, Hendricks House, 1952).

William Dean Howells, *Criticism and Fiction* (New York, Harper, 1891).

William Dean Howells, *My Literary Passions* (New York, Harper, 1895).

Stanley Edgar Hyman, *The Armed Vision: A Study in the Methods of Modern Literary Criticism* (New York, Knopf, 1948); revised and abridged (New York, Vintage Books, 1955).

Henry James, *The American Essays,* edited with an introduction by Leon Edel (New York, Vintage Books, 1956).

Henry James, *The House of Fiction: Essays on the Novel,* edited with an introduction by Leon Edel (London, Rupert Hart-Davis, 1957).

Henry James, *Literary Reviews and Essays on American, English and French Literature,* edited by Albert Mordell (New York, Twayne Publishers, 1959).

Alfred Kazin, *On Native Grounds: An Interpretation of Modern*

American Prose Literature (New York, Reynal and Hitchcock, 1942).

Francis Otto Matthiessen, *The Responsibilities of the Critic: Essays and Reviews,* selected by John Rackliffe (New York, Oxford, 1952).

John Paul Pritchard, *Criticism in America: An Account of the Development of Critical Techniques from the Early Period of the Republic to the Middle Years of the Twentieth Century* (Norman, Oklahoma, 1956).

Bernard Smith, *Forces in American Criticism: A Study in the History of American Literary Thought* (New York, Harcourt, 1939). A product of the liberal interests of the 1930's.

Robert Ernest Spiller, *The Cycle of American Literature: An Essay in Historical Criticism* (New York, Macmillan, 1955).

Robert Wooster Stallman, *Critiques and Essays in Criticism, 1920–1948, Representing the Achievement of Modern British and American Critics* (New York, Ronald, 1949).

Floyd Stovall, ed., *The Development of American Criticism* (Chapel Hill, North Carolina, 1955). Essays by Harry Hayden Clark and others.

Lionel Trilling, *The Liberal Imagination: Essays on Literature and Society* (New York, Viking, 1950).

Lionel Trilling, *The Opposing Self: Nine Essays in Criticism* (New York, Viking, 1955).

Morton Dauwen Zabel, ed., *Literary Opinion in America: Essays Illustrating the Status, Methods, and Problems of Criticism in the United States in the Twentieth Century,* 2 vols., 3rd edition, revised (New York, Harper, 1962).

J · BIOGRAPHY

Marion Dargan, *Guide to American Biography* (Albuquerque, University of New Mexico Press, 1949, 1952). In two parts. Part II covers the years 1815–1933. The *Biography Index* (1946—) covers biographical material in current books and magazines.

John Mark Longaker, *Contemporary Biography* (Philadelphia, University of Pennsylvania Press, 1934).

Dana Kinsman Merrill, *American Biography: Its Theory and Practice* (Portland, Maine, The Bowker Press, 1957).

Edward Hayes O'Neill, *Biography by Americans, 1658–1936: A Subject Bibliography* (Philadelphia, University of Pennsylvania Press, 1939).

Edward Hayes O'Neill, *A History of American Biography, 1800–1935* (Philadelphia, University of Pennsylvania Press, 1939).

K · THE MAGAZINES

Frederick John Hoffman, Charles Allen, and Carolyn Farquhar Ulrich, *The Little Magazine: A History and a Bibliography* (Princeton, 1947).

Index to Little Magazines (Denver, Alan Swallow, Publisher, 1949—). Commonly issued each year, but 1953–1955 appeared as one volume in 1956; 1956–1957 as one volume in 1958; 1958–1959 as one volume in 1960; 1960–1961 as one volume in 1962. There have been various compilers, the latest issue being put together by Eugene Paul Sheehy and Kenneth A. Lohf.

Frank Luther Mott, *A History of American Magazines* (Cambridge, Harvard, 1938—). There are four volumes, the first having been issued by another publisher in 1930. Volume IV (1957) covers the years 1885–1905, and a fifth volume is promised.

Theodore Bernard Peterson, *Magazines in the Twentieth Century* (Urbana, Illinois, 1956).

Paul Robert Stewart, *The Prairie Schooner Story: A Little Magazine's First 25 Years* (Lincoln, University of Nebraska Press, 1955).

Carolyn Farquhar Ulrich and Eugenia Patterson, *Little Magazines: A List* (New York, New York Public Library, 1947).

James Playsted Wood, *Magazines in the United States: Their Social and Economic Influence,* second edition (New York, Ronald, 1956).

L · AMERICAN PUBLISHING

1 · *General Books*

Bowker Lectures on Book Publishing (New York, Bowker, 1957). This contains the first seventeen Bowker Memorial Lectures, 1935–1956, delivered at the New York Public Library.

Pierce Butler, ed., *Librarians, Scholars, and Booksellers at Mid-Century: Papers Presented Before the Sixteenth Annual Conference of the Graduate Library School of the University of Chicago* (Chicago, University of Chicago Press, 1953).

Orion Howard Cheney, *Economic Survey of the Book Industry, 1930–1931* (New York, National Association of Book Publishers, 1931). Reprinted by Bowker in 1949 and 1961. A *Supplementary Report* by the Employing Bookbinders of America and a *Review* by the National Association of Book Publishers were issued in New York in 1932.

Chandler B. Grannis, ed., *What Happens in Book Publishing* (New York, Columbia, 1957).

Harold K. Guinzburg, Robert William Frase, and Theodore Waller, *Books and the Mass Market* (Urbana, Illinois, 1953). The fourth annual Windsor lectures.

Alice Payne Hackett, *Sixty Years of Best Sellers, 1895–1955* (New York, Bowker, 1956).

Henry Charles Link and Harry Arthur Hopf, *People and Books: A Study of Reading and Book-Buying Habits* (New York, Book Industry Committee of the Book Manufacturers' Institute, 1946).

William Miller, *The Book Industry* (New York, Columbia, 1949). Part of the investigation known as the Public Library Inquiry.

Donald Henry Sheehan, *This Was Publishing: A Chronicle of the Book Trade in the Gilded Age* (Bloomington, Indiana University Press, 1952).

Raymond Howard Shove, *Cheap Book Production in the United States, 1870–1891* (Urbana, University of Illinois Library, 1937).

Madeleine Bettina Stern, *Imprints on History: Book Publishers and American Frontiers* (Bloomington, Indiana University Press, 1956).

Albert Douglas Van Nostrand, *The Denatured Novel* (Indianapolis, Bobbs, 1960). A study of the relation between commercial pressures and artistic purposes in marketing books.

2 · *Particular Publishers*

Alfred A. Knopf: Quarter Century (New York, privately printed, 1940). Articles by Willa Cather, H. L. Mencken, and eight others.

Edward William Bok, *The Americanization of Edward Bok* (New York, Scribner, 1920). Often reprinted. The "success story" of the editor of *The Ladies' Home Journal.*

The Borzoi, 1925: Being a Sort of Record of Ten Years of Publishing (New York, Knopf, 1925). Concerns the house of Knopf.

George Britt, *Forty Years—Forty Millions: The Career of Frank A. Munsey* (New York, Farrar & Rinehart, 1935).

Roger Burlingame, *Of Making Many Books: A Hundred Years of Reading, Writing and Publishing* (New York, Scribner, 1946). Chiefly concerns Charles Scribner's Sons.

Edward Howard Dodd, *The First Hundred Years: A History of the House of Dodd, Mead, 1839–1939* (New York, Dodd, Mead & Co., 1939).

George Henry Doran, *Chronicles of Barabbas, 1884–1934* (New York, Harcourt, 1935). Chiefly concerns George H. Doran Co.

William Webster Ellsworth, *A Golden Age of Authors: A Publisher's Recollection* (Boston, Houghton, 1919). Chiefly concerns The Century Co.

E. McClung Fleming, *R. R. Bowker: Militant Liberal* (Norman, Oklahoma, 1952).

James Lauren Ford, *Forty-Odd Years in the Literary Shop* (New York, E. P. Dutton & Co., 1921). General reminiscences chiefly of New York literary life.

Charles Eliot Goodspeed, *Yankee Bookseller: Being the Reminiscences of Charles E. Goodspeed* (Boston, Houghton, 1937).

Ferris Greenslet, *Under the Bridge: An Autobiography* (Boston, Houghton, 1943). Chiefly concerns Houghton Mifflin Co.

Francis Whiting Halsey, *Our Literary Deluge and Some of its Deeper Waters* (New York, Doubleday, Page and Co., 1902). General reminiscences.

Joseph Henry Harper, *The House of Harper: A Century of Publishing in Franklin Square* (New York, Harper, 1912).

Joseph Henry Harper, *I Remember* (New York, Harper, 1934). Chiefly concerns Harper & Brothers.

Henry Holt, *Garrulities of an Octogenarian Editor* (Boston, Houghton, 1923). Chiefly concerns Henry Holt & Co.

Robert Underwood Johnson, *Remembered Yesterdays* (Boston, Little-B, 1923). By the editor of *The Century Magazine*.

Raymond Lincoln Kilgour, *Estes and Lauriat: A History, 1872–1898. With a Brief Account of Dana Estes and Company, 1898–1914* (Ann Arbor, University of Michigan Press, 1957).

Sidney Kramer, *A History of Stone & Kimball and Herbert S. Stone & Co., with a Bibliography of their Publications, 1893–1905* (Chicago, Norman W. Forgue, 1940).

Thomas Bonaventure Lawler, *Seventy Years of Textbook Publishing: A History of Ginn and Company* (Boston, Ginn & Co., 1938).

One Hundred and Twenty-Five Years of Publishing, 1837–1962 (Boston, Little-B, 1937). Concerns Little, Brown.

Grant Martin Overton, *Portrait of a Publisher: And the First Hundred Years of the House of Appleton, 1825–1925* (New York, D. Appleton and Co., 1925).

Walter Hines Page, *A Publisher's Confession*, new edition (Garden City, Doubleday, Page and Co., 1923). The publishing house is of course the house of Doubleday.

George Haven Putnam, *George Palmer Putnam: A Memoir, Together with a Record of the Earlier Years of the Publishing House Founded by Him* (New York, G. P. Putnam's Sons,

1912). This George Palmer Putnam should not be confused with George Palmer Putnam, the younger, named below.

George Haven Putnam, *Memories of a Publisher, 1865–1915,* second edition (New York, G. P. Putnam's Sons, 1923).

George Palmer Putnam, *Wide Margins: A Publisher's Autobiography* (New York, Harcourt, 1942).

Quentin Reynolds, *The Fiction Factory, or From Pulp Row to Quality Street: The Story of 100 Years of Publishing at Street & Smith* (New York, Random, 1955).

Frank Leopold Schick, *The Paperbound Book in America: The History of Paperbacks and Their European Background* (New York, Bowker, 1958).

Ellery Sedgwick, *The Happy Profession* (Boston, Little-B, 1946). By an editor of *The Atlantic Monthly.*

Frederick Abbot Stokes, *A Publisher's Random Notes, 1800–1935* (New York, New York Public Library, 1935). One of the Bowker lectures.

John William Tebbel, *George Horace Lorimer and The Saturday Evening Post* (Garden City, Doubleday, 1948).

Lewis Frank Tooker, *The Joys and Tribulations of an Editor* (New York, The Century Co., 1924). Concerns *The Century Magazine.*

John Hall Wheelock, *Editor to Author: The Letters of Maxwell E. Perkins* (New York, Scribner, 1950). Mr. Wheelock has not only selected and edited the letters of the famous editor at Scribner's but has also supplied a running commentary.

88

VI · CRITICAL LIST OF MAGAZINES

The following selective list includes magazines, of general character or of specifically literary, critical, ideational, or scholarly interest, of concern to the student of American literature; and magazines of opinion likely to illumine the thought and writing of the years covered by this handbook.

ACCENT: A QUARTERLY OF NEW LITERATURE (1940—). Published by the English Department of the University of Illinois, at Urbana.

AMERICAN HERITAGE: THE MAGAZINE OF HISTORY (1949—), New York. Bimonthly, but begun as a quarterly. Sponsored by the American Association for State and Local History and the Society of American Historians, Inc. It treats American history, from all angles, for the general intelligent reader.

AMERICAN LITERATURE (1929—), Durham, N.C. Quarterly. The official scholarly publication of the American Literature Group of the Modern Language Association. Useful for its current bibliographies of scholarly investigation. See Thomas Frederic Marshall, *An Analytical Index to American Literature, Volumes I–XXX*, March 1929–January 1959 (Durham, Duke University Press, 1963).

THE AMERICAN MAGAZINE (1905–1955), New York. Monthly. Originally the organ of the "Muckrakers," this magazine after a few years changed character and became simply another household periodical.

THE AMERICAN MERCURY (1929—), New York. Monthly. Founded by Alfred A. Knopf as a vehicle for H. L. Mencken and George Jean Nathan, this periodical was characteristic of the twenties, but by 1934, following the withdrawal of both men, it had changed character. Three numbers were entitled *The New American Mercury*, then the old title was restored. The present *American Mercury* is published in Texas by the Legion for the Survival of Freedom Inc., an extreme rightest organization.

AMERICAN QUARTERLY (1949—), Minneapolis; Philadelphia. Quarterly. Created at the University of Minnesota by the Program in American Studies, this quarterly aims to do for programs in American civilization what *American Literature* does for its field. In 1951 it moved to the University of Pennsylvania.

The AMERICAN REVIEW. See The (American) BOOKMAN.

The AMERICAN SCHOLAR (1932—), New York. Quarterly. Supported by Phi Beta Kappa, this magazine contains articles appraising the American scene, and debates on current political, economic, and cultural questions.

The AMERICAN SPECTATOR (1932–1937), New York. Monthly. Originally an organ for George Jean Nathan, Ernest Boyd, Van Wyck Brooks, this periodical changed character in 1935.

The ANTIOCH REVIEW (1941—), Yellow Springs, Ohio. A quarterly of opinion and criticism.

The ARENA (1889–1909), Boston. Monthly. Founded by Benjamin O. Flower and largely edited by him, this periodical fought for economic and social reform and for realism in the arts.

The ATLANTIC MONTHLY (1857—), Boston. Monthly. Still the leading general literary periodical, conservative in taste and outlook, the *Atlantic* is an institution. Recent editors include Horace E. Scudder, 1890–1898; Walter Hines Page, 1898–1899; Bliss Perry, 1899–1909; Ellery Sedgwick, 1909–1938; and Edward Weeks, 1938—.

The BILLBOARD (1894—), Cincinnati. Weekly. A theatrical trade paper with special emphasis upon the worlds of burlesque, carnivals, fairs, circus, popular music, night club entertainment, vaudeville, radio, and television. See *Variety*.

The (American) BOOKMAN (1895–1933), New York. Monthly. In its earlier years supposed to be the organ of genteel criticism, this magazine changed character under Burton Rascoe (1928–1929), who made it a magazine of controversy. Seward Collins (1930–1933) made it the organ of the Neohumanists. *The American Review* (1933–1937), New York, monthly except for July and August, continued and superseded the foregoing. There is also *The American Bookman* (1944—), New York, a quarterly.

MAGAZINES

BOOKS ABROAD (1927–), Norman, Oklahoma. Quarterly. A gallant attempt to keep abreast of and interpret foreign literature in terms relevant to American readers.

BROOM: AN INTERNATIONAL MAGAZINE OF THE ARTS (1921–1924), no fixed place. Monthly. Published successively in Rome, Berlin, and New York, this was an *avantgarde* magazine of the twenties.

The CENTURY ILLUSTRATED MAGAZINE (1881–1930), New York. Monthly. This magazine was preceded by *Scribner's Monthly* (1870–1881), not to be confused with the contemporary of the *Century, Scribner's Magazine* (q.v.). One of the great magazines of its time, the *Century* published a notable series of Civil War memoirs by generals and others; it did much to awaken Northern sympathy for the South after Reconstruction and an interest in national issues; and it was one of the leading periodicals in the encouragement of art, particularly through its own illustrations. Richard Watson Gilder edited it from 1881 to 1909. The title varies. It merged with *The Forum* in 1930.

The CHAP BOOK (1894–1898), Chicago. Semimonthly. This magazine contained material by Stephen Crane, Eugene Field, Henry James, William Vaughn Moody, Hamlin Garland, and others. It was finally merged with the (Chicago) *Dial*.

COLLEGE ENGLISH (1939–), Champaign, Illinois. Eight times a year (October through May). The official organ of the National Council of Teachers of English, it frequently carries interesting lead articles on current writers. (See *The English Journal*, below.)

The COMMONWEAL (1924–) New York. Weekly. A weekly magazine of opinion and review of literature and art and public affairs from the Catholic point of view.

The COSMOPOLITAN MAGAZINE (1866–), New York. Monthly. This magazine has suffered various changes of title, the most important coming in 1925 when it became *Hearst's International Cosmopolitan*. A vehicle for fiction in its earlier years, it is now mostly a household magazine.

The CRITIC (1881–1906), New York. Monthly. Later merged

into *Putnam's Magazine,* this periodical was an organ for the Genteel Tradition. *Putnam's* ceased publication in 1910.

The (Chicago) DIAL (1880–1929), Chicago; New York. Monthly; semimonthly; biweekly; monthly. Not to be confused with the transcendentalist *Dial* (1840–1844), this magazine was conservative in taste until 1916, when it removed to New York, where, for a time, it was in the vanguard of the new writing, under Conrad Aiken, Randolph Bourne, Van Wyck Brooks, and Thomas Mann. In 1925 Marianne Moore became the editor.

DIOGENES (1952—), Chicago. Published by the International Council for Philosophy and Humanistic Studies, this is the English-language edition of an international quarterly. The general editor is Roger Coullain, but the American edition is edited by Richard McKeon.

The DOUBLE-DEALER (1921–1926), New Orleans. Monthly. An *avant-garde* magazine for the South, including, however, Northern writers temporarily resident in New Orleans.

DRAMA MAGAZINE (1911–1931), Chicago. Quarterly; monthly; irregular. The organ of the Drama League of America, expressing the vague idealism of the theater "movement" of the period.

The ENGLISH JOURNAL (COLLEGE EDITION) (1928–1939), Chicago. Nine times a year. Founded in 1912, *The English Journal* is published by the National Council of Teachers of English for high schools. Founded in 1928, *The English Journal (College Edition)* was superseded in 1939 by *College English,* described above.

ESQUIRE (1933—), Chicago. Monthly. This "magazine for men" is distinguished by cartoons and drawings supposed to have a special masculine appeal. Its articles are rather obviously "sophisticated," but it occasionally publishes literary work of importance, such as F. Scott Fitzgerald's "The Crack-up." Latterly it has become more sober in tone as its articles improve in literary quality.

ETC: A REVIEW OF GENERAL SEMANTICS (1943—), Chicago. This quarterly, the nature of which is indicated by its subtitle, has been from its inception under the editorship of S. I. Hayakawa.

The FORUM (1886–1950), New York. Monthly; quarterly. Chiefly a magazine of debate on contemporary problems, it occasionally published fiction. Henry Goddard Leach was editor from 1923 to 1940. In 1930 it absorbed *The Century;* in 1940 it merged with *Current History* to become *Current History and Forum.* From 1945 to 1950 it was again published as an independent magazine.

The FREEMAN (1920–1924), New York. Weekly. This brilliant liberal magazine was founded by Van Wyck Brooks, Albert Jay Nock, Francis Nielson, and others. It contained excellent literary criticism. *The Freeman Book* (New York, 1924), is an anthology of gleanings from its pages.

The FRONTIER AND MIDLAND (1920–1939), Missoula, Montana. Three issues a year. Founded by H. G. Merriam at Montana State University as a medium for regionalism, *The Frontier* in 1933 took over *The Midland* (q.v.). It began life as *The Montanan* (1920) and acquired its *Frontier* title after a few issues.

The FUGITIVE (1922–1925), Nashville, Tennessee. Quarterly; bimonthly; quarterly. Devoted to poetry, principally that of Donald Davidson, Merrill Moore, John Crowe Ransom, Allen Tate, and Robert Penn Warren. *A Fugitive Anthology* (New York, 1928) was made from its pages.

HARPER'S MAGAZINE (1850—), New York. Monthly. Originally *Harper's Monthly Magazine* (to 1925), this magazine began chiefly as a reprint periodical containing British literature. Henry Mills Alden was editor from 1869 to 1919, probably the longest term of service of its kind in American history. Howells occupied the famous Editor's Easy Chair from 1901 to 1921. Bernard De Voto sat in it from 1935 until his death in 1955. Crucial changes of policy occurred in 1900 and in 1925. Recently the magazine has become less a literary vehicle than one of social and political discussion.

HOUND AND HORN (1927–1934), Portland, Maine; Cambridge, Mass. Quarterly. Founded at Harvard by Lincoln

Kirstein, this *avant-garde* publication included work by R. P. Blackmur, Kenneth Burke, T. S. Eliot, Katherine Anne Porter, Gertrude Stein, and Allen Tate. The editorial office was moved to New York in 1930.

The HUDSON REVIEW (1948—), New York. Quarterly. A literary periodical expressive of, though not dominated by, the "New Criticism."

JUDGE (1881–1939), New York. Weekly. One of the three great comic magazines of the period, regularly publishing cartoons, light verse, quips, short stories, and informal essays. See *Puck* and *Life,* below.

The KENYON REVIEW (1939—), Gambier, Ohio. Quarterly. Largely the creation of John Crowe Ransom, this magazine has been one of the more prominent periodicals of the "New Criticism."

LADIES' HOME JOURNAL (1883—), Philadelphia. Monthly. Under the editorship of Edward J. Bok, this characteristically American magazine rose to a circulation of over two million just when, after thirty years of editing, Bok turned to other fields, having persuaded the American housewife to want what he wanted her to want.

The LARK (1895–1897), San Francisco. Monthly. One of the famous "little magazines" of the nineties, its announced policy being "gaiety."

LIFE (before it became a picture magazine) (1883–1936), New York. Weekly. Disputed with *Puck* and *Judge* leadership in the field of humorous writing and drawing. Less political than either. It became a Luce publication in 1936.

The LITTLE REVIEW (1914–1929), Chicago; New York; Paris. Irregular. This famous and unbusinesslike periodical was the work of Margaret Anderson. See her book, *My Thirty Years' War* (1930).

The MASSES (1911–1917), New York. Monthly. Originally edited by Max Eastman, this magazine included among its contributors Floyd Dell and John Reed. It was the Marxist organ of its time, suppressed in World War I and revived as *The Liberator* (1918–1924). It contained some of the finest black-

and-white art work of the period. Unfortunately files are rare. See *New Masses*, below.

McCLURE'S MAGAZINE (1893–1929), New York. Monthly. Famous as a muckraking magazine, this periodical was also notable for its low price. It was the product of S. S. McClure and was edited from 1902 to 1906 by Lincoln Steffens, Ida M. Tarbell and Ray S. Baker being among the contributors. The title varies.

The MIDLAND (1915–1933), Iowa City, Iowa; Chicago. Monthly. Established by John T. Frederick as a regional magazine, this periodical suffered a variety of changes and was merged with *The Frontier* (q.v.).

M'LLE NEW YORK (1895–1899), New York. Fortnightly. Vance Thompson edited this magazine, supposed to be notably "Bohemian" and "French." James G. Huneker was an important contributor.

The MODERN QUARTERLY (1923–1940), Baltimore. Quarterly; monthly. Retitled in 1933 the *Modern Monthly*, this magazine "of the newer spirit" was edited by V. F. Calverton and was leftist in viewpoint.

The NATION (1865—), New York. Weekly. Founded by E. L. Godkin, editor from 1865 to 1881, *The Nation* did much for science, the acceptance of Darwinism, civil service reform, and literary criticism. Under Paul E. More, editor from 1909 to 1914, it became a conservative critical journal, but Oswald Garrison Villard (1918–1933) turned it into a leading liberal weekly. The current editor is Carey McWilliams.

NEW MASSES (1926–1948), New York. Monthly; weekly. Successor to *The Masses* (see above) and *The Liberator*, this magazine was edited by Joseph Freeman, Michael Gold, and other proletarian critics. It became the fighting organ of Marxism. In 1948 it merged with another Marxist journal under the name *Masses and Mainstream*.

The NEW MEXICO QUARTERLY (1931—), Albuquerque. Quarterly. A quiet and distinguished academic magazine. The title varies.

The NEW REPUBLIC (1914—), New York; Washington. Weekly. Founded by Herbert Croly, this liberal weekly had a brilliant staff during World War I, including Robert Morss Lovett, Malcolm Cowley, and Walter Lippmann. Its later years were less distinguished, but lately it has undergone a renaissance.

The NEW YORKER (1925—), New York. Weekly. The chief organ of "sophisticated" urban wit (with such contributors as James Thurber, Ogden Nash, and others), this magazine is also a crusader against intolerance and obscurantism. Harold Ross edited the magazine, 1925–1951.

NEWSWEEK (1933—), New York. Weekly. The chief rival of *Time*, this weekly newspaper has departments devoted to books, the movies, radio, the theater, music, and so on.

The OUTLOOK (1870–1935), New York. Weekly; monthly. This magazine was the organ of the liberal Protestant point of view, including the social gospel, and had for its contributors Hamilton Wright Mabie, Lyman Abbott, and Theodore Roosevelt, among others. Title varies.

The PACIFIC SPECTATOR (1947–1956), Stanford University. Quarterly. A quarterly of the humanities edited by a group with John W. Dodds as head.

The PARTISAN REVIEW (1934—), New York. Monthly; quarterly. Originally showing Marxist tendencies, this magazine is now a periodical of literary theory and criticism. It suspended publication in 1936–37, but is now the organ of the American Committee for Cultural Freedom.

POET LORE (1889–1953), Philadelphia; Boston. Quarterly. Edited originally by Charlotte Porter and Helen A. Clarke, this magazine has been a medium for genteel discussion of the art of literature, but even more importantly a vehicle for translating Continental drama into English. There has been talk of its revival.

POETRY (1912—), Chicago. Monthly. Founded by Harriet Monroe, this is the oldest and most important of the existing poetry magazines. It championed the "Poetic Renaissance."

PUBLISHERS' WEEKLY (1872—), New York. Weekly. The most neglected source material in the field of American literary history can be found in the files of this magazine.

MAGAZINES

PUCK (1877–1918), New York. Weekly. This comic magazine had a brilliant line of editors—Henry C. Bunner (1878–1896), Harry Leon Wilson (1896–1902), John Kendrick Bangs (1904–1905) among them. Keppel's political cartoons were influential.

The READER'S DIGEST (1922—), Pleasantville, New York. Monthly. This magazine, theoretically a parasite on other magazines, is the creation of De Witt Wallace and, in its various forms (there are American, British, Canadian, Spanish, Portuguese, Swedish, Arabian, Chinese, Finnish, Danish, and other editions, not to speak of one in Braille and a "talking record" edition for the blind) has the largest circulation in the world. See for a somewhat unsympathetic account, John Bainbridge, *Little Wonder; or, The Reader's Digest and How it Grew,* New York, Reynal & Hitchcock, 1946.

REEDY'S MIRROR (1891–1920), St. Louis. Weekly. The creation of William Marion Reedy (1862–1920), this wandering periodical, St. Louis being one of its homes, first published *The Spoon River Anthology* and work by John Gould Fletcher, Julia Peterkin, and others. Title varies.

The REPORTER (1949—), New York. Biweekly. Founded by Max Ascoli, who continues (1964) as editor and publisher, this magazine aims at disseminating facts and ideas chiefly political, but it also publishes critical reviews, literary essays, and occasionally fiction.

THE SATURDAY EVENING POST (1821—), Philadelphia. Weekly. *Not* founded by Benjamin Franklin, this famous weekly is too familiar to need description. Its special articles are well, if sometimes mechanically written; its fiction, though it frequently tends to type, is sometimes excellent; its poetry is negligible; and its politics are conservative.

The SATURDAY REVIEW (1924—), New York. Weekly. Originally *The Saturday Review of Literature,* this critical weekly sticks to a middle-of-the-road position in literary theory, now includes departments concerned with travel, education, drama, movies, and recorded music. Under the leadership of Norman Cousins and Harrison Smith, it also insists upon the desirability of better world organization. It was founded by Henry Seidel Canby, Amy Loveman, and others, seceders from the old *New York Post*.

SCIENCE AND SOCIETY: A MARXIAN QUARTERLY (1936—), New York. Quarterly. For the intellectual Marxists.

The SCIENTIFIC AMERICAN (1845—), New York. Monthly. This magazine is now the most intelligent magazine edited for the lay reader in the world of science. It is intended to fill the gap between the technical journals and the merely popular "science magazine." The original editor was Orson D. Munn, and it was once a magazine of invention as well as of scientific research. The mode of publication has varied over the years; and a *Scientific American Supplement* ran from 1876 to 1919. Title varies.

SCRIBNER'S MAGAZINE (1887–1939), New York. Monthly. This famous literary magazine was one of the chief cultural periodicals in the Genteel Tradition, many famous names appearing on its muster roll. It came to a sad end as *Scribner's Commentator* (1939–1942).

SECESSION (1922–1924), various places. Irregular. A characteristic expatriate periodical, this was edited by Gorham B. Munson and others. It published Hart Crane.

The SEVEN ARTS (1916–1917), New York. Monthly. Merged with *The Dial*. Short-lived but influential, this magazine had among its contributors Dreiser, Vachel Lindsay, Amy Lowell, Mencken, Sherwood Anderson, and Randolph Bourne.

SEWANEE REVIEW (1892—), Sewanee, Tenn. Quarterly. Founded at the University of the South and edited at first by William P. Trent, then by William S. Knickerbocker, this magazine devoted itself mainly to cultural material of interest to the South. Later it was captured by the "New Criticism."

The SMART SET (1900–1930), New York. Monthly. This influential magazine, neglected by librarians, was edited in its best days by H. L. Mencken and George Jean Nathan. No periodical did more for "sophistication" and realism. The title varies.

SOUTH ATLANTIC QUARTERLY (1902—), Durham, N. C. Quarterly. Highly academic, this quarterly is chiefly devoted to scholarly general articles. It was founded by John Spencer Bassett.

SOUTHWEST REVIEW (1915—), Dallas, Texas. Quarterly. Founded as *The Texas Review* at Austin and edited originally by Stark Young, this regional periodical moved to Southern Methodist University and changed its name in 1924.

SURVEY and SURVEY GRAPHIC (1897–1932; 1933–1949; 1949–1953), New York. Monthly. This magazine, ostensibly for the social worker, carried from time to time able and dispassionate reports on all sorts of social, economic, and educational problems. Mostly it was issued as a monthly. In 1933 it was superseded by two separate periodicals, which again combined in January 1949, continuing the volume numbering of *Survey Midmonthly*.

TEXAS QUARTERLY (1958—), Austin, Texas. This quarterly is unique in that the second section of each number in the first three volumes is devoted to a whole book, which can be detached from the magazine and bound separately. It is a magazine of general cultural comment.

THIS QUARTER (1925–1932), Paris. Irregular. An expatriate magazine.

TIME (1932—), New York. Weekly. This weekly newspaper, published by the Luce interests, prides itself on a special style and upon accuracy. Both have been severely attacked. It has special departments concerning books, the movies, the theater, music, etc., and occasionally publishes lengthy articles on prominent literary figures.

transition (1927–1938), Paris; The Hague. Irregular. Moved to Iowa in 1940. Originally edited by Eugene Jolas and Elliot Paul, this *avant-garde* magazine was superseded by *Vertical*.

VARIETY (1905—), New York. Weekly. A theatrical trade paper covering the legitimate theater, vaudeville, the films, popular music, nightclub entertainment, radio, and television. See *The Billboard*.

VIRGINIA QUARTERLY REVIEW (1925—), Charlottesville. Quarterly. This conservative quarterly is especially associated with the Upper South, though it is national (and even international) in its interests.

The YALE REVIEW (1892—), New Haven. Quarterly. Long edited by Wilbur L. Cross, this quarterly attained national prominence about 1910 as a relatively conservative journal of literature, politics, and opinion.

It should be noted that, especially during the last twenty-five or thirty years, most leading universities and colleges have founded magazines, commonly quarterlies, of criticism, opinion, and general literature, representative titles among which are included in the above list. But in view of limitations of space it has been impossible to include all these magazines, in most of which serious and thoughtful discussions of literary problems and of cultural trends may be found.

VII · CHIEF HISTORICAL EVENTS, 1890–1963

1889–1893 BENJAMIN HARRISON (R), PRESIDENT

1889–91 Invention of motion pictures.

1890 Ending of the American frontier. Sherman Anti-Trust Act. Sherman Silver Purchase Act. The McKinley Tariff. Pan-American Congress (James G. Blaine, Secretary of State). First electrocution for murder, Auburn, New York, prison. Ellis Island opened as immigration depot.

1892 Homestead steel strike. Dr. Rudolf Diesel patented an internal combustion engine operating on pulverized fuel.

1893–1897 GROVER CLEVELAND (D), PRESIDENT

1893 Panic of 1893. Repeal of Sherman Silver Purchase Act. World's Columbian Exposition, Chicago. Opening of the University of Chicago.

1894 First public showing of Edison's Kinetoscope in New York. March of "Coxey's Army" on Washington. Pullman Car Company strike. The Wilson-Gorman Tariff Act.

1895 Roentgen announced discovery of X-rays. Invention of the Vitascope. The Selden patent marked practical beginning of the automobile industry in the United States. Marconi sent first wireless message. Venezuelan boundary dispute.

1896 Completion of the Vitascope and first showing of motion pictures at Koster and Bials Music Hall, New York City. In Paris Becquerel announced the radioactivity of uranium. Creation of Greater New York (union of five boroughs). Bryan-McKinley campaign ("Sixteen to one").

1897–1901 WILLIAM MCKINLEY (R), PRESIDENT

1897 The Dingley Tariff.

1898 In Paris the Curies and associates announced the discovery of radium. Sending of the first radiogram. Spanish-American War (Battle of Manila Bay, San Juan Hill, destruction of the Spanish fleet in Cuban waters). Annexation of Puerto Rico, the Philippine Islands. Annexation of the Hawaiian Islands.

101

1899 Philippine Insurrection under Aguinaldo (to 1901). Tension with Germany over the Samoan Islands. Universal Peace Conference at The Hague. Beginning of the Boer War (to 1902).

1899–1901 The Boxer Rebellion in China; intervention by the Great Powers; beginning of agitation for an "Open Door" policy (John Hay, Secretary of State).

1900 Opening of the Paris Exposition. The Gold Standard Act. Beginning of the campaign by Dr. Walter Reed and associates to wipe out yellow fever.

1901 WILLIAM MCKINLEY (R), PRESIDENT

1901–1905 THEODORE ROOSEVELT (R), PRESIDENT

1901 President McKinley was shot at the Buffalo Exposition and died on September 14, 1901. He was succeeded by Vice-President Theodore Roosevelt. First radio signal sent across the Atlantic Ocean by Marconi.

1902 First radio message sent. Blockade of Venezuela by European powers. American occupation of Cuba ended and the Republic of Cuba proclaimed. First International Court of Arbitration opened at The Hague. Pennsylvania anthracite coal strike. Creation of the Reclamation Service.

1903 The Wright brothers announced the first successful flight of a heavier-than-air machine. "The Great Train Robbery," first successful American commercial motion picture. First transcontinental automobile trip, New York to San Francisco. Massacre of Jews at Kichinev, Russia. Republic of Panama recognized by the United States.

1904 New York subway opened. Northern Securities Case. Panama Canal brought under American auspices (completed 1914). Russo-Japanese War began (ended by the Treaty of Portsmouth, September 5, 1905).

1905–1909 THEODORE ROOSEVELT (R), PRESIDENT

1905 First motion picture theater ("nickelodeon") opened in Pittsburgh. Beginning of political battle between Speaker Joseph G. Cannon and conservative senators on the one hand, and a "progressive" group on the other, for control of the Republican party. First Russian parliament (Duma) opened.

1906 Trial of Harry K. Thaw for killing Stanford White. San Francisco fire and earthquake. Hepburn (Railway Rate) Act. Pure Food Act (amended 1912).

1907 Panic of 1907 checked by J. P. Morgan and Co., and by U.S. government. "Ben Hur," first multiple-reel motion picture, exhibited. Oklahoma became a state. Immigration Act checked entrance of Japanese into the United States. Second Hague Conference.

1908 American fleet sent around the world (1907–1909). Danbury Hatters' Case (1902–1914). Root-Takahira agreement admitted Japan's special interest in Asia. Austro-Hungary annexed Bosnia and Herzegovina.

1909–1913 WILLIAM HOWARD TAFT (R), PRESIDENT

1909 Admiral Robert E. Peary reached the North Pole. Louis Blériot flew across the English Channel. Payne-Aldrich Tariff Act. Agitation for "Conservation."

1910 Mann-Elkins Act increased the powers of the Interstate Commerce Commission. Hague Tribunal settled Newfoundland fisheries dispute between United States and Great Britain. "Insurgent" Republicans reduced powers of the speaker of the house. Return of Theodore Roosevelt from Africa and proclamation by him of the "New Nationalism." Boy Scouts of America founded.

1911 First transcontinental airplane flight (by O. P. Rogers). Roald Amundsen reached the South Pole. Supreme Court ordered dissolution of the Standard Oil "trust" and of the American Tobacco Company as monopolies. Commercial treaty with Japan. Mexican Revolution started.

1912 Captain R. F. Scott reached the South Pole. Creation of the Progressive ("Bull Moose") party. Eight-hour day for federal employees. New Mexico and Arizona became states (last territories within the borders of the continental United States). Taft-Roosevelt-Wilson election. Creation of the Republic of China. Sinking of the S.S. *Titanic*. First Balkan War (against Turkey). Founding of the Camp-Fire Girls. Renewal of the Triple Alliance.

BACKGROUNDS

1913–1917 WOODROW WILSON (D), PRESIDENT

1913 Ratification of the Sixteenth (income tax) Amendment. Ratification of the Seventeenth (popular election of U.S. senators) Amendment. Underwood Tariff Act. Creation of the Federal Reserve system. Dedication of the Peace Palace at The Hague. Second Balkan War.

1914 Showing of "The Birth of a Nation." First ship passed through the Panama Canal. Meeting of the Second International at Brussels. United States Marines landed at Vera Cruz. Murder of the Austrian Archduke Francis Ferdinand at Sarajevo (June 28) precipitated the First World War. Invasion of Belgium. First Battle of the Marne. Battle of Ypres. Stalemate on the Western front. American declaration of neutrality.

1915 Reorganization of the Ku Klux Klan. American recognition of the Carranza government in Mexico. Japan forced the "Twenty-one Demands" on China. Turkey entered the war on the German side. Italy entered the war on the side of the Entente. Failure of the Dardanelles expedition. Russian defeat on the Eastern front. Defeat and occupation of Serbia. Increasing importance of the Mesopotamian front. German submarine sank *S.S. Lusitania* (May 7). Preparedness movement in the United States.

1916 Federal statute closed interstate commerce to products of child labor. Mooney and Billings convicted of bomb outrage in San Francisco (freed 1939). Germans attacked Verdun. Russian successes against Austria. Romania conquered by the Central Powers. British advance in Palestine. Indecisive naval battle of Jutland.

1917–1921 WOODROW WILSON (D), PRESIDENT

1917 Copper strike at Bisbee, Arizona, settled by vigilance committee. Puerto Ricans became American citizens. Lansing note to Japan recognized Japan's "special interest in China." U.S. entered the war on the side of the Entente April 6. Second battle of Ypres. Italian disaster at Caporetto. Capture of Jerusalem by the British. Russian breakdown and revolution. Proclamation of Russian Republic and eventual capture of power by the Bolsheviki (March–November). Emergence of Lenin and Trotsky.

1918 Woodrow Wilson enunciated the Fourteen Points. Russian-German peace signed at Brest-Litovsk (March 3). Second Battle of the Marne (August 8–September 28). Collapse of Bulgaria and Turkey. American attack at St. Mihiel. Collapse of Austria. Abdication of the Kaiser and proclamation of the German Republic. Armistice declared, November 11.

1919 First "artificial disintegration of the nucleus" announced by Rutherford. First crossing of the Atlantic by air (Alcock and Brown). Boston police strike. Eighteenth (prohibition) Amendment adopted (effective 1920). Versailles Peace Conference (January 18–June 28), ending the war and creating the League of Nations. Civil war increased in Russia. U.S. Senate rejected the Versailles Treaty (November 19). Russian-Polish war (to October 1920).

1920 First commercial radio broadcasting station, KDKA, opened in Pittsburgh. Beginning of the Sacco-Vanzetti case (April 15; trial, May 21, 1921; execution August 22, 1927). Nineteenth (woman suffrage) Amendment went into effect. League of Nations founded at Geneva.

1921–1923 WARREN GAMALIEL HARDING (R), PRESIDENT
1923–1925 CALVIN COOLIDGE (R), PRESIDENT

1921 Successful extraction of insulin by Banting, Best, and MacLeod (made public in 1922). Joint resolution by Congress declared peace with Germany and Austria. Washington Conference on limitation of armaments (to 1922). Founding of Fascist party in Italy. Beginning of famine in Russia. Announcement of New Economic Policy by Lenin.

1922 Fordney-McCumber Tariff Act. Transfer of oil reserves (Teapot Dome) by presidential order from Navy Department to Department of Interior. Bonus bill vetoed by Harding. Fascists march on Rome. Mussolini became dictator. Creation of the U.S.S.R. (proclaimed July 6, 1923).

1923 First (partial) talking movies shown at Rivoli Theatre, New York. Hitler's abortive "Beerhall Putsch" at Munich. French and Belgian troops occupied the Ruhr. President

Harding died on August 2, and was succeeded by Vice-President Calvin Coolidge. Dictatorship established in Spain (Primo de Rivera).

1924 Soviet constitution adopted. First round-the-world air flight. First performance of Gershwin's "Rhapsody in Blue." Investigation, by the Walsh Committee of the U.S. Senate, of scandals in the Harding regime. Inauguration of the Dawes plan for Germany. Evacuation of the Ruhr by the French and Belgians. Death of Nikolai Lenin. British Labor Government recognized the Soviets. Accord between Soviet Russia and China (Sun Yat-sen).

1925–1929 CALVIN COOLIDGE (R), PRESIDENT

1925 Scopes trial in Dayton, Tennessee. Congress authorized contracts with airlines for carrying mail. Nine-Power Treaty for limitation of armaments.

1926 New York-London telephone service established. Admiral Byrd circled the North Pole by plane. Pilsudski became dictator of Poland. U.S. Senate refused to adhere to World Court without reservations. Germany admitted to the League of Nations.

1927 Charles A. Lindbergh made nonstop solo flight, New York to Paris. First successful sound picture, "The Jazz Singer," shown in New York. First television transmission, New York to Washington. First successful mediation of a railway strike since 1907. Battle in Nicaragua between U.S. Marines and rebels under Sandino. Disarmament conference at Geneva. Severance of diplomatic relations between Great Britain and Russia.

1928 All-talking motion picture, "The Lights of New York," shown at Strand Theatre, New York City. Signing of the Briand-Kellogg Pact in Paris (renouncing war as an instrument of national policy) by fifteen powers (U.S. Senate ratified January 15, 1929). Chiang Kai-shek became President of China. Trotsky and his followers exiled from Russia. Rise of Joseph Stalin.

1929–1933 HERBERT HOOVER (R), PRESIDENT

1929 Admiral Byrd flew to the South Pole. Conviction of Albert

B. Fall, former Secretary of the Interior, for accepting a bribe from E. L. Doheny. Stock market crash October 29 marked beginning of the Great Depression. The Papal State revived as Vatican City. The Five-Year Plan begun in Russia (proposed in 1928).

1930 Drought in Far Western states. Hawley-Smoot Tariff Act passed. Hoover plan for unemployment relief. London Naval Conference. Sinclair Lewis awarded Nobel Prize in Literature. The French evacuated Baden and the Rhineland. "Liquidation of the kulaks" in Russia.

1931 Report of the Wickersham Commission on law enforcement. Japan invaded Manchuria. Proclamation of the Spanish Republic. Banking crisis in Austria. Great Britain abandoned the gold standard.

1932 March of the "Bonus Army" on Washington. The Lindbergh kidnaping case. Reconstruction Finance Corporation authorized. The Scottsboro case before the Supreme Court. Manchuria became Japanese puppet state (Manchukuo). The Japanese attacked Shanghai. Salazar became dictator of Portugal. End of the first Five-Year Plan in Russia.

1933–1937 FRANKLIN D. ROOSEVELT (D), PRESIDENT

1933 The Twentieth ("Lame Duck") Amendment. The Twenty-First (prohibition repeal) Amendment. Closing of American banks and of stock exchanges. The "Hundred Days" of the New Deal (AAA, NRA, PWA, WPA, CCC, etc.). Creation of the Tennessee Valley Authority. Federal insurance of bank deposits. United States recognized the Soviet Union. Adolf Hitler became Chancellor of Germany. Beginning of persecution of the Jews in Germany. Failure of the London economic conference through refusal of the United States to join in an international agreement for stabilizing currency. The Reichstag fire.

1934 The Johnson Act forbade American loans to countries defaulting on debt payments. The Catholic Legion of Decency formed. Philippine Independence Act passed. Nazi storm troopers killed numerous party leaders in a "blood purge." On the death of Hindenberg, Hitler became President as well as Chancellor of Germany. Russia joined the League of Nations. Signing of the Polish-German nonaggression pact. Outbreak of the Italian-Ethiopian war (to 1935).

1935 Beginnings of the CIO. Passage of the Federal Social Security Act. Creation of the Resettlement Administration. Creation of National Labor Relations Board. The NRA declared unconstitutional. The Saar returned to Germany by plebiscite. Hitler repudiated the Treaty of Versailles. Jews lost citizenship in Germany. Economic sanctions against Italy. End of the Bolivia-Paraguay struggle for the Chaco.

1936 Vogue of Father Coughlin's "Union for Social Justice." Passage of the Bonus Act. The AAA declared unconstitutional. Nye investigation into the munitions industry. Outbreak of the Spanish Civil War (to 1939). Death of George V; abdication of Edward VIII; proclamation of George VI. Eugene O'Neill awarded Nobel Prize in Literature. Japan and Germany signed the anti-Comintern pact. Proclamation of the "Rome-Berlin Axis." Buenos Aires conference agreed to Latin-American neutrality in case of war between any two American nations.

1937–1941 FRANKLIN D. ROOSEVELT (D), PRESIDENT

1937 Economic "recession." Proposed reform of the Supreme Court precipitated controversy. Wagner Act declared constitutional. FDR's "quarantine" speech at Chicago. U.S. Neutrality Act. The "China" incident provoked by Japanese. Japanese bombed the U.S.S. *Panay*. Interference by European powers in the Spanish Civil War. Emergence of the Franco dictatorship in Spain.

1938 Formation of the Dies Committee. Pearl Buck awarded Nobel Prize in Literature. Hitler invaded Austria. Hitler demanded the Sudeten area from Czechoslovakia. Munich Conference.

1939 Fission of the uranium nucleus announced by Hahn and Strassman. Invasion of Czechoslovakia by Hitler. Italy annexed Albania. Border war on Manchurian frontier between Japan and Russia. Russian-German nonagression pact. Finno-Russian War and annexation by Russia of parts of Finland (1940). Pius XI succeeded by Pius XII. Germany invaded

Poland September 1 and thus began World War II. In the United States, declaration of national emergency.

1940 Selective Service Act passed (by one vote in the House). End of the "phoney" war as Germany successively invaded Denmark, Norway, the Low Countries, and France. Churchill became Prime Minister. British army rescued from Dunkirk. Formation of the Vichy government in France. Battle of Britain. Italy attacked Greece. The "destroyer deal" with Great Britain. Death of Trotsky in Mexico after an assassin's attack.

1941–1945 FRANKLIN D. ROOSEVELT (D), PRESIDENT

1941 Announcement of the "Four Freedoms" by Roosevelt and of the Atlantic Charter by Roosevelt and Churchill. Creation of lend-lease. United States Marines occupied Iceland. United States occupation of Greenland. FDR appealed to Japanese Emperor for peace. Germany invaded Russia. Overrunning of the Balkan countries, including Greece. Sneak attack on Pearl Harbor by the Japanese December 7. Declaration of war by the United States.

1942 Fall of Singapore. Loss of the Philippines. Struggle for the control of the Pacific. American-British invasion of North Africa. Twenty-six nations declared the desirability of creating the United Nations.

1943 Race riots in Detroit and Harlem. Repeal of the Chinese Exclusion Act. Establishment of UNRRA. German retreat from Stalingrad. German surrender in North Africa. Fall of Mussolini and occupation of much of Italy by the Germans.

1944 Supreme Court upheld constitutional right of Negroes to vote in primary elections. Invasion of Normandy under direction of General Dwight D. Eisenhower. Reconquest of the Philippines by General Douglas MacArthur.

1945 FRANKLIN D. ROOSEVELT (D), PRESIDENT
1945–1949 HARRY S. TRUMAN (D), PRESIDENT

1945 FDR died April 12, 1945 and was succeeded by Vice-President Harry S. Truman. Russians reached Berlin. German collapse and surrender May 7. Dropping of first atomic bomb on Hiroshima August 6. Surrender of Japan. United Nations conference held at San Francisco, creating that body and also UNESCO (United Nations Educational, Scientific and Cultural Organization). Discovery in Germany of the horrors of the concentration camps, followed by the arrest of chief criminals. General MacArthur took over the government of Japan.

1946 Establishment of the United States Atomic Energy Commission. Further tests of atomic bombs at Bikini. Radar beam reached the moon. Henry A. Wallace ousted as Secretary of Commerce for opposing a "get tough with Russia" policy. First meeting of the United Nations and of UNESCO. Abdication of Victor Emanuel III and proclamation of Italian republic. Ending of hostilities proclaimed December 31. Philippines became independent Republic July 4.

1947 Announcement of the Marshall Plan. Selective Service Act expired. Creation of the (unified) Department of Defense. Taft-Hartley Act passed. Pakistan and India became autonomous commonwealths. U.N. partition of Palestine.

1948 First peacetime selective service bill passed. E.C.A. established. Appearance in national politics of the "Dixiecrat" party in the South and the "Progressive" party (Henry A. Wallace) nationally. Beginning of the Alger Hiss case (conviction 1950). Mohandas K. Gandhi assassinated. Communists took over Czechoslovakia. Proclamation of the State of Israel. The Berlin blockade and airlift.

1949–1953 HARRY S. TRUMAN (D), PRESIDENT

1949 President Truman announced evidence of an atomic explosion in Russia. American Communist leaders convicted of conspiracy (Judge Medina); conviction upheld by the Supreme Court (1950). End of the Nuremberg trials and conviction of chief war criminals. War between Israel and other (Arab) nations. Chiang Kai-shek resigned as President of China. Western Powers ended military government of Western Germany. Beginning of Tito deviation from Russia. North Atlantic Treaty Organization agreement signed by ten nations March 18.

HISTORICAL EVENTS

1950 The Atomic Energy Commission directed to work toward creating a hydrogen bomb. Attempt to assassinate President Truman. Peace Treaty with Japan. Soviet boycott of the Security Council of the U.N. United States recalled all consular officers from Communist China. India proclaimed a Republic. Vietnam declared a sovereign nation within the French Union. Invasion of South Korea by forces from the North (June 25). Invasion of South Korea by Chinese "volunteers" (November). William Faulkner awarded Nobel Prize in Literature for 1949. In the United States proclamation of state of national emergency (December 16).

1951 Creation of a government Commission on Internal Security. Passage of a bill setting up machinery for Universal Military Service. The Twenty-Second Amendment, limiting the president to two terms, became effective. General MacArthur recalled from Korea. California teachers reinstated when the state courts voided special loyalty oath imposed upon university professors. The Conservatives regained control in Great Britain (October 25). Opening of NATO headquarters in Europe. Treaty of peace with Japan signed by forty-nine nations, but not by Soviets. Nationalization of the oil industry in Iran. Occupation of Tibet by Chinese Communists. Communist China branded as an aggressor by the U.N. Armistice negotiations opened in Korea.

1952 King George VI died (February 6); Elizabeth II proclaimed Queen of Great Britain and the Commonwealth. Increasing racial tensions in Africa (Union of South Africa, Tunisia, Egypt, The Sudan). Japanese Peace Treaty put in force (April 28). Formal establishment of the European Defense Community. Keel of the first atomic submarine laid (June 14). Puerto Rico made a Commonwealth (July 25). Chinese mission in Moscow (August 17). New York teachers dismissed under the Feinberg Law on suspicion of being Communists (September 8). Dwight D. Eisenhower and Richard M. Nixon elected over Adlai E. Stevenson and John J. Sparkman (November 4), the first Republicans elected to the presidency and the vice-presidency since the administration of Hoover (442 electoral votes against 89). U.S. Atomic Energy Commission announced hydrogen bomb test at Eniwetok (November 16).

1953 Stalin died (March 5). U.S. agreed to assist West Germany to rearm when the European Defense Community would become effective (April 9). Creation of the new Department of Health, Education, and Welfare in the Cabinet (April 12). United Nations passed resolution calling for peace in Korea (April 19). Top of Mt. Everest reached by Hillary and Tenzing (May 29). Elizabeth crowned Queen (June 2). Egypt proclaimed a Republic (June 18). Korean armistice signed at Panmanjom (July 7). Russia announced possession of the hydrogen bomb (July 8). Earl Warren made Chief Justice of the U.S. Supreme Court (October 5). Secretary of State Dulles accused Senator McCarthy of attacking the "heart" of American foreign policy (December 1). In an address at the U.N., President Eisenhower called for an international pool of fissionable materials for peaceful purposes.

1954 The *Nautilus,* the first nuclear-powered submarine in the U.S. Navy, launched at Groton (January 21). Nasser became Premier of Egypt (February 25). U.S. Senate defeated the "Bricker amendment" limiting the treaty-making power of the president (February 26). The "most powerful" U.S. thermonuclear device exploded at Bikini (March 1). Army-McCarthy dispute hearings opened in Washington (April 22). Nationwide test of Salk polio vaccine began (April 26). U.S. Supreme Court unanimously ruled that racial segregation in the public schools is unconstitutional (May 17). Security clearance denied Robert Oppenheimer by the Atomic Energy Commission (June 29). Senate voted to investigate charges of misconduct against Senator McCarthy (August 2). President Eisenhower signed bill outlawing the Communist Party (August 24); also bill opening the way for the private development of nuclear power (August 30). Ernest Hemingway awarded Nobel Prize in Literature. Censure of Senator McCarthy voted by the Senate (December 2). Great Britain agreed to transfer the Suez Canal Zone to Egypt by June 1956.

1955 Winston Churchill retired as Prime Minister of Great Britain (April 5). The Bandung Conference of Asiatic and

African nations held (April). The Federal Republic of Germany (West Germany) attained full sovereignty (May 15). U.S. Supreme Court ruled that the states must end racial segregation in public schools within a "reasonable time" (May 31). U.S. Air Force Academy dedicated in Colorado (July 11). Austria regained full sovereignty (July 27). The first international conference on the peaceful uses of atomic energy held in Geneva (August 8–20). An army-navy revolt ousted Peron from Argentina (September). Ford Foundation announced grant of $500,000,000 to 4157 colleges, hospitals, and universities (December 13).

1956 In Russia, Khrushchev attacked the Stalin legend and the cult of individualism (February 14). Pakistan formally became an Islamic republic (March 23). Molotov resigned as Russian Foreign Minister (June 1). The British evacuated the Suez Canal Zone (June 13). Nasser elected President of Egypt (June 23). U.S. and Great Britain withdrew offer to assist financially in the Aswan Dam project (July 19–20). Nasser proclaimed nationalization of the Suez Canal (July 26) and rejected the plan of a London Conference over Suez (September 9). Soviet-Japan peace treaty signed (October 19). Anti-Soviet riots in Hungary (October 24). Israel invaded the Sinai Peninsula (October 29); British and French forces bombarded Egyptian oilfields (October 31). U.N. General Assembly called for withdrawal of Israeli-British-French forces (November 2). Soviet troops crushed the Hungarian rebellion (November 4). Eisenhower and Nixon re-elected, but the Democrats won control of both houses of Congress. End of bus segregation in Montgomery, Alabama (December 21). British and French forces evacuated from Egypt (December 22).

1957–1961 DWIGHT D. EISENHOWER (R), PRESIDENT

1957 Anthony Eden resigned as Prime Minister of Great Britain (January 9). European Common Market formed (February 19–20). U.S. Congress passed civil rights legislation giving federal courts power to hold offenders on criminal contempt charges and creating a Civil Rights Division in the Department of Justice (August 29). In Little Rock, Arkansas,

Governor Faubus ordered the Arkansas National Guard to prevent integration at Central High School; President Eisenhower ordered federal troops to enforce the court order requiring integration (September 4–24). U.S.S.R. launched first artificial satellite (October 4) and the first intercontinental ballistic missile. U.S. submarine *Nautilus* made successful trip under Arctic ice (October 28). November elections gave Democrats control of both houses of Congress. U.S. atomic-power station opened at Shippingport, Pennsylvania (December 2). U.S. launched "Atlas," first American intercontinental ballistic missile (December 17). Afro-Asian Peoples' Conference held December 26–January 1.

1958 *Daily Worker* suspended publication (January 13). U.S.-U.S.S.R. cultural exchange pact signed (January 27). Van Cliburn winner of Tchaikovsky International Piano Contest in Russia (April 13). Suez Canal settlement (April 29). Khrushchev became premier of U.S.S.R. (May 27). Vice-President Nixon's tour of certain Latin-American republics met by mob violence. De Gaulle in full political control of France (June 1), which soon adopted the "De Gaulle" constitution. U.S. submarine *Skate* remained under water for more than 31 days. U.S. landed marines in Lebanon (July 15). Sherman Adams, Assistant to President Eisenhower, forced to resign (September 22). John XXIII became Pope (October 28). All-Africa People's Conference held December 9–13. U.S. launched first "talking satellite" (December 18).

1959 Castro in control of Cuba after first year; visited U.S. (April 15–26). France began weakening ties with NATO. Alaska (January 3) and Hawaii (March 18) became the 49th and 50th states. Communist China invaded and took over Tibet. Congressional investigation into "fixed" TV contests. Federal courts proclaimed legal failure of Virginia's "massive resistance" to integration. First U.S. weather station in space (February 17). Last Civil War veteran (John B. Salling) died (March 16). John Foster Dulles resigned as Secretary of state (April 15; died May 24); succeeded by Christian Herter. St. Lawrence Seaway opened for traffic April 25; dedicated June 26. *Lady Chatterley's Lover* freed from charge of pornography by federal court in New York (July 21).

Khrushchev visited U.S., beginning September 15. Antarctica became a "scientific preserve" by treaty signed by several nations (December 1). Strife-torn Cyprus became a republic; Archbishop Makarios elected first president (December 13).

1960 Construction of Aswan Dam begun in Egypt by Nasser. U.S.S.R.-Cuba Economic Pact (February 13). France became fourth nuclear power. First important Negro "sit-down" in Greensboro, N.C. (February). New racial outburst in Union of South Africa (March 21–22); attempt to kill Premier Verwoerd (April 9); South Africa condemned by U.N. Security Council. U.S. "spy" plane shot down by U.S.S.R. (May 5). Israelis captured Adolf Eichmann (May 23); Eichmann sentenced to death (December 15, 1961). Belgian Congo became independent (June 30); U.N. forces entered Congo (August 12). Eisenhower visit to Japan canceled. Castro seized oil refineries in Cuba (July 1); signed pact with Communist China (July 23). Khrushchev attacked Hammarskjold, Secretary-General of U.N. (September 23). TV debates between Nixon and Kennedy (September 26–October 21). Kennedy, first Roman Catholic to be elected president, won by narrow margin. Furor over integration of schools in New Orleans (November). Neutralist government in Laos collapsed (December).

1961–1963 JOHN F. KENNEDY (D), PRESIDENT
1963–1965 LYNDON B. JOHNSON (D), PRESIDENT

1961 U.S. broke diplomatic relations with Cuba (January 3). Formation of U.S. Peace Corps (March 1). Union of South Africa withdrew from British Commonwealth of Nations (March 15). "Bay of Pigs" invasion of Cuba failed (April). Soviet Astronaut Gagarin, first human space traveler, safely orbited the globe (April 12). Freedom Rider movements began in May; U.S. marshals forced to intervene because of riots in Montgomery, Alabama. U.S. Astronaut Shepard made successful trip 115 miles into space in suborbital rocket flight (May 5). Kennedy-Khrushchev conference in Vienna (June 3–4). Rift between U.S.S.R. and Communist China more and more evident. U.N. Secretary-General Hammarskjold died in plane crash September 18 in Northern Rhodesia. U.S.S.R. exploded biggest nuclear bomb (October

23). U Thant chosen to succeed Hammarskjold. Castro announced communist aims (December 2). India invaded and annexed Portuguese enclaves (December).

1962 Organization of American States ostracized Cuba (January–February). John H. Glenn, first American astronaut to orbit the earth, circled the globe three times (February 20). Truce in Algeria (March); Algerian independence approved by French vote (April); Algerian independence proclaimed (July 3). U.S. rocket hit the moon (April 23). U.S. troops sent to Thailand May 12 because of explosive situation in nearby countries. U.S. Supreme Court outlawed official prayer in New York schools (June 25). U.S.S.R. cast 100th veto in U.N. Telstar in orbit (July 10). James Meredith's admission into University of Mississippi enforced, despite rioting (September 10–October 1). Pope opened 21st Ecumenical Council (October 11). Crisis over Soviet bases in Cuba (October 22–November 2). John Steinbeck awarded Nobel Prize in Literature (October 25). New York newspaper strike began (November 1). Richard Nixon defeated for governorship of California (November 6).

1963 De Gaulle rejected Britain's membership in the European Common Market (January 14). Treaty of cooperation and reconciliation between France and West Germany. U.S. resumed underground nuclear testing (February 8). The 114-day-long New York newspaper strike ended (April 1). Pope John XXIII issued his encyclical "Pacem in Terris" ("Peace on Earth") outlining a plan for safeguarding the peace in the atomic age (April 9). Antisegregation drive in Birmingham, Alabama, led to arrest of Reverend Martin Luther King and 60 others (April 12). Five weeks of racial tension in Birmingham. Major L. Gordon Cooper completed a successful 22-orbit space flight (May 16). Heads of 28 independent African states met in Addis Ababa in their first unity conference (May 22). Governor Wallace of Alabama, confronted by National Guard troops, stepped aside to allow two Negroes to enroll at the University of Alabama (June 11). President Kennedy asked Congress to enact the most far-reaching civil rights legislation to date (June 19). Two Soviet cosmonauts, one a woman, landed after twin orbits around the earth (June 19). The U.S., Great Britain, and the Soviet Union initiated a test ban agreement in Moscow prohibiting nuclear testing on land, in space, and under water (July 25). The U.N. Security Council passed a resolution to bar arms shipments to South Africa in a move aimed against that country's apartheid policy (August 7). James Meredith received a degree from the University of Mississippi, becoming its first Negro alumnus (August 18). Some 200,000 persons, white and Negro, marched peacefully on Washington to dramatize the fight for civil rights legislation (August 28). Governor Wallace backed down and permitted the integration of public schools after President Kennedy federalized the National Guard (September 11). A bomb exploded in a Birmingham church, killing four Negro girls, and renewed racial tension ensued (September 15). The Senate ratified the limited test ban treaty (September 22). Chancellor Adenauer of West Germany retired after 14 years and Ludwig Erhard succeeded him (October 16). President Kennedy was assassinated in Dallas; Vice-President Lyndon Johnson was sworn in as the 36th President (November 22). Lee Harvey Oswald, the alleged assassin, was shot and killed by Jack Ruby (November 24). President Johnson pledged to continue the policies of President Kennedy and asked for early action on the civil rights and tax cut bills (November 27).

Reading Lists of
American Literature
Since 1890

I · AMERICAN LITERATURE, 1890–1919

A · THE GENTEEL TRADITION

1 · *The Genteel Tradition: "Culture"*

In 1890 the cultural life of the United States was largely dominated by a complex of inherited values now ironically called the Genteel Tradition, after George Santayana's use of the phrase in *The Genteel Tradition at Bay* (1931). This complex of values was in general satisfactory to the inheritors of the tradition of (1) Anglo-Saxon (2) Protestant (3) middle-class America. It involved, among other matters:

a. A strong belief in metaphysical and moral idealism, in origin partly Platonic and partly Christian.

b. An equally strong belief that the highest cultural sanction is ethical, both in education ("liberal" education) and in the arts.

c. The general assumption that culture was self-culture; i.e., that the individual has within him capacities for self-directed growth and maturation in the light of such examples as Goethe, Arnold, and James Russell Lowell, the ideal being that of a well-rounded individual of noble purpose and refined intelligence.

The doctrine of culture in the Genteel Tradition may be studied in such representative works as these:

James Thompson Bixby (1843–1921), *The Crisis in Morals*, 1891 (Reissued in 1900 as *The Ethics of Evolution*.)

George William Curtis (1824–1892), *From the Easy Chair*, 1892 (There are two subsequent volumes: *Other Essays from the Easy Chair*, 1893, and *From the Easy Chair, Third Series*, 1894, which also illustrate genteel values.)

Charles W. Eliot (1834–1926), *American Contributions to Civilization and other Essays and Addresses*, 1897

Charles W. Eliot, *Educational Reform: Essays and Addresses*, 1898

Robert Grant (1852–1940), *Reflections of a Married Man*, 1892

Robert Grant, *The Art of Living*, 1899

Robert Grant, *Search-Light Letters*, 1899

Life and Letters of Edward Everett Hale, 2 vols., 1917 (Hale lived from 1822 to 1909.)

Thomas Wentworth Higginson (1823–1911), *Cheerful Yesterdays*, 1898

Hamilton Wright Mabie (1845–1916), *Books and Culture*, 1896

Barrett Wendell (1855–1921), *Liberty, Union and Democracy*, 1906 (The discussion of democracy is especially revelatory.)

Barrett Wendell, *The Privileged Classes*, 1908 (Note the implications of the title essay.)

Woodrow Wilson (1856–1924), *Mere Literature and Other Essays*, 1896

George Edward Woodberry (1855–1930), *Studies in Letters and Life*, 1890

2 · *The Genteel Tradition: The Theory of the Arts*

In all the arts, but especially in painting and literature (and notably in poetry), upholders of the tradition clung to a set of canons regarding art. Four elements were especially important:

a. Art is the expression of the highest idealism, whether this be interpreted to mean purposefulness in the cosmos, purposefulness in the life of the soul, or purposefulness in the life of the state.

b. Although good work in both the classic and the romantic schools was acceptable to the Genteel Tradition, art was acceptable principally as an expression of the highest morality (nobility).

c. Since, however, the weakness of the romantic tradition was likely to be "excess" or else formlessness, art as discipline was central (restraint, workmanship, craftsmanship).

d. The business of criticism was steadily to hold before artist and audience ideal standards not so much dogmatically conceived as garnered from traditional practice in Western Europe, New England, and (in lesser degree) other parts of the United States.

The theory of art (and of criticism) can be gleaned from careful reading of such critics as these:

William C. Brownell (1851–1928), *French Art,* 1892 (Especially chapters 1, 3.)

William C. Brownell, *American Prose Masters,* 1909 (Note especially the fresh interpretation of James Fenimore Cooper.)

Edmund C. Stedman (1833–1908), *The Nature and Elements of Poetry,* 1892 (Especially chapters 2 and 8.)

William Wetmore Story (1819–1895), *Conversations in a Studio,* 2 vols., 1890

William Wetmore Story, *Excursions in Art and Letters,* 1891

Charles Dudley Warner (1829–1900), *The Relation of Literature to Life,* 1896

George Edward Woodberry (1855–1930), *The Heart of Man,* 1899 (Note the Platonic overtones of "A New Defence of Poetry.")

Edmund C. Stedman, ed., *American Anthology,* 1900

The practice of poetry in the Genteel Tradition may be studied in a great number of volumes. The appearance of Stedman's anthology, however, summed up a period. Characteristic poetry within the tradition may be read, *inter alia,* in such pieces as these:

Richard Watson Gilder, "Ode" (474–475); "The Celestial Passion," (475); "The Heroic Age" (478)

Louise Imogene Guiney, selections (664–667)

Lloyd Mifflin, sonnets (496–498)

Lizette Woodworth Reese, selections (609–612)

Characteristic books of poetry in the tradition are:

Thomas Bailey Aldrich (1836–1907), *Unguarded Gates and Other Poems,* 1895 (*Writings,* 8 vols., 1897; 9 vols., 1907.)

Richard Hovey (1869–1900), *Along the Trail: A Book of Lyrics,* 1898. Hovey was also the author of an ambitious cycle of verse dramas, never completed, on the Arthurian legends:
The Quest of Merlin, 1891
The Marriage of Guenevere, 1891
The Birth of Galahad, 1898
Taliesin, 1899
The Holy Grail, 1902 (Fragmentary.)

Harry Lyman Koopman (1860–1937), *Morrow-Songs,* 1898

George Cabot Lodge (1837–1909), *The Song of the Wave and Other Poems,* 1898

Louise Chandler Moulton (1835–1908), *Poems,* 1889

Lizette Woodworth Reese (1856–1935), *A Handful of Lavender,* 1891

George Santayana (1863–1952), *Sonnets and Other Verses,* 1894/96; 1906

George Santayana, *A Hermit of Carmel and Other Poems,* 1901

Trumbull Stickney (1874–1904), *Dramatic Verses,* 1902

Trumbull Stickney, *Poems,* 1905

George Edward Woodberry, *The North Shore Watch and Other Poems,* 1890

George Edward Woodberry, *Selected Poems,* 1933

B · LITERATURE WRITTEN WITHIN
THE GENTEEL TRADITION

3 · *The Regional and the Local*

Regionalism, cultural pluralism, or the doctrine that the United States is composed of culturally autonomous regions (New England, the South, the Far West, etc.) offered writers in the Genteel Tradition both a challenge and an opportunity. On the one hand localism, through its insistence upon recording actual speech and custom, seemed to deny the validity of universal or idealized art; on the other hand, if properly managed, localism revealed the ideal in the actual, the universal in the present, the general in the particular. (A title like "A Village Lear" by Mary E. Wilkins Freeman illustrates this attempt.)

Techniques were developed in local color by which the flavorsomeness of provinciality was fused with a general philosophy of ideal conduct, typicality of human nature, and the dominance of universal moral standards, usually Christian. Favorite forms were the short story and the tale, the novel and poetry being less successful.

Earlier, simpler, and more sentimentalized versions of local color may be illustrated from:

Rose Terry Cooke (1827–1892), *Huckleberries Gathered from New England Hills,* 1891

Characteristic volumes in the period, arranged by regions, are these:

NEW ENGLAND

Alice Brown (1857–1948), *Meadow-Grass,* 1895

Alice Brown, *Tiverton Tales,* 1899

Mary E. Wilkins Freeman (1862–1930), *A New England Nun and Other Stories,* 1891

Mary E. Wilkins Freeman, *Jane Field,* 1893

Sarah Orne Jewett (1849–1909), *A Native of Wimby and Other Tales,* 1893

Sarah Orne Jewett, *The Country of the Pointed Firs,* 1896

Sarah Orne Jewett, *The Queen's Twin and Other Stories,* 1899

Edith Wharton (1862–1937), *Ethan Frome,* 1911

NEW YORK AND PENNSYLVANIA

Margaret Deland (1857–1944), *Old Chester Tales,* 1898

Margaret Deland, *Dr. Lavendar's People,* 1903

Margaret Deland, *The Awakening of Helena Ritchie,* 1906

Edward N. Westcott (1846–1898), *David Harum,* 1898

THE MIDWEST

James Whitcomb Riley (1849–1916), *Poems Here at Home,* 1893

James Whitcomb Riley, *Neighborly Poems,* 1897

Booth Tarkington (1869–1946), *The Gentleman from Indiana,* 1899

"Octave Thanet" (Alice French, 1850–1934), *Stories of a Western Town,* 1893 (Arkansas.)

THE SOUTH

Kate Chopin (1851–1904), *Bayou Folk,* 1894

Kate Chopin, *A Night in Acadie,* 1897

Grace King (1852–1932), *Balcony Stories,* 1893

F. Hopkinson Smith (1838–1915), *Colonel Carter of Cartersville,* 1891

THE NEGRO

Charles W. Chestnutt (1858–1932), *The Conjure Woman,* 1899

Paul Laurence Dunbar (1872–1906), *Lyrics of Lowly Life,* 1896

THE FAR WEST

Mary Austin (1868–1934), *The Land of Little Rain,* 1903

4 · *Historical Romance*

The vogue of historical romance, especially after 1898, owed much to British success in the field (Stevenson, Conan Doyle, Rider Haggard, Stanley J. Weyman, etc.), and much to the nationalism ebullient after the Spanish-American War. It posed certain problems to the Genteel Tradition analogous to those presented by local color. How reconcile the *locus* of an historical event with universal idealism? For the tradition a usable past was soon created by equating the hero and heroine of the historical novel with a philosophy of ideal conduct, and then fusing ideal conduct with an interpretation of history, providential in fact, known as "American idealism."

The following novels are representative of the vogue:

Mary H. Catherwood (1847–1902), *The Romance of Dollard*, 1889 (French settlement and exploration in the Old Northwest.)

Winston Churchill (1871–1947), *Richard Carvel*, 1899 (American Revolution.)

Winston Churchill, *The Crisis*, 1901 (Civil War.)

Winston Churchill, *The Crossing*, 1904 (The George Rogers Clark expedition.)

"Charles E. Craddock" (Mary Noailles Murfree, 1850–1922), *The Story of Old Fort Loudon*, 1899 (Colonial Tennessee.)

Paul Leicester Ford (1865–1902), *Janice Meredith*, 1899 (The Revolutionary period in the Middle Colonies.)

Thomas A. Janvier (1849–1913), *The Aztec Treasure House: A Romance of Contemporaneous Antiquity*, 1890 (Mexico.)

Mary Johnston (1870–1936), *Prisoners of Hope*, 1898 (Colonial Virginia.)

Mary Johnston, *To Have and To Hold*, 1900 (Colonial Virginia.)

Mary Johnston, *Audrey*, 1902 (Colonial Viriginia.)

S. Weir Mitchell (1829–1914), *Hugh Wynne, Free Quaker*, 1897 (Revolutionary Philadelphia.)

S. Weir Mitchell, *The Red City*, 1907 (The presidency of Washington.)

Thomas Nelson Page (1853–1922), *Red Rock*, 1898 (Civil War and Reconstruction in Virginia.)

Maurice Thompson (1844–1901), *Alice of Old Vincennes*, 1900 (The Old Northwest.)

5 · *Travel*

Although travel literature has been from the earliest period an important element in American letters, the Genteel Tradition put its special stamp upon this branch of nonfictional prose. Not the scientific expedition, not the voyage of geographical exploration, not the pragmatical book of advice to emigrants, but the travel book as the record of a "broadening" experience, the result of being exposed to an older, richer, or alien culture, was the theme of volumes characteristic of the tradition. Such a book was an explication of an alien culture (a) in terms of life older, richer, or wiser than that in the United States; and (b) in terms of social controls usually seen from the point of view of a governing class —the "gentlemen and ladies" of the alien culture. But it might also explicate the exotic or the far away.

Typical volumes of the period are these:

Charles A. Dana (1819–1897), *Eastern Journeys,* 1898

Richard Harding Davis (1864–1916), *About Paris,* 1895

Charles M. Flandrau (1871–1938), *Viva Mexico!* 1908

Lafcadio Hearn (1850–1904), *Two Years in the French West Indies,* 1890

Lafcadio Hearn, *Glimpses of Unfamiliar Japan,* 1894

William Dean Howells (1837–1920), *London Films,* 1905

William Dean Howells, *Certain Delightful English Towns,* 1906

William Dean Howells, *Roman Holidays,* 1908

William Dean Howells, *Seven English Cities,* 1909

Henry James (1843–1916), *Essays in London and Elsewhere,* 1893

Henry James, *English Hours,* 1905

Henry James, *The American Scene,* 1907

John La Farge (1835–1910), *An Artist's Letters from Japan,* 1897

Percival Lowell (1855–1916), *Occult Japan,* 1895

Edward Sylvester Morse (1838–1925), *Glimpses of China and Chinese Homes,* 1902

Edward Sylvester Morse, *Japan Day By Day,* 1917

F. Hopkinson Smith (1838–1915), *A White Umbrella in Mexico* 1889

Charles Warren Stoddard (1843–1909), *A Cruise under the Crescent: From Suez to San Marco,* 1898

Edith Wharton (1862–1937), *Italian Villas and their Gardens,* 1904

Edith Wharton, *Italian Backgrounds,* 1905

Edith Wharton, *A Motor-Flight Through France,* 1908

6 · *The Literature of Entertainment*

The phrase "literature of entertainment" is misleading. No attitude of condescension, however, is implied. In an era not yet affected by the movies, the radio, or television, writers faced problems resulting from the fact that the theater and the novel were two chief means of rational amusement, both dominated by the supposed requirements of women of the middle and upper classes, notably the young girl, whom H. H. Boyesen called "the iron virgin." Literature as purified entertainment for this purpose was both theorized and exemplified during the period.

The theory of literature as entertainment may be read in these books:

Francis Marion Crawford (1854–1909), *The Novel: What It Is,* 1893

Brander Matthews (1852–1929), *Aspects of Fiction and Other Ventures in Criticism,* 1896 (Note the emphasis upon technique as a mode of securing attention.)

Brander Matthews, *The Historical Novel and Other Essays,* 1901 (Note especially the implications of the title essay.)

Characteristic examples of fiction as entertainment are these:

Thomas Bailey Aldrich (1836–1907), *Two Bites at a Cherry,* 1894

Henry Cuyler Bunner (1855–1896), *Short Sixes,* 1890

Francis Marion Crawford, *Sant' Ilario,* 1889

Francis Marion Crawford, *A Cigarette Maker's Romance,* 1890

Francis Marion Crawford, *Don Orsino,* 1892 (The Saracinesca series, probably Crawford's most enduring claim to fame, consists of *Saracinesca,* 1887; *Sant' Ilario,* 1889; *Don Orsino,* 1892; and *Corleone,* 1896.)

Francis Marion Crawford, *Casa Braccio,* 2 vols., 1894

Francis Marion Crawford, *Via Crucis,* 1898

Francis Marion Crawford, *In the Palace of the King,* 1900 (A story of Philip II of Spain.)

Paul Leicester Ford (1865–1902), *The Great K & A Train Robbery*, 1897

Henry Blake Fuller (1857–1929), *The Chevalier of Pensieri Vani*, 1890

George Barr McCutcheon (1866–1928), *Graustark*, 1901

George Barr McCutcheon, *Brewster's Millions*, 1903

Booth Tarkington (1869–1946), *Monsieur Beaucaire*, 1900

7 · *The Literature of Childhood*

Following upon the success of Louisa May Alcott (*Little Women,* 1868–69; *Little Men,* 1871) and Mark Twain (*Tom Sawyer,* 1876; *Huckleberry Finn,* 1885), the last third of the nineteenth century and the opening decades of the twentieth century produced a library of fiction that treated childhood gravely or sympathetically. Most such material was written within the Genteel Tradition in the sense that the ethical and religious prepossessions of the cultured group were made the canons by which childhood was judged. The following volumes, of varying degree of literary merit or complexity, are relevant:

L. Frank Baum (1865–1919), *The Wonderful Wizard of Oz,* 1900

John Bennett (1865–1956), *Master Skylark: A Story of Shakespeare's Time,* 1897

Gelett Burgess (1866–1951), *Goops and How to Be Them,* 1900

Stephen Crane (1871–1900), *Whilomville Stories,* 1900

Charles G. Finney (1905–   ), *Past the End of the Pavement,* 1939

Henry James (1843–1916), *What Maisie Knew,* 1897

Owen M. Johnson (1878–1952), *The Varmint,* 1910

Owen M. Johnson, *The Tennessee Shad,* 1911

James Whitcomb Riley (1849–1916), *Rhymes of Childhood,* 1891

Booth Tarkington (1869–1946), *Penrod,* 1914

Jean Webster (1876–1916), *Daddy Long-Legs,* 1912

William Allen White (1868–1944), *The Court of Boyville,* 1899

Kate Douglas Wiggin (1856–1923), *Rebecca of Sunnybrook Farm,* 1903

8 · *Humor*

Two traditions have dominated the development of humor in American literature: (a) urbane humor, represented by a succession of authors extending from Benjamin Franklin and Washington Irving to Dorothy Parker and E. B. White; and (b) folk humor, represented by folk tales about Paul Bunyan and Tony Beaver, and by "literary" humorists who have sought to exploit popular humor. Among these are Mark Twain, Artemus Ward, "Josh Billings," and, eventually, Will Rogers. The problem before the Genteel Tradition was to "gentle" folk humor while retaining its tang. Among the instruments working toward this end were the three great comic magazines of the later nineteenth and early twentieth century: *Puck,* 1877–1918, *Judge,* 1881–1939, and *Life,* 1883–1936.

Humorists in the Genteel Tradition engaged in reconciling these two traditions (omitting Mark Twain) are represented by the following titles:

George Ade (1866–1944), *Fables in Slang,* 1900

George Ade, *More Fables,* 1900

John Kendrick Bangs (1862–1922), *A Houseboat on the Styx,* 1896

Guy Wetmore Carryl (1873–1904), *Fables for the Frivolous,* 1898

Guy Wetmore Carryl, *Grimm Tales Made Gay,* 1902

Finley Peter Dunne (1867–1936), *Mr. Dooley in Peace and War,* 1898

Finley Peter Dunne, *Mr. Dooley's Opinions,* 1901

John A. Mitchell (1845–1918), *The Last American,* 1889

Frank R. Stockton (1834–1902), *The Great War Syndicate,* 1889

Frank R. Stockton, *The Great Stone of Sardis,* 1898

Edward W. Townsend (1855–1942), *Chimmie Fadden, Major Max and Other Stories,* 1895

Harry Leon Wilson (1867–1939), *Ruggles of Red Gap,* 1915

9 · *The West*

Until the rise of Hollywood and the resultant easy connection between California and New York, the antinomy of East and West had been constant in American culture. The West was at once jealous of, and subservient to, the more experienced East; the East was both condescending and terrified before the lawless energy of the West—an area defined in the 1890's as the Great Plains, the Rocky Mountains, the intervening area, and the Pacific Coast. An image of the West was formed, in which at least five elements can be ascertained:

a. Surprise

b. Plenitude

c. Vastness

d. Melancholy

e. Incongruity—especially the incongruity of the petty human element against the naked grandeur of God's handiwork as exemplified in the Yosemite Valley, the Grand Canyon, and other characteristic Western natural phenomena.

On the whole, though not uniformly, the expression of Western life was kept uneasily in check by the imposition of genteel standards of achievement and control, which, by no means unsympathetic to Western energy and Western democracy, nevertheless evaluated Western ebullience by its eventual acquiescence in Eastern standards. In varying degree this can be studied in such books as the following:

Andy Adams (1859–1935), *The Log of a Cowboy,* 1903

Thomas Hornsby Ferril (1896–   ), *New and Selected Poems,* 1952

Zane Grey (1875–1939), *Riders of the Purple Sage,* 1912

Alfred Henry Lewis (1857–1914), *Wolfville,* 1897

Alfred Henry Lewis, *Wolfville Days,* 1902

John Muir (1838–1914), *The Mountains of California,* 1894

John Muir, *Our National Parks,* 1901
Eugene Manlove Rhodes (1869–1934), *Stepsons of Light,* 1921
Eugene Manlove Rhodes, *Copper Streak Trail,* 1922.
Theodore Roosevelt (1858–1919), *The Wilderness Hunter,* 1893
Owen Wister (1860–1938), *The Virginian,* 1902

C · FORCES HOSTILE TO THE GENTEEL TRADITION

10 · *The Fin de Siècle Spirit*

The Genteel Tradition eventually lost its cultural dominance. The reasons for its decline are complex, but among them was the emergence of new values and forces in art and thought, with which the tradition was unprepared to cope. Three outstanding elements of "revolt" were these:

a. The acceptance in the United States, at least in cities having some pretension to cosmopolitanism ("sophistication"), of the *fin de siècle* spirit.

b. The acceptance among educated Americans of the evolutionary hypothesis, an acceptance that, despite the emergence of the "Social Gospel" as a practical *via media* between Darwinism and Christianity, deepened the difficulties of the idealist position.

c. The enthusiastic proclamation of realistic and naturalistic theories of art, especially by the rising generation of novelists.

By the *fin de siècle* spirit one means, briefly, the emotional attitudes consequent upon the pessimistic belief that civilization was inevitably declining. Sensitive souls could find existence bearable only by throwing themselves into a life of sensation and of art. The philosophic attitude of pessimism was encouraged by the discovery of Schopenhauer, von Hartmann, Omar Khayyám, Wagner, Nordau, and Nietzsche; and the prestige of the Decadent and Art-for-Art's-Sake movements in London, coupled with desultory information about an analogous development in French, German, and Italian poetry, helped to sustain an American aesthetic revolt.

One or another phase of American pessimism may be studied in the following books:

Ignatius Donnelly (1831–1901), *Caesar's Column,* 1891

Edgar Saltus (1855–1921), *The Philosophy of Disenchantment,* 1885

Edgar Saltus, *The Anatomy of Negation,* 1886

George Santayana (1863–1952), *Lucifer,* 1899

"Mark Twain" (Samuel L. Clemens, 1835–1910), *The Mysterious Stranger*, 1916

The aesthetic and impressionist movements can be studied in these titles:

Bliss Carman (1861–1929) and Richard Hovey (1864–1900), *Songs from Vagabondia*, 1894

Chap-Book Essays, 1896

H. C. Chatfield-Taylor (1865–1945), *Two Women and a Fool*, 1895

Lafcadio Hearn (1850–1904), *Chita, A Memory of Last Island*, 1889

Lafcadio Hearn, *Exotics and Retrospectives*, 1898

Lafcadio Hearn, *Shadowings*, 1900

Lafcadio Hearn, *Fantastics and Other Fancies*, 1914

James Gibbons Huneker (1860?–1921), *Melomaniacs*, 1902

James Gibbons Huneker, *Iconoclasts*, 1905

James Gibbons Huneker, *Promenades of an Impressionist*, 1910

James Gibbons Huneker, *Painted Veils*, 1920

Harry Thurston Peck (1856–1914), *The Personal Equation*, 1898

Percival Pollard (1869–1911), *Their Day in Court*, 1909

Edgar Saltus, *Imperial Purple*, 1892

Vance Thompson (1863–1925), *French Portraits*, 1900

11 · *The American Interpretation of Evolution*

Although the work of Lyell (*Principles of Geology,* 1830–1833 and often re-edited and reprinted) was known to American geologists, and although Darwin's *Origin of Species* (1859) was immediately debated by American scientists and theologians, discussion did not grow heated over the problem of evolution until the publication of Huxley's *Man's Place in Nature* (1863) and Darwin's *The Descent of Man* (1871). The appearance of Huxley at the ceremonies opening The Johns Hopkins University (1876), and the virtual underwriting of Herbert Spencer (1820–1903) by American money so that he might complete the Synthetic Philosophy (the last volume of *Principles of Sociology* appeared in 1896) were events of importance in the controversy. Spencer's sweeping generalizations appealed to the American love of broad statement; his distrust of state action pleased industrial leaders; and his vague assurance that progress was virtually assured to man by evolution pleased reformers and labor leaders, committed as they were to a principal of voluntarism.

The American parallel to Spencer is *Outlines of Cosmic Philosophy,* 2 vols., 1874, by John Fiske. Less formal but equally cogent treatments of the evolutionary hypothesis may be read in such works as the following:

John Fiske (1842–1901), *Excursions of an Evolutionist,* 1884 (Note the essay, "Our Aryan Forefathers," and the one on "The Meaning of Infancy." This last is Fiske's original contribution to evolutionary theory.)

John Fiske, *The Destiny of Man,* 1884 (Key chapters are I–V, X, XV–XVI.)

John Fiske, *The Idea of God as Affected by Modern Knowledge,* 1886 (Key chapters are V–VII, XI, XIV.)

John Fiske, *A Century of Science,* 1899

John Fiske, *Through Nature to God,* 1899 (Note the evolutionary implications in "The Cosmic Roots of Love and Self-Sacrifice.")

William James (1842–1910), *The Principles of Psychology,* 2 vols., 1890 (Note especially the theory of the function of the brain and the theory of instincts.)

Henry F. Osborn (1857–1935), *From the Greeks to Darwin,* 1894

Josiah Royce (1855–1916), *Fugitive Essays,* 1920 (Note the essay on "The Nature of Voluntary Progress.")

Andrew D. White (1832–1918), *A History of the Warfare of Science with Theology in Christendom,* 2 vols., 1896

12 · *The Application of Evolutionary Theory*

The evolutionary hypothesis affected and still affects all departments of American culture. Those who struggled with the problem of the relation of the evolutionary hypothesis to the social present and to the probable future of American life may be divided into two broad categories: one group which, imaginatively or philosophically, interpreted evolution as supporting a doctrine of loyalty to idealism, social progress, and religious "modernism," usually taking shape as the "Social Gospel"; and another, more disillusioned, group which tended to the point of view that progress was an illusion, state action for ameliorative purposes a piece of sentimentality, and altruism a cloak for ruthless competition in the struggle for existence.

The following writers interpreted evolution as a challenge to a more heroic loyalty to the ideal:

William Vaughn Moody (1869–1910), *Poems and Plays*, 2 vols., 1912 (See especially *The Masque of Judgment*, 1900, *The Fire-Bringer*, 1904, and the unfinished *Death of Eve* among the poetic dramas; and, among the poems, "Gloucester Moors," "The Menagerie," "Ode on a Soldier Fallen in the Philippines," "Ode in Time of Hesitation," and "The Troubling of the Waters.")

Josiah Royce (1855–1916), *The Philosophy of Loyalty*, 1908

The Catholic position as to social amelioration is well expressed in:

John L. Spaulding (1840–1916), *Socialism and Labor*, 1902

The general doctrine of the Social Gospel may be studied in:

Lyman Abbott (1835–1922), *The Evolution of Christianity*, 1892 (Note especially chapters 1, 8–9.)

Washington Gladden (1836–1918), *Ruling Ideas of the Present Age*, 1895

Washington Gladden, *How Much Is Left of the Old Doctrines?* 1899

Walter Rauschenbusch (1861–1918), *Christianity and the Social*

Crisis, 1907 (Note especially the chapters on "The Present Crisis" and "The Stake of the Church in the Social Movement.")

Walter Rauschenbusch, *Christianizing the Social Order,* 1912 (Key chapters are those on "The Case of Christianity against Capitalism," "Economic Democracy," and "The Economic Basis for Fraternity.")

Among novels dramatizing the Social Gospel are:

Winston Churchill (1871–1947), *The Inside of the Cup,* 1913

Charles M. Sheldon (1857–1946), *In His Steps,* 1896

Albion W. Tourgée (1838–1905), *Murvale Eastman, Christian Socialist,* 1890

The view of progress under evolution is less roseate in such writers as these:

Oliver Wendell Holmes (1841–1935), *Collected Legal Papers,* 1920 (See especially "The Path of the Law," "The Theory of Legal Interpretation," and "Law in Science and Science in Law.")

William James (1842–1910), *Varieties of Religious Experience,* 1902 (See especially chapters 4, 10, 20.)

Alfred Thayer Mahan (1840–1914), *The Influence of Sea Power upon History, 1600–1783,* 1890

Theodore Roosevelt (1858–1919), *The Winning of the West,* 4 vols., 1889–1896 (In the competition of races the "Anglo-Saxons" must conquer to live.)

Theodore Roosevelt, *The Rough Riders,* 1899

William Graham Sumner (1840–1910), *Essays,* 2 vols., eds. Keller and Davie, 1934 (In Volume I, see especially "Religion and Mores," "War," "Earth Hunger," "The Forgotten Man"; in Volume II, "What Makes the Rich Richer and the Poor Poorer?" and "The Conquest of the United States by Spain.")

William Graham Sumner, *Folkways,* 1907 (On the relativity of morals.)

Frederick Jackson Turner (1861–1932), *The Frontier in American History*, 1920 (An expansion of his famous paper of 1893, "The Significance of the Frontier in American History.")

Thorstein Veblen (1857–1929), *The Theory of the Leisure Class*, 1899 (See especially chapters 3, 4, 14.)

Thorstein Veblen, *The Theory of Business Enterprise*, 1904

13 · *The Forces of Realism: William Dean Howells*

If the phases of American literary history were denominated by the names of their principal authors, the period covered by this part of the outline would be the Age of Howells. Chief exponent of a theory of realism, cultured exponent during the period of a mild but sincere form of gradualistic socialism, Howells befriended younger and more daring authors and himself exemplified a quality of fictional realism which devoted itself to the sympathetic presentation of average middle-class American life and its problems. Representative works by him are these:

LITERARY THEORY

William Dean Howells (1837–1920), *Criticism and Fiction,* 1891

Heroines of Fiction, 2 vols., 1901 (In the course of these amiable comments on fictional heroines Howells also uttered a great deal of valuable technical advice on the writing of fiction.)

Literature and Life, 1902

FICTION

The Rise of Silas Lapham, 1885

Annie Kilburn, 1888

A Hazard of New Fortunes, 1890

The Shadow of a Dream, 1890

The Quality of Mercy, 1892

The World of Chance, 1893

The Landlord at Lion's Head, 1897

The Son of Royal Langbrith, 1904

The Vacation of the Kelwyns, 1920

SOCIALISTIC UTOPIANISM

A Traveler from Altruria, 1894

Through the Eye of a Needle, 1907

14 · *The Forces of Realism: The Contemporaries of Howells*

From 1890 to his death in 1916, Henry James, in the eyes of present-day criticism a greater writer than Howells, lived principally in England or on the Continent except for occasional visits to his native land, which he observed almost with the eyes of an alien. In 1915 he became a British subject. His influence was to be greater after World War I than before, but so far as it was felt by writers in the period 1890–1920 it was a technical influence upon psychological fiction. Probably his most influential work of literary theory was *Notes on Novelists* (1914).

Putting aside the more difficult later works, titles of novels that contributed to American realism from 1890 to 1920 are these:

Henry James (1843–1916), *The Tragic Muse,* 1890
Henry James, *The Spoils of Poynton,* 1897
Henry James, *What Maisie Knew,* 1897
Henry James, *The Awkward Age,* 1899
Henry James, *The Wings of the Dove,* 1902
Henry James, *The Ambassadors,* 1903

Other lesser writers, more immediately in touch with American life, advanced the cause of realism. Representative writers and representative novels by them follow:

Gertrude Atherton (1857–1948), *Patience Sparhawk and Her Times,* 1897
Gertrude Atherton, *Senator North,* 1900
Gertrude Atherton, *Black Oxen,* 1923
Arlo Bates (1850–1918), *The Puritans,* 1898 (This novel of Boston should be read in conjunction with its predecessors, *The Pagans,* 1888, and *The Philistines,* 1889.)
H. H. Boyesen (1848–1895), *The Mammon of Unrighteousness,* 1891
Francis Marion Crawford (1854–1909), *Katharine Lauderdale,* 1894 (A sequel, *The Ralstons,* appeared the following year.)
Francis Marion Crawford, *Adam Johnstone's Son,* 1896

Margaret Deland (1857–1944), *John Ward, Preacher,* 1888

Edward Eggleston (1837–1902), *The Faith Doctor,* 1891

Harold Frederic (1856–1898), *The Lawton Girl,* 1890

Harold Frederic, *The Copperhead,* 1893

Harold Frederic, *The Damnation of Theron Ware,* 1896

Robert Grant (1852–1940), *Unleavened Bread,* 1900

Robert Grant, *The Chippendales,* 1909 (A sequel, *The Dark Horse,* appeared in 1931.)

"Mark Twain" (Samuel L. Clemens, 1835–1910), *Pudd'nhead Wilson,* 1894

"Mark Twain," *The Man That Corrupted Hadleyburg,* 1900

Charles Dudley Warner (1829–1900), *The Golden House,* 1894

Charles Dudley Warner, *That Fortune,* 1899

15 · *The Forces of Naturalism: The Meliorists*

Distinctions between realism and naturalism are hard to make. Naturalism, however, tends to concentrate upon the concept of man as a superior animal rather than as an individual soul and upon his more elemental motives and therefore upon the more disagreeable or physiologically unpleasant events of life. Naturalism often adopts a theory of physical determinism that strikes alike at the roots of idealism and of altruism. Many American novelists, however, though accepting "naturalistic" themes and even naturalistic concepts of character, felt that naturalism, by discarding hampering (because unrealistic) supernatural or idealistic presuppositions, would open the road to necessary reforms in society, supposedly based on "scientific" truth. American naturalists, therefore, tend to fall into two divisions: the meliorists or "soft" naturalists, who are but imperfect exponents of rigorous naturalism; and the determinists (in greater or less degree), who follow with greater consistency the logic of nineteenth-century science, in which events in a closed universe are beyond the control of an individual. The present list gives representative work by "soft" naturalists (some critics deny they are naturalists at all); the following list (16) gives representative work by the "hard" naturalists.

An imperfect theory of fictional naturalism may be read in:

Hamlin Garland (1860–1940), *Crumbling Idols,* 1894 (Much light is thrown both upon Garland and upon his contemporaries by his *Son of the Middle Border,* 1917; *Roadside Meetings,* 1930.)

Frank Norris (1870–1902), *The Responsibilities of the Novelist,* 1903

Representative works of fiction which, naturalistic in part, nevertheless seek improvement in the social and political order are these:

Hamlin Garland, *Main-Travelled Roads,* 1891

Hamlin Garland, *A Spoil of Office,* 1892

Hamlin Garland, *Prairie Folks,* 1893

Hamlin Garland, *Rose of Dutcher's Coolly,* 1895

Hamlin Garland, *Jason Edwards,* 1897
Jack London (1876–1916), *The Call of the Wild,* 1903
Jack London, *The Sea-Wolf,* 1904
Jack London, *The Iron Heel,* 1907
Jack London, *Martin Eden,* 1909
Frank Norris, *McTeague,* 1899
Frank Norris, *The Octopus,* 1901
Frank Norris, *The Pit,* 1903

16 · *The Forces of Naturalism: The Determinists*

For comment, see the headnote to list 15 above.

Ambrose Bierce (1842–1914?), *In the Midst of Life,* 1898 (Originally published in 1891 as *Tales of Soldiers and Civilians.*)

Ambrose Bierce, *Can Such Things Be?* 1893

Stephen Crane (1871–1900), *Maggie: A Girl of the Streets,* 1893; 1896 (First published privately under the pseudonym "Johnston Smith," it was revised for the 1896 printing under his own name.)

Stephen Crane, *The Red Badge of Courage,* 1895

Stephen Crane, *George's Mother,* 1896

Stephen Crane, *The Monster and Other Stories,* 1899 (Contains "The Blue Hotel.")

Theodore Dreiser (1871–1945), *Sister Carrie,* 1900 (First printed in 1900, it was withheld from circulation by the publisher; in 1912 it was reissued.)

Theodore Dreiser, *Jennie Gerhardt,* 1911

Theodore Dreiser, *The Financier,* 1912

Theodore Dreiser, *The Titan,* 1914

Theodore Dreiser, *The "Genius,"* 1915

Theodore Dreiser, *An American Tragedy,* 1925

Theodore Dreiser, *The Stoic,* 1947 (With *The Financier* and *The Titan* this book constitutes the "Trilogy of Desire." The main character, Frank Cowperwood, is a fictional treatment of the Philadelphia tycoon Charles T. Yerkes.)

AMERICAN LITERATURE

D · MOVEMENTS OF RECONSTRUCTION

17 · *New Viewpoints in Social Interpretation*

From 1893 to 1897–98 the country suffered from "The Panic of
1893." The American experiment seemed to be headed for
disaster, industrial democracy looked impossible, and American
society appeared to be "sick." By and large the middle classes
were unaware of the nature of the sociological puzzle before the
country; consequently an important library of books appeared
designed to describe sympathetically a variety of American
"underdogs" and to indicate ways and means of improving both
the condition of the misfits and of the American commonwealth.
The "tramp" was discovered; the slums were dramatized; problems of the Negro and of the immigrant were posed. A selected
list of such books follows:

Jane Addams (1860–1935), *Twenty Years at Hull-House,* 1910
Jane Addams, *The Second Twenty Years at Hull-House,* 1930
Mary Antin (1881–1949), *The Promised Land,* 1912
George Washington Cable (1844–1925), *The Negro Question,*
    1888
Josiah Flynt (Willard) (1869–1907), *Tramping with the
    Tramps,* 1899
Josiah Flynt (Willard), *Notes of an Itinerant Policeman,* 1900
Laurence Gronlund (1846–1899), *Our Destiny,* 1891
Laurence Gronlund, *The New Economy,* 1898
Jack London (1876–1916), *The People of the Abyss,* 1903
Simon N. Patten (1852–1922), *The New Basis of Civilization,*
    1907
Jacob A. Riis (1849–1914), *How the Other Half Lives,* 1890
Jacob A. Riis, *The Making of an American,* 1901
Upton Sinclair (1878–   ), *The Jungle,* 1906 (Fiction.)
Lester Frank Ward (1841–1913), *The Psychic Factors of Civili-
    zation,* 1893 (This, though a commentary on his *Dynamic
    Sociology,* 1883, can be read independently.)
Booker T. Washington (1856–1915), *Up from Slavery,* 1901
Walter A. Wyckoff (1865–1908), *The Workers: The East,* 1897
Walter A. Wyckoff, *The Workers: The West,* 1898

18 · *Social Reform: Program and Experience*

The disturbing discovery that large classes of Americans and of persons resident in America were not enjoying the fruits of an ideal democratic society led to considering ways and means to achieve practical reform within the existing political order. The climax of this movement was of course the Progressive ("Bull Moose") Movement, which reached its height in the election of 1912 when Theodore Roosevelt battled successfully to defeat Taft and unsuccessfully to defeat the "New Freedom" of Woodrow Wilson. The characteristic literary expression corresponding to the political movement was the literature of muckraking, which, except for the name, was not new in the twentieth century. Much of the muckraking library was ephemeral, although some of it has lasting value. The most sagacious volume rising out of the "progressivism" of the early twentieth century, a key book for the interpretation of American life before World War I, is:

> Herbert D. Croly (1869–1930), *The Promise of American Life,* 1909

Other general books of more than ephemeral value include:

> Henry Demarest Lloyd (1847–1903), *Wealth against Commonwealth,* 1894 (See especially chapters 5, 14, 24, 25.)
> Lincoln Steffens (1866–1936), *The Shame of the Cities,* 1904

Autobiographical writings by the progressives are at once documents of primary importance for understanding the doctrine of change within the American system, and books of value as revelations of character or personality. Among these are:

> Tom L. Johnson (1854–1911), *My Story,* 1911
> Robert M. LaFollette (1855–1925), *Autobiography,* 1913
> Lincoln Steffens, *Autobiography,* 1931

Insight into the general mood of progressivism may be gained from:

> John Jay Chapman (1862–1933), *Causes and Consequences,* 1898

AMERICAN LITERATURE

Theodore Roosevelt (1858–1919), *The Strenuous Life,* 1900
Woodrow Wilson (1856–1924), *The New Freedom,* 1913
The Public Papers of Woodrow Wilson, eds. Ray Stannard
  Baker and William E. Dodd, 6 vols., 1925–1927 (Particularly
  the two volumes entitled *The New Democracy.*)

19 · *Novels of Social and Political Reform*

Like *Pilgrim's Progress,* the novel of political exposure, designed to dramatize the conflict between political righteousness and moral idealism, and the sinister forces of political corruption, amoral business enterprise, and the gangster, the grafter, the briber, the bribe-taker, and the boss, assured readers of the eventual victory of what is good and pure. Many of these books contain vivid and sympathetic studies of political personalities or record in fictional guise dramatic, political, and economic struggles. Representative works of this sort are here listed:

Winston Churchill (1871–1947), *Coniston,* 1906

Winston Churchill, *My Crewe's Career,* 1908

Paul Leicester Ford (1865–1902), *The Honorable Peter Stirling,* 1894

Ellen Glasgow (1874–1945), *The Voice of the People,* 1900

Ellen Glasgow, *The Romance of a Plain Man,* 1909

Robert Herrick (1868–1938), *The Web of Life,* 1900

Robert Herrick, *Memoirs of an American Citizen,* 1905

Robert Herrick, *Clark's Field,* 1914

Alfred Henry Lewis (c. 1858–1914), *The Boss,* 1903

David Graham Phillips (1867–1911), *The Cost,* 1904

David Graham Phillips, *The Plum Tree,* 1905

David Graham Phillips, *The Deluge,* 1905

David Graham Phillips, *Light-Fingered Gentry,* 1907

David Graham Phillips, *The Second Generation,* 1907

David Graham Phillips, *Susan Lenox: Her Fall and Rise,* 1917

Brand Whitlock (1869–1934), *The 13th District,* 1902

20 · *The Interpretation of Fiction*

Other novelists dug deeper and saw further. They were gravely alarmed by the transition out of an agrarian into an industrial society, out of a social order having relatively fixed moral codes into a society living by the spending standard, and out of an epoch still retaining the heroic flavor of the pioneer into an era which in William James's phrase was dedicated to the worship of the bitch goddess, Success.

In New York City the slow corruption of the "natural" aristocracy of Little Old New York by the intrusion of vulgar wealth was chronicled by Edith Wharton (1862–1937) in such novels as these:

> *The House of Mirth*, 1905
> *The Reef*, 1912
> *The Custom of the Country*, 1913
> *The Age of Innocence*, 1920
> *Hudson River Bracketed*, 1929

What Mrs. Wharton did for a city, Ellen Glasgow (1874–1945) in some sense did for a whole commonwealth, her native state of Virginia, as in:

> *The Deliverance*, 1904
> *The Miller of Old Church*, 1911
> *Virginia*, 1913
> *Life and Gabriella*, 1916
> *Barren Ground*, 1925
> *They Stooped to Folly*, 1929
> *The Sheltered Life*, 1932
> *Vein of Iron*, 1935

In the Middle West, Booth Tarkington (1869–1946) broadened the lens to take in a whole region moving from a village republic to a megalopolitan culture in:

1890–1919

The Turmoil, 1915
The Magnificent Ambersons, 1918
Alice Adams, 1921
The Midlander, 1923

And for the Great Plains, Willa Cather (1876–1947) chronicled a similar transition, although hope arose (as in the case of the other novelists) through the appearance of characters of integrity, even amid vulgarity:

The Song of the Lark, 1915
My Ántonia, 1918
A Lost Lady, 1923
The Professor's House, 1925
Death Comes for the Archbishop, 1927

21 · *Governing Philosophies*

While novelists were penetrating deeper into American life, American philosophy, now fully mature, was digging deeper still, posing the problem of relativism against the absolute, and endeavoring to fuse the implications of nineteenth-century science, notably physics and biology, with some of the traditional postulates of the metaphysician. Not all the authors listed below were technical philosophers. Moreover, the kind of information necessary to grasp the relation between professional philosophical systems and the impact or influence of a point of view upon the general intellectual life of the country does not necessarily require expertise in logic and metaphysics. The titles which follow seem to be more readable and less difficult volumes by writers whose formal treatises, if they wrote any, may lie beyond the comprehension of readers untrained in epistemology and logic.

Thus the most important of Royce's philosophical works seems to be *The World and the Individual*, 1900, 1901 (two successive volumes), yet the following titles are easier reading and give at least a working acquaintance with him:

Josiah Royce (1855–1916), *The Spirit of Modern Philosophy*, 1892 (Note especially the "General Introduction" and, *inter alia*, the discussions of Hegel and Schopenhauer.)

Josiah Royce, *Studies of Good and Evil*, 1898

Josiah Royce, *The Hope of the Great Community*, 1916

Interesting in connection with Royce is a book by an opponent of his:

Francis Ellingwood Abbot (1836–1903), *The Way Out of Agnosticism*, 1890

A darker interpretation of the course of history appears in the following:

Brooks Adams (1848–1927), *The Law of Civilization and Decay*, 1895

Brooks Adams, *America's Economic Supremacy*, 1900

Brooks Adams, *The New Empire*, 1902

Henry Adams (1838–1918), *Mont St.-Michel and Chartres,* 1904

Henry Adams, *The Education of Henry Adams,* 1907 (1918)

Brooks Adams and Henry Adams, *The Degradation of the Democratic Dogma,* 1919 (This is Henry Adams' *Letter to Teachers of American History,* 1910, plus "The Tendency of History," 1909, with introductory matter by Brooks Adams.)

A greater degree of affirmation, even of optimism, was expressed, however, by two philosophers thought to be more characteristic of the twentieth century than any of the above:

John Dewey (1859–1952), *The School and Society,* 1899

John Dewey, *Democracy and Education,* 1916

Joseph Ratner (1901–   ), *Intelligence in the Modern World: John Dewey's Philosophy,* 1939 (This is an anthology of characteristic writings by Dewey, prefaced by an elaborate introduction. Section 11, "Science and Philosophy of Education," is informative.)

William James (1842–1910), *The Will to Believe and Other Essays,* 1897

William James, *Pragmatism,* 1907

Influenced by evolution but standing aloof from the others is George Santayana (1863–1952). Representative volumes by him are these:

George Santayana, *Interpretations of Poetry and Religion,* 1900

George Santayana, *The Life of Reason,* 5 vols., 1905–1906

George Santayana, *Scepticism and Animal Faith,* 1923

George Santayana, *The Realm of Being,* 4 vols., 1942 (Includes the four "realms" concerning which volumes were published as follows: *Essence,* 1927; *Matter,* 1930; *Truth,* 1937; *Spirit,* 1940.)

Logan P. Smith, ed., *Little Essays Drawn from the Writings of George Santayana,* 1920

AMERICAN LITERATURE

F · NEW DIRECTIONS

22 · The Drama

Before the advent of Eugene O'Neill (1888–1953), American theaters prospered on melodrama, sensationalism, domestic drama, the star system, and Shakespeare. From 1895, they were controlled by the Theatrical Syndicate and later by the United Booking Office. New York City was the center and the rest of the nation was "The Road." Realism was slow to be accepted on the stage in spite of the advances in American fiction, between 1890 and World War I, and the appearance abroad of Ibsen, Strindberg, Hauptmann, Wedekind, and other naturalists (who often turned into symbolists). Much of what entertained American audiences in these years is subliterary though good theater; but a few playwrights tried to break new ground with problem plays, witty satire, fantasy, political issues, and the inevitable psychological analyses.

James A. Herne (1838–1901), *Margaret Fleming*, 1890
Augustus Thomas (1857–1934), *Alabama*, 1891
Clyde Fitch (1865–1909), *The Climbers*, 1901
David Belasco (1859–1931), *The Girl of the Golden West*, 1905
William Vaughn Moody (1869–1910), *The Great Divide*, 1906
Langdon Mitchell (1862–1935), *The New York Idea*, 1906
Edward Sheldon (1886–1946), *The Nigger*, 1907

Eugene O'Neill's first productions were one-act plays of the sea, notably *The Long Voyage Home* (1917) and *The Moon of the Caribbees* (1918). When he moved from Provincetown to Broadway, he began a career which firmly established him as America's most gifted playwright. His best early plays are:

The Emperor Jones, 1920
Anna Christie, 1921
"The Hairy Ape," 1921

The major works of the next decade include:

Desire Under the Elms, 1924

158

1890–1919

The Great God Brown, 1928
Strange Interlude, 1928
Mourning Becomes Electra, 1931

O'Neill broke a long silence with *The Iceman Cometh* in 1946. After his death in 1953, Broadway saw three more of his plays, the first of which, *Long Day's Journey into Night* (1956), sparked an O'Neill revival.

23 · *The Poetic Renaissance: Preliminary*

Just prior to World War I the most forward-looking movement in American letters, judged from the point of view of subsequent developments, was probably the "poetic renaissance" which may be dated from the founding of *Poetry: A Magazine of Verse* by Harriet Monroe (1860–1936) in Chicago in 1912. This movement not only sought to end the whole nineteenth-century manner in verse, but served also as a bridge into the development of poetry in the twentieth century subsequent to World War I. One of the poets is still (1964) alive; most of them were affected by both World Wars and by the world events of the thirties. As a whole, however, the names grouped here may be thought of as constituting a transition movement between the first half of the period under survey and the later portion.

The initial struggle concerned poetic language, figures of speech, and the subject matter of verse, a struggle which swirled around the doctrine of "Imagism," which was for a time an international matter, part of the conflict occurring in London and part of it in the United States.

The two leaders (and combatants) were Amy Lowell and Ezra Pound:

Amy Lowell (1874–1925), *Six French Poets,* 1915

Amy Lowell, *Tendencies in Modern American Poetry,* 1917

Amy Lowell, *Selected Poems,* ed. John Livingston Lowes, 1928

Ezra Pound (1885–   ), *Personae,* 1909

Ezra Pound, *The Spirit of Romance,* 1910

Ezra Pound, *Ripostes,* 1912

Ezra Pound, *Instigations,* 1920

Ezra Pound, *Hugh Selwyn Mauberley,* 1920

Ezra Pound, *Poems, 1918–21,* 1921

Ezra Pound, *Personae: The Collected Poems of Ezra Pound,* 1926

Ezra Pound, *Make It New,* 1934

The Letters of Ezra Pound, 1907–1941, ed. D. D. Paige, 1950

1890–1919

The movement of Imagism in the United States can be followed in:

Some Imagists Poets, 1915
Some Imagists Poets, 1916
Some Imagists Poets, 1917 (These three volumes were under the general supervision of Amy Lowell.)
An Imagist Anthology, 1930

The English poets of the group were Richard Aldington, T. E. Hulme, F. S. Flint, and, briefly, D. H. Lawrence. The Americans, in addition to Pound and Lowell, were:

"H.D." (Hilda Doolittle [Aldington], 1886–1961), *Collected Poems,* 1925; reprinted 1940
John Gould Fletcher (1886–1950), *Preludes and Symphonies,* 1922; reprinted 1930
John Gould Fletcher, *Selected Poems,* 1938
William Carlos Williams (1883–1963), *Collected Earlier Poems,* 1951; *Collected Later Poems,* 1950

24 · *The Poetic Renaissance: Fulfillment*

The lasting achievements of the poetic renaissance, so far as popular favor is concerned, must be distinguished from their lasting achievements among the passionate few devoted to "advanced" poetry. The four or five names most generally known achieved a general audience denied to the others. These poets fall into two groups: those from the Middle West and those associated with New England.

Vachel Lindsay (1879–1931), *General William Booth Enters into Heaven and Other Poems,* 1913

Vachel Lindsay, *The Congo and Other Poems,* 1914

Vachel Lindsay, *Collected Poems,* 1925

Vachel Lindsay, *Selected Poems,* 1931

Edgar Lee Masters (1869–1950), *Spoon River Anthology,* 1915

Carl Sandburg (1878–   ), *Chicago Poems,* 1916

Carl Sandburg, *Cornhuskers,* 1918

Carl Sandburg, *Smoke and Steel,* 1920

Carl Sandburg, *Slabs of the Sunburnt West,* 1922

Carl Sandburg, *The People, Yes,* 1936

The two poets associated with New England are:

Robert Frost (1875–1963), *A Masque of Reason,* 1945

Robert Frost, *A Masque of Mercy,* 1947

Robert Frost, *Complete Poems,* 1949

Edwin Arlington Robinson (1869–1935), *Collected Poems,* 1937 (This replaces earlier volumes by the same title issued in 1921, 1927, 1929, and 1931; and includes, *inter alia, The Town Down the River,* 1910; *The Man Against the Sky,* 1916; *Merlin,* 1917; *Lancelot,* 1920; *Roman Bartholow,* 1923; *The Man Who Died Twice,* 1924; *Tristram,* 1927; *Cavender's House,* 1929; *King Jasper,* 1935.)

25 · *The Impact of World War I*

Perhaps the most difficult job of the historical imagination among students of American literature too young to have lived through the period is to envision the profound shock that World War I gave to America.

There had been other recent wars, often bloody and determined—that between Russia and Japan and the two Balkan wars—but these were in remote places. Suddenly Western Europe burst into flame; and it is hard to say whether the Americans were more disturbed by the revelation of international perfidy on a grand scale or by reports of the vast, gray-green German army as it poured through Belgium. However, the war was shortly interpreted in familiar fashion as a conflict between good and evil. In this melodrama Germany was the villain, France was thought of in terms of Joan of Arc, and Great Britain appeared as the old bulldog full of pluck, losing campaigns but winning the last battle. The fact that the Archduke Francis Ferdinand of Austria had been murdered in Serbia was passed over, the "scrap of paper" having obliterated other moral considerations. The sinking of the *Lusitania* underlined the moral issues. That the war was far more complex, deadly, destructive, monotonous, and self-seeking than this simple pattern of right and wrong was only gradually understood, and the contrast between the theory of an age-old struggle of good and evil and the later revelation of military stupidities and diplomatic irresponsibility produced in the twenties a new cynical spirit.

The following list of representative books by American writers reporting on the war or supporting the interpretation of the conflict as a simple moral issue is representative. It ignores books by British and French writers which were equally influential in shaping American opinion.

Mildred Aldrich (1853–1928), *A Hilltop on the Marne*, 1915
Gertrude Atherton (1857–1948), *Life in the War Zone*, 1916

Richard Harding Davis (1864–1916), *With the Allies,* 1914 (This contains the great picture of the German armies marching endlessly through Brussels. See chapters 1, 3, 6, 10.)

Arthur Guy Empey (1883–   ), *Over the Top,* 1917 (Vastly popular, this book narrated with *sang-froid* the experiences of an American who enlisted in the British army. See the useful "Tommy's Dictionary of the Trenches," pp. 281 ff.)

Floyd Gibbons (1887–1939), *And "They Thought We Wouldn't Fight,"* 1918 (Gibbons was an immensely influential war correspondent. For characteristic passages see chapters 1, 7, 8.)

Robert Herrick (1868–1938), *The World Decision,* 1916 (Interpretation by an enthusiast for the cause of the Allies. See especially the section on France.)

Frederick Palmer (1873–1958), *My Year of the Great War,* 1915 (Palmer was a correspondent and military historian. Note especially chapters 2, 9–11.)

Edith Wharton (1862–1937), *Fighting France,* 1915

Brand Whitlock (1869–1934), *Belgium,* 1918/19 (By the American minister to Belgium.)

Brand Whitlock, *Letters and Journal,* ed. Allan Nevins, 2 vols., 1936 (The material on the German march into Belgium illuminates the American attitude.)

Woodrow Wilson (1856–1924), *In Our First Year of War,* 1918 (See the following especially: Speech asking Congress to declare war, April 2, 1917; Address to Congress, December 4, 1917; Address to Congress giving terms of peace, January 9, 1918. These speeches can be found in other collections. Note, however, the interpretation of the war as a moral crusade.)

Owen Wister (1860–1938), *The Pentecost of Calamity,* 1915 (Virtually a little classic, this influential book persuaded Americans that Germany was wrong.)

26 · *The New Spirit and the War Novels*

Even before disillusioned young Americans returned from Europe to write a library of war novels, a sense of stir, vaguely referred to as the "New Spirit" was felt by a younger generation in revolt against their elders. Partly this was directed against the still powerful Genteel Tradition; partly this was caused by the American discovery of Freud and his contemporary psychologists (A. A. Brill published a translation of Freud's *The Interpretation of Dreams* in 1913 and followed this by other works); partly the movement represented an awareness of new movements in painting (the Armory Show of 1913 was the discovery by America of such European developments in painting as distortion, nonrepresentational art, and similar "radical ideas"), poetry (the French symbolists enjoyed a new vogue), Continental drama, and new experiments in prose, particularly in fiction (the stream-of-consciousness method). The war novels capitalized upon the sense of the failure of the elder generation to understand the world, and drove American fiction farther in the direction of naturalism.

The books here listed are accordingly divided into two sections: (i) books expressing the feeling of the younger generation in revolt; (ii) novels reporting on the part of participants in the war that life was not in the least like the orthodox American interpretation of battle, sex, idealism, or democracy.

I

New writers appeared to question traditional American postulates about literary values, idealism as a social force, and the traditional classics of American letters. These may be roughly divided into critics of society and critics of literature. But most writers were both.

EMPHASIS ON LITERARY CRITICISM

Max Eastman (1883–), *The Enjoyment of Poetry,* 1913 (Poetry must either disappear or change its nature in an age of science.)

Henry L. Mencken (1880–1956), *A Book of Prefaces,* 1917

Henry L. Mencken, *Selected Prejudices,* 1927 (Chosen from successive volumes of *Prejudices*, 1919, 1920, 1922, 1924, 1926, 1927.)

Joel E. Spingarn (1875–1939), *The New Criticism*, 1911

Joel E. Spingarn, *Creative Criticism: Essays on the Unity of Genius and Taste*, 1917 (Includes the preceding.)

EMPHASIS ON CULTURAL AND SOCIAL CRITICISM

Randolph Bourne (1886–1918), *Youth and Life*, 1913

Randolph Bourne, *Untimely Papers*, 1919

Randolph Bourne, *The History of a Literary Radical*, 1920

Waldo Frank (1889–   ), *Our America*, 1919

Waldo Frank, *The Rediscovery of America*, 1928

George Santayana (1863–1952),*The Genteel Tradition at Bay*, 1931

EXPERIMENTATION BASED ON EUROPEAN INFLUENCES

William E. Leonard (1876–1944), *Two Lives* (1922), 1925

Gertrude Stein (1874–1946), *Selected Writings*, edited by Carl Van Vechten, 1946

FICTION REPRESENTING THE "NEW MANNER,"
THE "NEW PSYCHOLOGY"

Sherwood Anderson (1876–1941), *Winesburg, Ohio*, 1919

Sherwood Anderson, *Poor White*, 1920

Sherwood Anderson, *Dark Laughter*, 1925

Floyd Dell (1887–   ), *Mooncalf*, 1920

Floyd Dell, *The Briary Bush*, 1921

Floyd Dell, *Janet March*, 1923

Zona Gale (1874–1938), *Miss Lulu Bett*, 1920

Ernest Poole (1880–1950), *The Harbor*, 1915

II. THE WAR NOVELS

Thomas Boyd (1898–1935), *Through the Wheat*, 1923

E. E. Cummings (1894–1962), *The Enormous Room*, 1922

John Dos Passos (1896–   ), *One Man's Initiation*, 1920

John Dos Passos, *Three Soldiers,* 1921
William Faulkner (1897–1962), *Soldiers' Pay,* 1926
William Faulkner, *Sartoris,* 1929
F. Scott Fitzgerald (1896–1940), *This Side of Paradise,* 1920
  (Listed here because, although Fitzgerald saw no fighting, it
  represents the disruption caused by the draft, enlistment, etc.)
Ernest Hemingway (1898–1961), *The Sun Also Rises,* 1926
Ernest Hemingway, *A Farewell to Arms,* 1929
"William March" (William Edward March Campbell, 1893–
  1954), *Company K,* 1933

27 · *The New Spirit in Fiction and Poetry*

The general stir in twentieth-century American letters cannot be closely defined, but in a broad sense the shift from the older basis of an art conceived as representation and as governing by ethical idealism to a new theory of art resulted from the fusion, during World War I and after, of (a) renewed awareness of contemporary or recent European experimentation in all the arts; (b) the long-run effects of American participation in the war and of such aftermaths as the Russian Revolution and world-wide anarchy; and (c) an increasing awareness that the psychology of the irrational (Freud, Jung, Adler) was but part of a universal revolt away from the intellectual premises of rationalism into a movement that was to reach its climax in the philosophy of existentialism. In the latter respect the American response to the philosophy of Bergson ("creative evolution") is an unassessed element of some importance. Eventually Bergson yielded to more dramatic philosophic outlooks of Europeans like Kierkegaard. The shift conditioned all serious American writing, but may be especially traced in novelists less concerned with social commentary (than the writers in list 29, for instance) and, of course, in the poets.

THE "NEW FICTION"

Conrad Aiken (1889–   ), *Blue Voyage*, 1927

Conrad Aiken, *Great Circle*, 1933

Maxwell Bodenheim (1893–1954), *Replenishing Jessica*, 1925

William Faulkner (1897–1962), *The Sound and the Fury*, 1929

William Faulkner, *As I Lay Dying*, 1930

William Faulkner, *Sanctuary*, 1931

William Faulkner, *Light in August*, 1932

William Faulkner, *Absalom, Absalom!* 1936

William Faulkner, *The Hamlet*, 1940

F. Scott Fitzgerald (1896–1940), *The Beautiful and Damned,* 1922

F. Scott Fitzgerald, *Tender is the Night*, 1934

Waldo Frank (1889–   ), *Rahab*, 1922

Ludwig Lewisohn (1882–1955), *The Case of Mr. Crump*, 1926

Thomas Wolfe (1900–1938), *Look Homeward, Angel,* 1929
Thomas Wolfe, *Of Time and the River,* 1935
Thomas Wolfe, *The Web and the Rock,* 1939
Thomas Wolfe, *You Can't Go Home Again,* 1940

POETRY IN THE "NEWER" MANNER

Léonie Adams (1899–   ), *Poems, A Selection,* 1954
Conrad Aiken, *The Jig of Forslin,* 1916
Conrad Aiken, *The Charnel Rose, Senlin (A Biography) and Other Poems,* 1918
Conrad Aiken, *Collected Poems,* 1953
Conrad Aiken, *The Morning Song of Lord Zero,* 1963
Louise Bogan (1897–   ), *Collected Poems, 1923–1953,* 1954
Hart Crane (1899–1932), *Collected Poems,* 1933
E. E. Cummings (1894–1962), *Poems, 1923–1954,* 1954
T. S. Eliot (1888–   ), *Poems,* 1920
T. S. Eliot, *The Waste Land,* 1922
T. S. Eliot, *Ash-Wednesday,* 1930
T. S. Eliot, *Four Quartets,* 1943 (*Burnt Norton* completed the series. The earlier parts, published separately, are *East Coker,* 1940; *The Dry Salvages,* 1941; *Little Gidding,* 1942.)
T. S. Eliot, *Collected Poems, 1909–1962,* 1963
Thomas Hornsby Ferril (1896–   ), *New and Selected Poems,* 1952
Edna St. Vincent Millay (1892–1950), *Collected Poems,* compiled by Norman Millay, 1956
Wallace Stevens (1879–1955), *Collected Poems,* 1954

AMERICAN LITERATURE

28 · The Fictional Attack on "Puritanism"

Skepticism about the social pattern of American life quickly appeared in fiction. The formula of business life seemed to many novelists to produce only a smothered dissatisfaction, inasmuch as economic success was no guarantee of individual happiness. The commonly accepted pattern of bourgeois respectability came to be dubbed "Puritanism." Already under attack in other categories of fiction, "Puritanism" was identified with social hypocrisy — marriage and a happy ending were no longer the climax of the novel. In some novels it was assumed that the ordinary American belief that class distinction was unknown in this country was a fallacy, and in others the identification of felicity with materialistic comfort was exposed as hypocritical. Still others led a crusade for a return to old-fashioned idealism and the rights of man, particularly in the Sacco-Vanzetti case, against the crushing pressures of city life.

Bernard De Voto (1897–1955), *We Accept with Pleasure,* 1934 (Turns on the Sacco-Vanzetti case.)

John Dos Passos (1896–   ), *Manhattan Transfer,* 1925

John Dos Passos, *USA,* 1937 (Composed of *The 42nd Parallel,* 1930; *1919,* 1932; *The Big Money,* 1936.)

F. Scott Fitzgerald (1896–1940), *The Great Gatsby,* 1925

F. Scott Fitzgerald, *The Last Tycoon,* 1941 (Unfinished. Published in an edition including *The Great Gatsby* and *Selected Stories.*)

Sinclair Lewis (1885–1951), *Main Street,* 1920

Sinclair Lewis, *Babbitt,* 1922

Sinclair Lewis, *Arrowsmith,* 1925

Sinclair Lewis, *Elmer Gantry,* 1927

Sinclair Lewis, *Dodsworth,* 1929

Sinclair Lewis, *It Can't Happen Here,* 1935 (Against incipient Fascism.)

John P. Marquand (1893–1960), *The Late George Apley,* 1937

John P. Marquand, *Wickford Point,* 1939

John P. Marquand, *H. M. Pulham, Esq.,* 1941

John P. Marquand, *Sincerely Willis Wayde,* 1955

Edmund Wilson (1895–   ), *I Thought of Daisy,* 1929

1920–1963

29 · *The Revaluation of American Culture*

The tremendous shock given to traditional mores by the forces outlined in the three foregoing sections disturbed complacency and necessitated a reassessment of American values. Some of this reassessment appears in the books in lists 26 and 27. Deeper problems were also raised. Were the traditional religious and philosophic assumptions of the national culture no longer viable? Ought the bases of modern life to be shifted to some new set of postulates more in keeping with twentieth-century science? Or should the thoughtful citizen simply assume that the error originated in the nineteenth century with its romantic belief in human goodness? If so, was not the solution of the modern problem a return to a more ancient wisdom—the traditional humanism of the West? During World War I, the twenties and thirties, and into World War II and its aftermath, the discussion continued— if, indeed, it has ever ceased. Characteristic documents are here listed:

Robert M. Hutchins (1899–   ), *The Higher Learning in America,* 1936

Matthew Josephson (1899–   ), *Portrait of the Artist as an American,* 1930

Joseph Wood Krutch (1893–   ), *The Modern Temper,* 1929

Joseph Wood Krutch, *The Twelve Seasons,* 1949

Walter Lippmann (1899–   ), *A Preface to Politics,* 1913

Walter Lippmann, *A Preface to Morals,* 1929

Henry L. Mencken, (1880–1956), *The American Credo,* 1920 (With George Jean Nathan.)

Henry L. Mencken, *Notes on Democracy,* 1926

Henry L. Mencken, *Treatise on Right and Wrong,* 1934

James Harvey Robinson (1863–1936), *The Mind in the Making,* 1921

Harold E. Stearns (1891–1943), *America and the Young Intellectual,* 1921

The conservative position tended to be either that of the Neo-Humanists or of the Neo-Confederates. Representative books by the Neo-Humanists are these:

171

Irving Babbitt (1865–1933), *Rousseau and Romanticism,* 1919

Irving Babbitt, *Democracy and Leadership,* 1924

William C. Brownell (1851–1928), *Standards,* 1917

William C. Brownell, *Democratic Distinction in America,* 1927

John Jay Chapman (1862–1933), *Learning and Other Essays,* 1910

John Jay Chapman, *Greek Genius and Other Essays,* 1915

Paul Elmer More (1864–1937), *The Drift of Romanticism,* 1913

Paul Elmer More, *Aristocracy and Justice,* 1915

Paul Elmer More, *The Demon of the Absolute,* 1928

Albert Jay Nock (1872?–1945), *The Theory of Education in the United States,* 1932

Stuart Pratt Sherman (1881–1926), *On Contemporary Literature,* 1917

Stuart Pratt Sherman, *The Main Stream,* 1927

Two representative books in the Neo-Confederate or Neo-Agrarian formula, out of which was to come an important movement in criticism, follow:

[Twelve Southerners], *I'll Take My Stand,* 1930

Donald Davidson (1893–   ), *The Attack on Leviathan,* 1938

Following World War II, the reassessment of our culture concentrated less on ancient wisdom than on survival in "one world," political debates, urban ills, and minority rights. Some observers, however, have been able to stand apart from immediate issues, or at least discuss these issues in a larger framework. Their commentary is frequently more harsh than the criticism of the twenties but none the less valuable as a reflection of the times.

James Baldwin (1924–   ), *Notes of a Native Son,* 1955

James Baldwin, *Nobody Knows My Name: More Notes of a Native Son,* 1961

Francis Biddle (1886–   ), *The Fear of Freedom,* 1952

William O. Douglas (1898–   ), *America Challenged,* 1960

Leslie Fiedler (1917–   ), *An End to Innocence: Essays on Culture and Politics,* 1955

Eli Ginzberg (1911–   ), *The Optimistic Tradition and American Youth*, 1962

Herbert Gold (1924–   ), *The Age of Happy Problems*, 1962

Sidney Hook (1902–   ), *Heresy, Yes—Conspiracy, No!* 1953

Sidney Hook, *The Paradoxes of Freedom*, 1962

Dwight Macdonald (1906–   ), *Against the American Grain*, 1962

Marya Mannes (1904–   ), *More in Anger*, 1958

Richard Rovere (1915–   ), *The American Establishment and Other Reports, Opinions, and Speculations*, 1962

Philip Wylie (1902–   ), *Generation of Vipers*, 1942

Van Wyck Brooks' famous phrase, "the search for a usable past," may be taken to describe another turn in the cultural revolution that began in the second decade of the century. It was insufficient to find fault with the present state of American culture because of a supposedly bad tradition; it was necessary, paradoxically enough, to find a new tradition, or to reinterpret an old one so that it could lend support to the new valuations, hazy as these valuations might be. American history, especially American cultural history, was critically viewed in the light of suppositions agreeable to the postwar world. Among the results was the dethronement of many "classic" American authors (like Longfellow, Whittier, and Lowell), an enlarged sense of the importance of others (Melville, Thoreau, and Henry James), and a search for relevant values in the fine arts as these have developed in the New World (including architecture), in politics, and in cultural history. History ceased to be political or military history in the older sense, and was rewritten in social terms; and biography came to dwell upon the humanizing imperfections of the subject no less than upon his achievements. A kind of amused tolerance for human weakness was for a time characteristic of much exploration of the past.

Carl Becker (1873–1945), *The Declaration of Independence,* 1922 (A distinguished example of the "history of ideas.")

Gamaliel Bradford (1863–1932), *American Portraits,* 1922

Gamaliel Bradford, *Damaged Souls,* 1923 (These books represent the method known as "psychography.")

Van Wyck Brooks (1886–1962), *The Wine of the Puritans,* 1908

Van Wyck Brooks, *America's Coming-of-Age,* 1915

Van Wyck Brooks, *Letters and Leadership,* 1918

Van Wyck Brooks, *The Ordeal of Mark Twain,* 1920

Van Wyck Brooks, *The Pilgrimage of Henry James,* 1925 (The general thesis of the last two volumes is that the subjects of the studies were frustrated by forces in American culture analyzed in the three preceding volumes.)

Ludwig Lewisohn (1882–1955), *Expression in America,* 1932

(A survey of American literature in terms of emotional and psychic energy and frustration.)

Alfred Lief, ed., *The Dissenting Opinions of Mr. Justice Holmes*, 1929 (Holmes, because he interpreted the law in terms of social development rather than of metaphysical absolutes, was highly satisfactory to this group, which did not realize he was a conservative at heart.)

John Macy (1877–1932), *The Spirit of American Literature* (1908), 1913 (The earliest of the "debunking" literary histories.)

Lewis Mumford (1895–   ), *Sticks and Stones*, 1924 (A history of architecture in America in its social and cultural context.)

Lewis Mumford, *The Golden Day*, 1926 (On American literature in the earlier nineteenth century.)

Lewis Mumford, *The Brown Decades*, 1931 (A reinterpretation of the culture of the brownstone-front period.)

Vernon L. Parrington (1871–1929), *Main Currents in American Thought*, 3 vols., 1927–1930 (The most influential of the histories of ideas, despite its tendency to thesis-writing.)

James Harvey Robinson (1863–1936), *The New History*, 1912 (A plea for "social" history.)

Constance Rourke (1885–1941), *American Humor*, 1931 (Cultural history from an unorthodox point of view.)

31 · *The New Method in the Historical Novel*

Even after the success of *The Red Badge of Courage* (1895) the American historical novel clung to the formula of romance. The hero was at the right hand of some great figure in some great historical crisis, and helped to bring about the victory of righteousness in American terms; the villain was invariably on the losing side; the heroine, unsoiled, fell into the hero's arms in the last chapter, when wedding bells brought history and fiction to a successful climax.

In the new novel of history, events were not seen in pattern but as they must have appeared to an ordinary human being only vaguely aware of their outcome and far from aware of their historical significance. This central character is, moreover, filled with human frailty, comes into contact with greatness only casually and not always comprehendingly, and at the end does not necessarily succeed in either his own purposes or the historical mission he is supposed to further. In one sense the new method was dedicated to determinism, since it assumed that human nature doesn't change; in another sense it showed the American past as the free creation of countless forgotten human beings.

James Boyd (1888–1944), *Drums,* 1925

James Boyd, *Marching On,* 1927

James Boyd, *Long Hunt,* 1930

Walter Van Tilburg Clark (1909–   ), *The Ox-Bow Incident,* 1940

Paul Corey (1903–   ), *Three Miles Square,* 1937

Paul Corey, *The Road Returns,* 1940

Clifford Dowdey (1904–   ), *Bugles Blow No More,* 1939

Walter D. Edmonds (1903–   ), *Rome Haul,* 1929

Walter D. Edmonds, *Drums Along the Mohawk,* 1936

Howard Fast (1914–   ), *The Unvanquished,* 1942

Esther Forbes (1894?–   ), *O Genteel Lady!* 1926

Esther Forbes, *A Mirror for Witches,* 1928

Esther Forbes, *Paradise,* 1937

Michael Foster (1904–   ), *American Dream,* 1937

A. B. Guthrie, Jr. (1901–   ), *The Big Sky,* 1947

Emerson Hough (1857–1923), *The Covered Wagon,* 1922

MacKinlay Kantor (1904–   ), *Long Remember,* 1934

MacKinlay Kantor, *Andersonville,* 1955

Ross F. Lockridge (1914–1948), *Raintree County,* 1948

Joseph Stanley Pennell (1908–   ), *The History of Rome Hanks and Kindred Matters,* 1944

Kenneth Roberts (1885–1957), *Arundel,* 1930

Kenneth Roberts, *Rabble in Arms,* 1933

Kenneth Roberts, *Northwest Passage,* 1937

O. E. Rölvaag (1876–1931), *Giants in the Earth,* 1927

Mari Sandoz (1901–   ), *Slogum House,* 1937

Evelyn Scott (1893–   ), *The Wave,* 1929

Wallace Stegner (1909–   ), *The Big Rock Candy Mountain,* 1943

Robert Penn Warren (1905–   ), *Brother to Dragons,* 1953 (Verse)

Robert Penn Warren, *Band of Angels,* 1955

Glenway Wescott (1901–   ), *The Grandmothers,* 1927

32 · *The Revival of the Exotic*

The twenties have become fabulous, but in addition to being the decade of H. L. Mencken, F. Scott Fitzgerald, Edna St. Vincent Millay, and other writers thought to represent rebellion against the inherited mores of the previous century, they also continued a tradition of the nineties—the mood and manner of the esoteric writing of the *fin de siècle* group. This approach to literature emphasized manner, liked to be knowledgeable about persons and places not revealed to the multitude, pretended to accept sex as an amusing game, and determined at all costs to enjoy an existence rescued from tediousness by an incessant parade of novelty, snobbery, and the recherché. Not all the authors listed below exhibit all these qualities, but they have in common what is known as *manner*—that is, an unusual or excessive interest either in style for its own sake, in novelties in literary construction for their own sake, or in a dandiacal attitude toward art, human beings, or life in general.

James Branch Cabell (1879–1958), *The Soul of Melicent,* 1913 (Revised and republished as *Domnei,* 1920.)

James Branch Cabell, *The Rivet in Grandfather's Neck,* 1915

James Branch Cabell, *The Cream of the Jest,* 1917

James Branch Cabell, *Beyond Life,* 1919

James Branch Cabell, *Jurgen,* 1919

James Branch Cabell, *Figures of Earth,* 1921

John Erskine (1879–1951), *The Private Life of Helen of Troy,* 1925

Joseph Hergesheimer (1880–1954), *The Three Black Pennys,* 1917

Joseph Hergesheimer, *Linda Condon,* 1919

Joseph Hergesheimer, *Java Head,* 1919

Joseph Hergesheimer, *Cytherea,* 1922

Joseph Hergesheimer, *The Bright Shawl,* 1922

Joseph Hergesheimer, *Balisand,* 1924

Robert Nathan (1894–   ), *The Bishop's Wife,* 1928
Robert Nathan, *One More Spring,* 1933
Robert Nathan, *Winter in April,* 1938
Robert Nathan, *Journey of Tapiola,* 1938
Robert Nathan, *Portrait of Jennie,* 1940
Dorothy Parker (1893–   ), *The Portable Dorothy Parker,* 1944
Carl Van Vechten (1880–   ), *Peter Whiffle,* 1922
Carl Van Vechten, *The Tattooed Countess,* 1924
Thornton Wilder (1897–   ), *The Cabala,* 1926
Thornton Wilder, *The Bridge of San Luis Rey,* 1927
Thornton Wilder, *The Woman of Andros,* 1930
Elinor Wylie (1885–1928), *The Venetian Glass Nephew,* 1925
Elinor Wylie, *The Orphan Angel,* 1926
Elinor Wylie, *Mr. Hodge and Mr. Hazard,* 1928

33 • *Drama in the Twenties and After*

Eugene O'Neill continued to build his reputation during the twenties and thirties (see list 22), but he was not alone in producing work of literary merit. The theater had progressed technically for almost a century; now the playwrights were catching up and growing up. Outspoken on social, political, and marital issues, they educated as well as entertained their audiences. They borrowed techniques from German expressionists and American vaudeville for satire. They abandoned the illusion of the fourth wall by extending the stage over the footlights; and by incorporating masks and music into serious drama they reinforced symbolic action. The temptation to classify their work is great, but it is wiser simply to list major successful playwrights and some of their representative plays:

Elmer Rice (1892–   ), *The Adding Machine,* 1923

Owen Davis (1874–1956), *Icebound,* 1923

Maxwell Anderson (1888–1959), *What Price Glory?* (with Laurence Stallings) 1924

Maxwell Anderson, *Winterset,* 1935

George Kaufman (1889–1961), *Beggar on Horseback* (with Marc Connelly), 1924

George Kaufman, *You Can't Take It With You* (with Moss Hart), 1936

George Kelly (1887–   ), *The Show-off,* 1924

Sidney Howard (1891–1939), *They Knew What They Wanted,* 1924

Sidney Howard, *The Silver Cord,* 1926

John Howard Lawson (1895–   ), *Processional,* 1925

Paul Green (1894–   ), *In Abraham's Bosom,* 1927

Philip Barry (1896–1949), *Holiday,* 1929

Philip Barry, *Hotel Universe,* 1930

Marc Connelly (1890–   ), *The Green Pastures,* 1930

S. N. Behrman (1893–   ), *Biography,* 1932

Robert E. Sherwood (1896–1955), *The Petrified Forest,* 1935

Robert E. Sherwood, *Idiot's Delight,* 1936

Sidney Kingsley (1906–   ), *Dead End,* 1935
Clifford Odets (1906–1963), *Waiting for Lefty,* 1935
Clifford Odets, *Awake and Sing!,* 1935
Thornton Wilder (1897–   ), *Our Town,* 1938
Lillian Hellman (1905–   ), *The Little Foxes,* 1939

After the brilliance of the American drama, 1920–1940, a decline was inevitable. Only three playwrights of distinction emerged after the war years. Television has made obvious inroads, and economic problems seem forever incurable; yet drama survives and shows signs of new life in the little theaters off Broadway and in the college and community theaters across the country. The veteran playwrights contributed several plays worthy of their early work during these years:

Robert E. Sherwood, *There Shall Be No Night,* 1940
Lillian Hellman, *Another Part of the Forest,* 1946
Lillian Hellman, *Toys in the Attic,* 1960
Thornton Wilder, *The Skin of Our Teeth,* 1942

Three younger playwrights show staying power as well as talent:

Tennessee Williams (1914–   ) *The Glass Menagerie,* 1945
Tennessee Williams, *A Streetcar Named Desire,* 1947
Tennessee Williams, *The Night of the Iguana,* 1961
Arthur Miller (1915–   ), *Death of a Salesman,* 1949
Arthur Miller, *The Crucible,* 1953
Arthur Miller, *A View from the Bridge,* 1955
William Inge (1913–   ), *Come Back, Little Sheba,* 1950
William Inge, *Picnic,* 1953

A still younger generation of playwrights emerged in the fifties, some of them trained in television, all of them intent on commenting boldly on our times:

Robert Anderson (1917–   ), *Tea and Sympathy,* 1953
Gore Vidal (1925–   ), *Visit to a Small Planet,* 1957

Paddy Chayefsky (1923–   ), *The Middle of the Night*, 1959
Jack Gelber (1932–   ), *The Connection*, 1959
Edward Albee (1928–   ), *The American Dream*, 1959
Edward Albee, *Who's Afraid of Virginia Woolf?* 1962
Tad Mosel (1922–   ), *All the Way Home*, 1960
Jack Richardson (1934–   ), *The Prodigal*, 1960

34 · *Poetry in the Twenties and After*

Under the impetus of T. S. Eliot and of the issues raised by the war and the postwar world, the writers of the Poetic Renaissance ceased to be novel. American poetry began a slow drift away from verse characterized by formality of pattern, a "public" style, and the acceptance of the traditional vocabulary. The new movement produced verse characterized by growing difficulty of style, an extreme use of allusion, private symbolism, and the loosening of stanza structure within the patterns of regular meter. The influence of seventeenth-century English verse, particularly that of the metaphysicals, was strongly felt; and towards the end of the phase, some of the verse of this order was written by the "New Critics."

In the present list of titles older or more conservative poets are named under I, and representatives of the newer phase under II.

I

Léonie Adams (See list 27.)

Conrad Aiken (See list 27.)

Witter Bynner (1881–   ), *Selected Poems,* 1936

Robert P. Tristam Coffin (1892–1955), *Collected Poems,* new and enlarged edition, 1948

Robert S. Hillyer (1895–1961), *Collected Verse,* 1933

Edna St. Vincent Millay (See list 27.)

John G. Neihardt (1881–   ), *Collected Poems,* 1926

Lizette Woodworth Reese (1856–1935), *Selected Poems,* 1926

George Santayana (1863–1952), *Poems,* revised edition, 1923

Ridgely Torrence (1875–1950), *Poems,* 1941

Mark Van Doren (1894–   ), *Collected and New Poems, 1924–1963,* 1963

Elinor Wylie (1885–1928), *Collected Poems,* 1932

William Carlos Williams (See list 23.)

II

John Peale Bishop (1892–1944), *Selected Poems,* 1941

E. E. Cummings (See list 27.)

Kenneth Fearing (1902–1961), *New and Selected Poems,* 1956

Archibald MacLeish (1892–   ), *Collected Poems, 1917–1952,*
1952

Marianne Moore (1887–   ), *Collected Poems,* 1951

John Crowe Ransom (1888–   ), *Selected Poems,* revised and
enlarged edition, 1963

Allen Tate (1899–   ), *Poems, 1922–1947,* 1948, revised under
the title *Poems,* 1960

Robert Penn Warren (1905–   ), *Selected Poems, 1923–1943,*
1944

I · THE THIRTIES

35 · *The New Criticism*

Like any other fecund literary movement, the "New Criticism" is difficult to define. It shared with the movement of Neo-Humanism, which is one of its roots, a belief in the moral integrity of the work of art in its own right, but differed from that movement by insisting that the act of moral judgment was not synchronous with the creative act. The creative act (that is, art) is a serious human activity, to be judged in its own right and in its own light. Therefore the New Critics repudiated the sociological interpretation of literature, subordinated historical scholarship to the scanning of the text, adopted a good many of the tenets of irrational psychology, and insisted that the meaning of a work of art lies in the text of the work of art. If the New Critics thus returned criticism to a proper function, they made reading more difficult for average readers who, when they discoverd in the New Criticism so many latent difficulties in comprehending poetry agreeable to adherents of the new approach, tended to turn elsewhere for good reading.

The movement was strongly influenced by T. S. Eliot and I. A. Richards, began in the twenties, flowered in the thirties, and has now apparently made its contribution and is on the wane.

Mark Schorer, Josephine Miles, and Gordon McKenzie, eds., *Criticism: The Foundations of Modern Literary Judgment,* 1948 (A good general introduction to the critical situation; the later selections in Part Two, "Form," are especially relevant.)

Conrad Aiken (1889–   ), *Scepticisms,* 1919 (An important predecessor of the New Criticism.)

R. P. Blackmur (1904–   ), *The Double Agent,* 1935

R. P. Blackmur, *The Expense of Greatness,* 1940

R. P. Blackmur, *Language as Gesture,* 1952

Cleanth Brooks (1906–   ), *Modern Poetry and the Tradition,* 1939

Cleanth Brooks, *The Well-Wrought Urn,* 1947

Kenneth Burke (1897–   ), *Counter-Statement,* 1931
Kenneth Burke, *The Philosophy of Literary Form,* 1941
Kenneth Burke, *A Grammar of Motives,* 1945
T. S. Eliot (1888–   ), *Selected Essays,* 1932
T. S. Eliot, *The Use of Poetry and the Use of Criticism,* 1933
William Empson (1906–   ), *Seven Types of Ambiguity,* 1930
John Crowe Ransom (1888–   ), *The World's Body,* 1938
John Crowe Ransom, *The New Criticism,* 1941
I. A. Richards (1893–   ), *Principles of Literary Criticism,* 1924
I. A. Richards, *Practical Criticism: A Study of Literary Judgment,* 1929
Allen Tate (1899–   ), *Reactionary Essays,* 1931
Allen Tate, *Reason in Madness,* 1941
Yvor Winters (1900–   ), *Primitivism and Decadence,* 1937
Yvor Winters, *Maule's Curse,* 1938
Yvor Winters, *In Defence of Reason,* 1947

36 · *The Proletarian Movement*

The Great Depression and the New Deal turned the thirties into a period that at times seemed to forbode revolutionary change, and at other times promised a great fulfillment of American life as managed capitalism. There has always been a tradition of social radicalism in American literature; in the thirties this kind of writing tended to take shape as Marxian writing. American Marxist writing was either Marxist criticism or proletarian fiction. In Marxist criticism American literary development was interpreted as enlisting all the American literary classics it could on the side of left-wing change; proletarian fiction tended to make a member of the laboring class the hero-victim of class war. By the forties the Marxist critics had lost their vogue or changed their views, and the proletarian novelists, by dint of reiterating the same theme, had lost their following.

I

Victor F. Calverton (1900–1940), *The Newer Spirit: A Sociological Criticism of Literature,* 1925

Victor F. Calverton, *The Liberation of American Literature,* 1932

James T. Farrell (1904–   ), *A Note on Literary Criticism,* 1936

Joseph Freeman (1897–   ), *An American Testament,* 1936

Granville Hicks (1901–   ), *The Great Tradition,* 1933

Granville Hicks and others, eds., *Proletarian Literature in the United States,* 1935

Bernard Smith (1906–   ), *Forces in American Criticism,* 1939

II

Robert Cantwell (1908–   ), *Laugh and Lie Down,* 1931

Robert Cantwell, *Land of Plenty,* 1934

John Dos Passos (See lists 26 and 28.)

"Michael Gold" (Irving Granich, 1894–   ), *Jews Without Money,* 1930

Albert Halper (1904–   ), *Union Square,* 1933

Josephine Herbst (1897–   ), *Pity Is Not Enough*, 1933
Josephine Herbst, *The Executioner Waits*, 1934
Josephine Herbst, *Rope of Gold*, 1939
Meyer Levin (1905–   ), *The Old Bunch*, 1937
Grace Lumpkin (? –   ), *To Make My Bread*, 1932
John Steinbeck (1902–   ), *In Dubious Battle*, 1936
John Steinbeck, *The Grapes of Wrath*, 1939

37 · *Neo-Naturalism in the Thirties and After*

Scarcely to be distinguished from much proletarian fiction was the neo-naturalistic novel developed in the thirties and after. Emphasis was placed upon environment; and against social conditions it was useless to struggle, especially in the case of the "little man." Even at higher levels freedom of the will was felt to be illusory. An especially grim phase of Neo-Naturalism was a small library of novels exposing the plight of the Negro in American life, hemmed in as he was not only by a crippling economic environment but also by racial tensions. It was felt to be inevitable, therefore, that the Negro should retaliate by an outburst of hatred against the white man, the subject of some of this fiction.

Nelson Algren (1909–   ), *Never Come Morning,* 1942

Nelson Algren, *The Man with the Golden Arm,* 1949

John Peale Bishop (1892–1944), *Act of Darkness,* 1935

James M. Cain (1892–   ), *The Postman Always Rings Twice,* 1934

Erskine Caldwell (1903–   ), *Tobacco Road,* 1932

Erskine Caldwell, *God's Little Acre,* 1933

Erskine Caldwell, *Journeyman,* 1935

Erskine Caldwell, *Trouble in July,* 1940

Erskine Caldwell, *Georgia Boy,* 1943

John Dos Passos (See lists 28 and 42.)

Ralph Ellison (1914–   ), *Invisible Man,* 1952

James T. Farrell (1904–   ), *Studs Lonigan,* 1935 (Composed of *Young Lonigan,* 1932; *The Young Manhood of Studs Lonigan,* 1934; *Judgment Day,* 1935.)

William Faulkner (See lists 27 and 42.)

John O'Hara (1905–   ), *Appointment in Samarra,* 1934

John O'Hara, *A Rage to Live,* 1949

John O'Hara, *Elizabeth Appleton,* 1963

Budd Schulberg (1914–   ), *What Makes Sammy Run,* 1941

Budd Schulberg, *The Disenchanted,* 1950 (A fictional life of F. Scott Fitzgerald.)

Lillian Smith (1897–   ), *Strange Fruit,* 1944
Jerome Weidman (1913–   ), *I Can Get It For You Whole-sale,* 1937
Nathanael West (1904–1940), *Miss Lonelyhearts,* 1933
Nathanael West, *The Day of the Locust,* 1939
Ira Wolfert (1908–   ), *Tucker's People,* 1943
Maritta Wolff (1918–   ), *Night Shift,* 1942
Richard Wright (1908–1961), *Native Son,* 1940
Richard Wright, *The Outsider,* 1953
Richard Wright, *Lawd Today,* 1963

1920–1963

J · WORLD WAR II AND AFTER

38 · *Prelude to World War II*

As in the case of World War I (see list 25) the understanding of a vast cultural convulsion takes the student beyond the realm of belles-lettres into an area in which intelligent writing is important, although the book in question may lack the stigmata of literature. Perhaps the best way to solve the dilemma is to confront it boldly.

The outbreak of World War II and subsequent American participation in the conflict found the nation far more aware of intellectual, cultural, and spiritual issues than was true in 1914. If this was true, warnings addressed to the American public by poets, novelists, and foreign correspondents, no less than by public men, were responsible. Probably no part of serious American writing since about 1935 is not conditioned, in some degree, by the world issues of fascism, communism, and democracy; the dictator state versus the democratic state; materialism, agnosticism, or atheism versus religious faith, spiritual values, or faith in immaterial things. It is an area in which sides are chosen under emotional pressures and points of view attacked with venom.

The following list, chronologically arranged, mingles both the prose of information and the prose of imagination to suggest the vast library discussing or presenting the nature of the world struggle up to the time World War II was transformed into the Cold War. Books are listed by a kind of rule-of-thumb process. Partisans of no point of view will be satisfied with the list, but here, as elsewhere, the intention is to suggest trends and movements rather than to be definitive.

Louis Adamic (1899–1951), *The Native's Return,* 1934
Walter Duranty (1884–1957), *I Write As I Please,* 1935
Frederic Prokosch (1908–   ), *The Asiatics,* 1935
Frederic Prokosch, *The Seven Who Fled,* 1937
Frederic Prokosch, *The Skies of Europe,* 1941
George Seldes (1890–   ), *Sawdust Caesar,* 1935
John Gunther (1910–   ), *Inside Europe,* 1936

191

Marvin Lowenthal (1890–   ), *The Jews of Germany*, 1936

Elliot Paul (1891–1958), *The Life and Death of a Spanish Town*, 1937

Herbert L. Matthews (1900–   ), *Two Wars and More to Come*, 1938

Stephen H. Roberts (1901–   ), *The House That Hitler Built*, 1937

Edgar Snow (1905–   ), *Red Star Over China*, 1938

Edgar Snow, *The Battle for Asia*, 1941

Vincent Sheean (1899–   ), *Not Peace but a Sword*, 1939

Nora Waln (1895–   ), *Reaching for the Stars*, 1939

Ernest Hemingway (1898–1961), *For Whom the Bell Tolls*, 1940

Edmund Wilson (1895–   ), *To the Finland Station*, 1940

William E. Dodd (1869–1940), *Ambassador Dodd's Diary*, 1941

Emily Hahn (1905–   ), *The Soong Sisters*, 1941

Joseph C. Harsch (1905–   ), *Pattern for Conquest*, 1941

Douglas P. Miller (1892–   ), *You Can't Do Business with Hitler*, 1941

William L. Shirer (1904–   ), *Berlin Diary*, 1941

Howard K. Smith (1914–   ), *Last Train from Berlin*, 1942

Alexander Werth (1901–   ), *Moscow War Diary*, 1942

Joseph C. Grew (1880–   ), *Ten Years in Japan*, 1944

Sumner Welles (1892–1961), *The Time for Decision*, 1944

39 · *The Literature of World War II*

An enormous library of printed material was produced and is still being produced about American participation in World War II. This library is at once too vast and too recent to be evaluated. If, however, one confines one's attention to selecting records of combat that seem to have directly influenced the American reading public, the task, although still insoluble, becomes smaller. Two varieties of battle report had this influence: (i) nonimaginative work by participants or reporters or by those in charge of great actions in the war; and (ii) imaginative reports, usually in the form of fiction. The following lists represent these two divisions; and each could of course be indefinitely extended.

I

Vannevar Bush (1890–   ), *Modern Arms and Free Men,* 1949

Dwight D. Eisenhower (1890–   ), *Crusade in Europe,* 1948

John Hersey (1914–   ), *Into the Valley,* 1943

John Hersey, *Hiroshima,* 1946

Ralph Ingersoll (1900–   ), *The Battle Is the Pay Off,* 1943

George C. Marshall (1880–1959), *General Marshall's Report,* 1945

Samuel Eliot Morison (1887–   ), *History of U.S. Naval Operations in World War II,* Vol. I., *The Battle of the Atlantic, 1939–1943,* 1947 (The first of fifteen volumes.)

"Ernie" (Ernest T.) Pyle (1900–1945), *Here Is Your War,* 1943

Robert E. Sherwood (1896–1955), *Roosevelt and Hopkins,* 1948

Edgar Snow (1905–   ), *The Pattern of Soviet Power,* 1945

William L. White (1900–   ), *Report on the Russians,* 1945

II

Lester Atwell (1908–   ), *Private,* 1958

Robert O. Bowen (1920–   ), *The Weight of the Cross,* 1951

Harry Brown (1917–   ), *A Walk in the Sun,* 1944

John Horne Burns (1916–1953), *The Gallery,* 1947

James Gould Cozzens (1903–   ), *Guard of Honor,* 1948

William Wister Haines, (1908–), *Command Decision*, 1947
Alfred Hayes (1911–), *The Girl on the Via Flaminia*, 1949
Thomas Heggen (1919–1949), *Mr. Roberts*, 1946
Joseph Heller (1923?–), *Catch-22*, 1955
John Hersey, *A Bell for Adano*, 1944
James Jones (1921–), *From Here to Eternity*, 1951
E. J. Kahn, Jr. (1916–), *The Peculiar War: Impressions of a Reporter in Korea*, 1952 (Not fiction, but gives an atmosphere not unlike war fiction.)
Norman Mailer (1923–), *The Naked and the Dead*, 1948
John P. Marquand (1893–1960), *So Little Time*, 1943
Carson McCullers (1917–), *Reflections in a Golden Eye*, 1941 (Concerns the "peacetime" army.)
James A. Michener (1907–), *Tales of the South Pacific*, 1947
Edward Newhouse (1912–), *The Iron Chain*, 1946
Lionel Shapiro (1908–), *The Sixth of June*, 1955
Irwin Shaw (1913–), *The Young Lions*, 1948
William Styron (1925–), *The Long March*, 1952
Herman Wouk (1915–), *The Caine Mutiny*, 1951

1920–1963

40 · *The Cold War and the Political Problem*

No victory ever left a nation less at ease than did victory in Asia and Europe. The problems remaining or newly appearing after VE-Day and VJ-Day seem in retrospect more complex than those before 1945. The evil of Fascism and Nazism was patent; so, too, was the sneak attack on Pearl Harbor. But the use of the atom bomb raised great questions, not only of power politics, espionage, and the like problems of policy, but also huge questions of morality. What good was science if it led the human race to destruction? What, moreover, was the nature of man if his latest performances were so doubtful or so evil? What was the nature of the democratic state if, on the one hand, it lay open to communist penetration and, on the other, produced the weak governments of France or the Labor government in Great Britain? And, above all, what was man's place in what seemed to be a hostile universe?

These philosophical or general questions were crisscrossed by problems of investigation into "un-American" activities, many of the investigators being more interested in publicity than truth; and by questions centering upon loyalty oaths, loyalty checks, and similar dubious modes of securing loyalty. Was loyalty the same as patriotism? Was patriotism inimical to or sympathetic with the United Nations? Could free men survive in a liberal state when the manipulation of "suspicion" proved to be politically possible? Such were some of the puzzles of the Cold War.

The following lists of books are, again, suggestive only. But beginning with these as a base the student can go further in almost any direction, finding a vast library in which to read.

Other aspects of the moral problem of the late forties and fifties affected belles-lettres, and may be traced in the imaginative writing of the last ten years. This is dealt with in list 41.

I · THE PROBLEM OF SCIENCE

Vannevar Bush (1890–   ), *Science, the Endless Frontier,* 1945
Rachel L. Carson (1907–   ), *The Sea Around Us,* 1951
James B. Conant (1893–   ), *On Understanding Science,* 1947
James B. Conant, *Science and Common Sense,* 1951 (Revision of the title above.)

AMERICAN LITERATURE
AMERICAN LITERATURE

Fairfield Osborn (1887–   ), *Our Plundered Plant*, 1948

Hans Zinsser (1878–1940), *Rats, Lice and History*, 1935

II · THE PROBLEM OF POLITICS AND DIPLOMACY

Herbert Agar (1897–   ), *A Time for Greatness*, 1942

Alan Barth (1906–   ), *The Loyalty of Free Men*, 1951

Elmer Davis (1890–1958), *But We Were Born Free*, 1954

George F. Kennan (1904–   ), *American Diplomacy, 1900–1950*, 1951

Owen Lattimore (1900–   ), *Ordeal by Slander*, 1950

Walter Lippmann (1889–   ), *Essays in the Public Philosophy*, 1955

Edgar A. Mowrer (1892–   ), *The Nightmare of American Foreign Policy*, 1948

Henry A. Wallace (1888–   ), *The Century of the Common Man*, 1943

Wendell Willkie (1892–1944), *One World*, 1943

III · THE NEW NATIONALISM

Duncan Aikman (1889–1955), *The Turning Stream*, 1948

Stephen Vincent Benét (1898–1943), *John Brown's Body*, 1928 (Listed here because its general influence came later than the date of publication.)

Jonathan Daniels (1902–   ), *A Southerner Discovers the South*, 1938

Marshall B. Davidson (1907–   ), *Life in America*, 2 vols., 1951 (A pictorial history.)

Paul Engle (1908–   ), *American Song*, 1934

John Gunther (1901–   ), *Inside USA*, 1947

Oscar Handlin (1915–   ), *The Uprooted*, 1951

Archibald MacLeish (1892–   ), *Conquistador*, 1932

Archibald MacLeish, *The Irresponsibles*, 1940

Ralph Barton Perry (1876–1957), *Characteristically American*, 1949

"Ernie" (Ernest T.) Pyle (1900–1945), *Home Country*, 1947

41 · *The Cold War and the Moral Problem*

See the discussion in list 40.

Stringfellow Barr (1897–   ), *The Pilgrimage of Western Man,* 1949

Stringfellow Barr, *Let's Join the Human Race,* 1950

James Burnham (1905–   ), *The Managerial Revolution,* 1941

Norman Cousins (1912–   ), *Modern Man Is Obsolete,* 1945

T. S. Eliot (1888–   ), *The Idea of a Christian Society,* 1939

John Hersey (1914–   ), *The Wall,* 1950

Robinson Jeffers (1887–1962), *Roan Stallion, Tamar, and Other Poems,* 1925

Robinson Jeffers, *The Women at Point Sur,* 1927

Robinson Jeffers, *Selected Poetry,* 1938 (Jeffers anticipated an important later attitude toward culture and civilization.)

Joseph Wood Krutch (1893–   ), *The Measure of Man,* 1954

Joshua Loth Liebman (1907–1948), *Peace of Mind,* 1946

Henry C. Link (1889–   ), *The Rediscovery of Man,* 1938

Henry C. Link, *The Rediscovery of Morals,* 1947

Lewis Mumford (1895–   ), *Technics and Civilization,* 1934

Lewis Mumford, *The Culture of Cities,* 1938

Lewis Mumford, *Faith for Living,* 1940

Lewis Mumford, *The Condition of Man,* 1944

Reinhold Niebuhr (1892–   ), *Moral Man and Immoral Society,* 1932

Reinhold Niebuhr, *The Nature and Destiny of Man,* 2 vols., 1941–1943

F. S. C. Northrop (1893–   ), *The Meeting of East and West,* 1946

George Santayana (1863–1952), *The Last Puritan,* 1936

Fulton J. Sheen (1895–   ), *Peace of Soul,* 1949

Walter Terence Stace (1886–   ), *Religion and the Modern Mind,* 1952

Paul Tillich (1886–   ), *The Protestant Era,* 1948

Lionel Trilling (1905–   ), *The Liberal Imagination,* 1950

42 · *The Novel in the Period of the Cold War*

Nothing is more difficult than to follow "trends" in fiction during the last few years, and the following list is more an act of desperation than the result of complete knowledge. Readers may find in the annual accounts of American literature in the *Americana* or the *Britannica Yearbook* surveys of fiction more detailed than this. Many novels appearing in the last decade have, for one reason or another, been placed in other categories in this handbook. But it is at least possible that the present list may be suggestive of what is happening in the most elusive of literary forms. Some novels placed here appeared before Pearl Harbor but are put in this category because they seem to indicate interests characteristic of the last quarter century.

Some established novelists seemed to take a new turn in certain instances:

John Dos Passos (1896–   ), *District of Columbia*, 1939–1949 (Composed of *Adventures of a Young Man*, 1939, *Number One*, 1943, and *The Grand Design*, 1949.)

William Faulkner (1897–1962), *Intruder in the Dust*, 1948

William Faulkner, *Requiem for a Nun*, 1951

William Faulkner, *A Fable*, 1954

William Faulkner, *The Town*, 1957. (With *The Hamlet*, 1940, and *The Mansion*, 1959, it forms the Snopes trilogy.)

Ernest Hemingway (1898–1961), *The Old Man and the Sea*, 1952

The "hard-boiled" school continued to produce novels:

John Kerouac (1922–   ), *On the Road*, 1957
Norman Mailer (1923–   ), *The Deer Park*, 1955
Willard Motley (1912–   ), *Knock on Any Door*, 1947
John O'Hara (1905–   ), *Ten North Frederick*, 1955

One or another aspect of the "psychological" novel is exemplified in such titles as these:

James Baldwin (1924–   ), *Go Tell It on the Mountain*, 1953

198

Saul Bellow (1915–   ), *The Adventures of Augie March,* 1953
Saul Bellow, *Henderson the Rain King,* 1959
Paul Bowles (1911–   ), *The Sheltering Sky,* 1949
Truman Capote (1924–   ), *Other Voices, Other Rooms,* 1948
James Gould Cozzens (1903–   ), *By Love Possessed,* 1957
George Garrett (1929–   ), *Which Ones Are the Enemy?* 1961
Caroline Gordon (1895–   ), *The Strange Children,* 1951
William Goyen (1915–   ), *The House of Breath,* 1950
Shirley Jackson (1920–   ), *The Haunting of Hill House,* 1959
Randall Jarrell (1914–   ), *Pictures from an Institution,* 1954
William Maxwell (1908–   ), *They Came Like Swallows,* 1937
Mary McCarthy (1912–   ), *The Groves of Academe,* 1952
Carson McCullers (1917–   ), *The Heart Is a Lonely Hunter,*
1940
Wright Morris (1910–   ), *The Field of Vision,* 1956
Flannery O'Connor (1925–   ), *The Violent Bear It Away,*
1960
James Purdy (1923–   ), *Malcolm,* 1959
J. D. Salinger (1919–   ), *The Catcher in the Rye,* 1951
Jean Stafford (1915–   ), *The Mountain Lion,* 1947
William Styron (1925–   ), *Lie Down in Darkness,* 1951
John Updike (1932–   ), *Rabbit, Run,* 1960

Novelists of social comment have been listed elsewhere, and they number a goodly company. Other representative titles are:

Herbert Gold (1924–   ), *The Prospect Before Us,* 1954
Laura Z. Hobson (1896–   ), *Gentleman's Agreement,* 1947
Bernard Malamud (1914–   ), *The Assistant,* 1957
Arthur Miller (1915–   ), *Focus,* 1945
Philip Roth (1933–   ), *Letting Go,* 1962
Elizabeth Spencer (1921–   ), *The Voice at the Back Door,*
1956
Jean Stafford, (1915–   ), *Boston Adventure,* 1944
Harvey Swados (1920–   ), *Out Went the Candle,* 1951

43 · *Criticism: Latest Phase*

Literary criticism in America seems to be still under the influence of the "New Criticism," no later school having arisen to challenge its supremacy. Volumes in which American literature is made to relate more closely to American cultural history than the New Criticism allows for have, indeed, appeared; and some of these are listed below. It is also to be noted that the pursuit of myth and symbol has occupied a good many interpreters of poetry.

Conrad Aiken (1899–   ), *Collected Criticism from 1916 to the Present: A Reviewer's ABC*, 1958

John W. Aldridge (1922–   ), *After the Lost Generation*, 1951

Louise Bogan (1897–   ), *Selected Criticism*, 1955

Cleanth Brooks (1906–   ), *The Hidden God: Studies in Hemingway, Faulkner, Yeats, Eliot, and Warren*, 1963

James T. Farrell (1904–   ), *The League of Frightened Philistines*, 1945

James T. Farrell, *The Fate of Writing in America*, 1946

James T. Farrell, *Literature and Morality*, 1947

Charles Feidelson, Jr. (1918–   ), *Symbolism and American Literature*, 1953

Stanley Edgar Hyman (1919–   ), *The Armed Vision*, 1948

Randall Jarrell (1914–   ), *Poetry and the Age*, 1953

Alfred Kazin (1915–   ), *Contemporaries*, 1962

Harry Levin (1912–   ), *The Power of Darkness*, 1958

R. W. B. Lewis, (1917–   ), *The American Adam*, 1955

F. O. Matthiessen (1902–1950), *The Responsibility of the Critic*, 1952

Wright Morris (1910–   ), *The Territory Ahead*, 1958

Philip Rahv (1908–   ), *Image and Idea*, 1940 (A revised and enlarged edition was published in 1957.)

Karl Shapiro (1913–   ), *Essay on Rime*, 1945

Karl Shapiro, *In Defense of Ignorance*, 1960

Lionel Trilling (1905–   ), *The Opposing Self*, 1955

Edmund Wilson (1895–   ), *Axel's Castle*, 1931

Edmund Wilson, *The Triple Thinkers,* 1938
Edmund Wilson, *The Wound and the Bow,* 1941
Edmund Wilson, *The Boys in the Back Room,* 1941
Edmund Wilson, *Patriotic Gore,* 1962
W. K. Wimsatt, Jr. (1907–   ), *The Verbal Icon: Studies in the Meaning of Poetry,* 1954

44 · *Poetry: Latest Phases*

Generally speaking, the movement in poetry during the last two decades has been a movement away from the elliptic verse of T. S. Eliot and his contemporaries. Under the influence of Auden, Spender, and other British poets, verse has been restored to the duty of immediate communication in terms of living language; and though more difficult of apprehension than was true of the generation of Robert Frost, verse now tends to avoid the studied difficulties of Pound and his admirers. The later movements seem to endorse the practice of the Poetic Renaissance (see lists 23 and 24) in believing that public communication is part of the duty of literature. The following list is suggestive and concentrates on poets who began publishing before World War II.

W. H. Auden (1907–), *Collected Poetry*, 1945

W. H. Auden, *The Age of Anxiety*, 1947

W. H. Auden, *Homage to Clio*, 1960

John Berryman (1914–), *Homage to Mistress Bradstreet*, 1956

Richard Eberhart (1904–), *Collected Poems, 1930–1960*, 1960

Robert Fitzgerald (1910–), *In the Rose of Time: Poems 1931–1956*, 1956

Stanley Kunitz (1905–), *Selected Poems: 1928–1958*, 1959

Theodore Morrison (1901–), *The Dream of Alcestis*, 1950

Muriel Rukeyser (1913–), *Poems 1935–1961*, 1961

Delmore Schwartz (1913–), *Summer Knowledge: New and Selected Poems, 1938–1958*, 1959

Winfield Townley Scott (1910–), *Collected Poems*, 1962

A younger group of poets earned their reputations through volumes published during the late forties and fifties.

Elizabeth Bishop (1911–), *Poems: North and South, A Cold Spring*, 1962

John Malcolm Brinnin (1916–), *Selected Poems*, 1963

John Ciardi (1916–), *As If: Poems New and Selected*, 1955

1920–1963

Randall Jarrell (1914–   ), *Selected Poems*, 1955

Robert Lowell (1917–   ), *Poems, 1938–1949*, 1950

Robert Lowell, *Life Studies*, 1959

William Meredith (1919–   ), *The Open Sea*, 1958

Howard Moss (1921–   ), *A Winter Come, A Summer Gone: Poems 1946–1960*, 1960

Howard Nemerov (1920–   ), *New and Selected Poems*, 1960

Theodore Roethke (1908–1963), *Words for the Wind*, 1959

Karl Shapiro (1913–   ), *Poems, 1940–1953*, 1953

Peter Viereck (1916–   ), *Terror and Decorum: Poems, 1940–1948*, 1948

Richard Wilbur (1921–   ), *Things of This World*, 1956

Richard Wilbur, *Advice to a Prophet and Other Poems*, 1961

A still younger group of poets can be sampled in two paper-bound collections, both of which claim to be the "new" poetry of the last decade. No one poet is included in both volumes. The more academic group appears in *The New Poets of England and America*, ed. by Donald Hall, Robert Pack, and Louis Simpson (Meridian, 1957). The best experimental poets are collected in *The New American Poetry, 1945–1960*, ed. by Donald M. Allen (Grove, 1960). The following list, representative of both groups, could easily be expanded.

Robert Creeley (1926–   ), *For Love—Poems 1950–1960*, 1962

Alan Dugan (1923–   ), *Poems*, 1961

Robert Duncan (1919–   ), *Selected Poems*, 1959

Lawrence Ferlinghetti (1919–   ), *A Coney Island of the Mind*, 1958

Thom Gunn (1929–   ), *Selected Poems*, 1962

Donald Hall (1928–   ), *Exiles and Marriages*, 1955

Daniel Hoffman (1923–   ), *A Little Geste, and Other Poems*, 1960

John Hollander (1929–   ), *A Crackling of Thorns*, 1958

Galway Kinnell (1927–   ), *What a Kingdom It Was*, 1960

Denise Levertov (1923–), *With Eyes at the Back of Our Heads*, 1959

James Merrill (1926–), *Selected Poems*, 1961

W. S. Merwin (1927–), *The Dancing Bears*, 1954

Charles Olson (1910–), *The Distances*, 1960

Louis Simpson (1923–), *A Dream of Governors*, 1959

William Jay Smith (1918–), *Poems, 1947–1957*, 1957

W. D. Snodgrass (1926–), *Heart's Needle*, 1959

May Swenson (1927–), *To Mix with Time: New and Selected Poems*, 1963

III · SOME CONTINUING ELEMENTS

45 · *The Short Story in the Twentieth Century*

Basic changes in the concept of literary art, changes in the nature and costs of American magazines, and changes in the interests and caliber of the reading public affected the short story, sometimes thought to be a particularly American contribution to literary form. The "slick" story continued in the popular magazines, whether as a love story, a story of adventure or mystery, or a story of humor, but as the century advanced, the formula story tended to recede among serious writers in favor of the "unfinished" or slice-of-life story, often pessimistic, sometimes confined to a single inconclusive episode, and occasionally twisted in the direction of an enigmatic or ironical ending.

The arrangement of titles in this section is not alphabetical by authors, but is in a general sense chronological, the stories of O. Henry serving as a base line. Other volumes of short stories are of course to be found on other lists in this guide.

"O. Henry" (William Sydney Porter, 1862–1910), *The Four Million,* 1906

Ring Lardner (1885–1933), *Gullible's Travels,* 1917

Ring Lardner, *How to Write Short Stories (with Samples),* 1924

Ring Lardner, *The Love Nest and Other Stories,* 1926

Sherwood Anderson (1876–1941), *The Triumph of the Egg,* 1921

Wilbur Daniel Steele (1886–   ), *The Man Who Saw Through Heaven,* 1927

Ruth Suckow (1892–1960), *Iowa Interiors,* 1926

Katherine Anne Porter (1894–   ), *Flowering Judas,* 1930

Katherine Anne Porter, *Pale Horse, Pale Rider,* 1939

Katherine Anne Porter, *The Leaning Tower,* 1944

William Faulkner (1897–1962), *Doctor Martino and Other Stories,* 1934

William Faulkner, *Go Down, Moses, and Other Stories,* 1942

William Faulkner, *Knight's Gambit,* 1949

Erskine Caldwell (1903–   ), *Kneel to the Rising Sun,* 1935

Kay Boyle (1903–   ), *The White Horses of Vienna and Other Stories*, 1936

Ernest Hemingway (1898–1961), *The Fifth Column and the First Forty-Nine Stories*, 1938

William Saroyan (1908–   ), *My Name is Aram*, 1940

Eudora Welty (1909–   ), *The Wide Net*, 1943

Eudora Welty, *The Bride of the Innisfallen and Other Stories*, 1955

Caroline Gordon (1895–   ), *The Forest of the South*, 1945

Caroline Gordon, *Old Red and Other Stories*, 1963

John O'Hara (1905–   ), *Pipe Night*, 1945

John O'Hara, *The Hat on the Bed*, 1963

Peter Taylor (1917–   ), *The Long Fourth and Other Stories*, 1948

Truman Capote (1924–   ), *A Tree of Night*, 1949

Paul Goodman (1911–   ), *The Break-Up of Our Camp*, 1949

Shirley Jackson (1919–   ), *The Lottery; or, The Adventures of James Harris*, 1949

Wallace Stegner (1909–   ), *The Women on the Wall*, 1950

Carson McCullers (1917–   ), *The Ballad of the Sad Café*, 1951

Jean Stafford (1915–   ), *Children Are Bored on Sunday*, 1953

John Cheever (1912–   ), *The Enormous Radio and Other Stories*, 1953

J. D. Salinger (1919–   ), *Nine Stories*, 1953

Shirley Ann Grau (1929–   ), *The Black Prince and Other Stories*, 1955

Flannery O'Connor (1925–   ), *A Good Man is Hard to Find*, 1955

James Purdy (1923–   ), *The Color of Darkness*, 1957

George Garrett (1929–   ), *King of the Mountain*, 1958

Bernard Malamud (1914–   ), *The Magic Barrel*, 1958

Philip Roth (1933–   ), *Goodbye, Columbus*, 1959

William Goyen (1915–   ), *The Faces of Blood Kindred*, 1960

John Updike (1932–   ), *Pigeon Feathers*, 1962

46 · *Conventional Fiction in the Twentieth Century*

Not all writers of talent yielded to the mood of experimentation that characterized much fiction in the second quarter of the present century. Many were content to keep the usual conventions of the novel, borrowing from the experimenters a wider range of topics, a deeper richness of psychology, a distrust of classifying human beings into types, and a greater flexibility of style, while retaining some of the older concepts of novel-writing, that fiction has a primary duty of story-telling and another duty of pleasing the intelligent reader. Literary histories are commonly unkind to novels of this sort, which, in some other era, might have drawn to themselves a greater degree of critical attention. It is a mark of critical imperceptivity to assume, because a writer produces a "conventional" novel, that he is therefore an inferior writer. The following titles vary greatly in literary art, but the best of them are quite as excellent as the "advanced" or "experimental" fiction.

James Agee (1909–1955), *A Death in the Family,* 1957

Hervey Allen (1889–1949), *Anthony Adverse,* 1933

Louis Auchincloss (1917–   ), *The Great World and Timothy Colt,* 1956

Margaret Ayer Barnes (1886–   ), *Years of Grace,* 1930

Margaret Ayer Barnes, *Within This Present,* 1933

Gerald Warner Brace (1901–   ), *The Garretson Chronicle,* 1947

Louis Bromfield (1896–1956), *The Green Bay Tree,* 1924

Louis Bromfield, *The Strange Case of Miss Annie Spragg,* 1928

John Brooks (1920–   ), *A Pride of Lions,* 1954

Mary Ellen Chase (1887–   ), *Mary Peters,* 1934

John Cheever (1912–   ), *The Wapshot Chronicle,* 1957

Peter De Vries (1910–   ), *The Tunnel of Love,* 1954

Edna Ferber (1887–   ), *Show Boat,* 1926

Edna Ferber, *American Beauty,* 1931

Dorothy Canfield Fisher (1879–1959), *The Bent Twig,* 1915

Hiram Haydn (1907–   ), *The Time is Noon,* 1948

Charles Jackson (1903–   ), *The Lost Weekend,* 1944

Elizabeth Janeway (1913–   ), *The Walsh Girls,* 1943

Victoria Lincoln (1904–   ), *February Hill,* 1934
Helen MacInnes (1907–   ), *Above Suspicion,* 1941
Margaret Mitchell (1900–1949), *Gone with the Wind,* 1936
Christopher Morley (1890–1957), *Kitty Foyle,* 1939
Theodore Morrison (1901–   ), *The Stones of the House,* 1953
Edwin O'Connor (1918–   ), *The Last Hurrah,* 1956
William Saroyan (1908–   ), *The Human Comedy,* 1942
Betty Smith (1904–   ), *A Tree Grows in Brooklyn,* 1943
John Steinbeck (1902–   ), *Tortilla Flat,* 1935
John Steinbeck, *Of Mice and Men,* 1937
Robert Lewis Taylor (1912–   ), *The Travels of Jamie McPheeters,* 1958
Lionel Trilling (1905–   ), *The Middle of the Journey,* 1947
Sloan Wilson (1920–   ), *The Man in the Gray Flannel Suit,* 1955

47 · The Twentieth-Century Regional Novel

After 1920 the regional novel also benefited from experimentation in other fields, particularly in the writing of historical fiction and in a renewed interest in the psychology of uneducated persons. The tendency to lyricism in the style of regional fiction already evident in earlier examples (see list 3) did not vanish, but character became more credible in twentieth-century terms, the happy ending disappeared, and the enforced comparison between the supposed superiority of city ways and that of country folk tended to vanish. The Negro was treated with tenderness vaguely recalling some of the "Yes, Massa" fiction, and the same mixture of envy and condescension was sometimes felt; but, on the whole, regional fiction after 1920 is better art than was regional fiction in the 1890's.

Again it is difficult to distinguish regional fiction from other sorts (is J. P. Marquand, for example, a regional writer because he is chiefly concerned with New England?), but the following list is suggestive. Other novelists who might be classed as regional may be found in almost any other list containing fiction titles in this guide.

Carl Carmer (1893–), *Stars Fell on Alabama*, 1934

Carl Carmer, *Listen to a Lonesome Drum*, 1936

Homer Croy (1883–), *West of the Water Tower*, 1923

August Derleth (1909–), *Still is the Summer Night*, 1937
(The first of four novels concerning the Prairie du Sac region of Wisconsin.)

Rachel Field (1894–1942), *All This and Heaven, Too*, 1938

Berry Fleming (1899–), *Siesta*, 1935

Shelby Foote (1916–), *Shiloh*, 1952

Daniel Fuchs (1909–), *Summer in Williamsburg*, 1934

Paul Green (1894–), *This Body the Earth*, 1935

DuBose Heyward (1885–1940), *Porgy*, 1925

Oliver La Farge (1901–1963), *Laughing Boy*, 1929

Rose Wilder Lane (1887–), *Free Land*, 1938

Harper Lee (1926–), *To Kill a Mockingbird*, 1960

Andrew Lytle (1902–), *The Velvet Horn*, 1957

Wright Morris (1910–   ), *The Home Place*, 1948

Julia Peterkin (1880–1961), *Black April*, 1927

Julia Peterkin, *Scarlet Sister Mary*, 1928

James Purdy (1923–   ), *The Nephew*, 1960

Marjorie Kinnan Rawlings (1896–1954), *The Yearling*, 1938

Elizabeth Madox Roberts (1886–1941), *The Time of Man*, 1926

Elsie Singmaster (1879–1958), *Ellen Levis*, 1921

Elsie Singmaster, *The Magic Mirror*, 1934

Elizabeth Spencer (1921–   ), *Fire in the Morning*, 1948

Robert Penn Warren (1905–   ), *Night Rider*, 1939

Eudora Welty (1909–   ), *Delta Wedding*, 1946

Eudora Welty, *The Ponder Heart*, 1954

CONTINUING ELEMENTS

48 · *Autobiography in the Twentieth Century*

Although autobiographies were occasionally written in the nineteenth century, they do not constitute an important literary genre, the *Memoirs* of Ulysses S. Grant being one of the few that aspires to literary merit. In the twentieth century, however, perhaps because of a change in publishing conditions, perhaps because of an alteration of the reading public, but above all because of the devouring interest of the twentieth century in personality, the autobiography is an important mode of literary expression. Where formerly a public figure expected to have an official biography written by someone else, he now anticipates this by publishing his own account of himself. These books, which picture all kinds of human beings in all sorts of situations, are of varying literary merit. The following titles are suggestive of an endless field.

Conrad Aiken (1899–   ), *Ushant*, 1952

Margaret Anderson (? –   ), *My Thirty Years' War*, 1930

Margaret Anderson, *The Fiery Fountains*, 1951

Sherwood Anderson (1876–1941), *Memoirs*, 1942

Mary Austin (1868–1934), *Earth Horizon*, 1932

S. N. Behrman (1893–   ), *The Worcester Account*, 1954

Henry Seidel Canby (1878–1961), *American Memoir*, 1947 (Composed of *The Age of Confidence*, 1934; *Alma Mater*, 1936; and later material.)

Hodding Carter (1907–   ), *Where Main Street Meets the River*, 1953

David L. Cohn (1897–1961), *Where I Was Born and Raised*, 1948

Malcolm Cowley (1898–   ), *Exile's Return*, 1934; revised edition, 1951

Wilbur L. Cross (1862–1948), *Connecticut Yankee*, 1943

John Erskine (1879–1951), *The Memory of Certain Persons*, 1947

Edna Ferber (1887–   ), *A Peculiar Treasure*, 1939

Joseph Freeman (1897–   ), *An American Testament,* 1936
Hamlin Garland (1860–1940), *A Son of the Middle Border,* 1917
Hamlin Garland, *A Daughter of the Middle Border,* 1921
Hamlin Garland, *Trailmakers of the Middle Border,* 1926
Hamlin Garland, *Backtrailers of the Middle Border,* 1928
(There is a second series of four books, running from *Roadside Meetings,* 1930, to *Afternoon Neighbors,* 1934.)
Ellen Glasgow (1874–1945), *The Woman Within,* 1954
Robert Grant (1852–1940), *Fourscore,* 1934
Hutchins Hapgood (1869–1944), *A Victorian in the Modern World,* 1939
Moss Hart (1904–1961), *Act One,* 1959
Alfred Kazin (1915–   ), *A Walk in the City,* 1951
Charles A. Lindbergh (1902–   ), *The Spirit of St. Louis,* 1953
Mabel Dodge Luhan (1879–1962), *Intimate Memories,* 1933–1937 (Composed of *Background,* 1933; *European Experiences,* 1935; *Movers and Shakers,* 1936; and *Edge of Taos Desert,* 1937.)
H. L. Mencken (1880–1956), *The Days of Henry L. Mencken,* 1947 (Composed of *Happy Days,* 1940; *Newspaper Days,* 1941; *Heathen Days,* 1943.)
Albert Jay Nock (1872?–1945), *Memoirs of a Superfluous Man,* 1943
William Alexander Percy (1885–1942), *Lanterns on the Levee,* 1941
Bliss Perry (1860–1954), *And Gladly Teach,* 1935
William Lyon Phelps (1865–1943), *Autobiography and Letters,* 1939
Eleanor Roosevelt (1884–1962), *This Is My Story,* 1937
Carl Sandburg (1878–   ), *Always the Young Strangers,* 1952
George Santayana (1867–1952), *Persons and Places,* 1944–1953 (Composed of *The Background of My Life,* 1944; *The Middle Span,* 1945; and *My Host the World,* 1953.)
Vincent Sheean (1899–   ), *Personal History,* 1935

CONTINUING ELEMENTS

Lincoln Steffens (1866–1936), *Autobiography*, 1931

Gertrude Stein (1874–1946), *The Autobiography of Alice B. Toklas*, 1933

Carl Van Doren (1885–1950), *Three Worlds*, 1936

Edith Wharton (1862–1937), *A Backward Glance*, 1934

Hans Zinsser (1878–1940), *As I Remember Him*, 1940

AMERICAN LITERATURE

49 · *Biography in the Twentieth Century*

One of the oldest forms of writing in what was to become the
United States, American biography dates from 1658, when the
Rev. John Norton published in Cambridge a brief life of the Rev.
John Cotton. In the eighteenth and nineteenth centuries biogra-
phy wavered between two poles: the popular book teaching by
example, of which the most famous is probably Mason L.
Weems's life of Washington (1800), and stately public memorials of the
life-and-times or life-and-letters category. James Parton (1822-
1891) combined scholarship with literary skill in biographies of
Aaron Burr, Andrew Jackson, Benjamin Franklin, and Thomas
Jefferson that still have primary value. The creation of the
"American Men of Letters" series under Charles Dudley Warner
in 1881 and of the "American Statesmen" series under John T.
Morse, Jr., in 1882 marked a firm union of historical scholarship
and literary skill, but did nothing for the intimate lives of the
subjects. But in the 1920's, as part of the drive toward "liberation"
and under the influence of Lytton Strachey in England and
Gamaliel Bradford in America, informality and exposure became
the rule. A spate of "debunking" biographies appeared at the
same time that the influence of theories of irrational psychology
altered the conventional view of motives. In the last twenty or
thirty years biography has tended to return to more responsible
notions of scholarship; it has also developed the multi-volume
biography of great figures.

What is "good" biography from the point of view of historical
scholarship may not be a work of literary art; and, contrariwise,
a biography that ranks higher as literature because it persuasively
sets forth a character may require constant correction as fact.
The following list tries to select representative biographies appearing since 1890 that keep a good balance between art and
information. Since American biographers have ranged widely,
the list includes only lives of American subjects by American
writers. This does injustice to American biographies of subjects
from other lands and earlier times.

Since only important figures attract biographies, and since
these figures are likely to be complex personalities, biographers
will vary in their approaches to the truth of a life. Some of these

214

titles have been "superseded," or so later writers feel; some have aroused controversy; and some are as characteristic of the biographer as they are of the subjects chosen. Should anyone have the time and patience to read all the list, however, he would gain considerable insight into biographical methodology and its changes since the 1890's. The titles are arranged chronologically.

Moncure D. Conway (1832–1907), *The Life of Thomas Paine,* 1892

Henry James (1843–1916), *William Wetmore Story and His Friends,* 2 vols., 1903

George Edward Woodberry (1855–1930), *Ralph Waldo Emerson,* 1907

William Dean Howells (1837–1920), *My Mark Twain,* 1910

Albert Bigelow Paine (1861–1937), *Mark Twain: A Biography,* 3 vols., 1912

Herbert Croly (1869–1930), *Marcus Alonzo Hanna: His Life and Work,* 1912

Harvey Cushing (1869–1939), *The Life of Sir William Osler,* 2 vols., 1925

Kenneth B. Murdock (1895–   ), *Increase Mather: The Foremost American Puritan,* 1925

Hervey Allen (1889–1949), *Israfel: The Life and Times of Edgar Allan Poe,* 1926

Carl Sandburg (1878–   ), *Abraham Lincoln: The Prairie Years,* 2 vols., 1926 (Followed in 1939 by *Abraham Lincoln: The War Years,* 4 vols.)

Rupert Hughes (1872–1956), *George Washington,* 3 vols., 1926–1930 (Never completed.)

Paxton Hibben (1880–1928), *Henry Ward Beecher: An American Portrait,* 1927

Robert H. Fuller (1865–1927), *Jubilee Jim: The Life of Colonel James Fisk,* 1928

Allan Nevins (1890–   ), *Frémont: The West's Greatest Adventurer,* 2 vols., 1928

Emanie Louise (Nahm) Sachs (? –   ), *"The Terrible Siren," Victoria Woodhull, 1838–1927,* 1928

Edwin F. Dakin (1898–   ), *Mrs. Eddy: The Biography of a Virginal Mind,* 1929

Marquis James (1891–1955), *The Raven: A Biography of Sam Houston,* 1929

Lloyd Paul Stryker (1885–   ), *Andrew Johnson: A Study in Courage,* 1929

Claude M. Fuess (1885–   ), *Daniel Webster,* 2 vols., 1930

John K. Winkler (1891–   ), *Morgan The Magnificent: The Life of J. Pierpont Morgan (1837–1913),* 1930

Burton J. Hendrick (1870–1949), *The Life of Andrew Carnegie,* 2 vols., 1932

Gilbert Chinard (1881–   ), *Honest John Adams,* 1933

Parker Morell (1906–1943), *Diamond Jim: The Life and Times of James Buchanan Brady,* 1934

Douglas Southall Freeman (1866–1953), *R. E. Lee: A Biography,* 4 vols., 1935

Mari Sandoz (1907–   ), *Old Jules,* 1935

Odell Shepard (1884–   ), *Pedlar's Progress: The Life of Bronson Alcott,* 1937

Carl Van Doren (1885–1950), *Benjamin Franklin,* 1938

Henry Seidel Canby (1878–1961), *Thoreau,* 1939

Allan Nevins, *John D. Rockefeller: The Heroic Age of American Enterprise,* 2 vols., 1940

Mason Wade (1913–   ), *Margaret Fuller: Whetstone of Genius,* 1940

Wheaton J. Lane (1902–   ), *Commodore Vanderbilt: An Epic of the Steam Age,* 1942

Muriel Rukeyser (1913–   ), *Willard Gibbs,* 1942

DeLancey Ferguson (1888–   ), *Mark Twain: Man and Legend,* 1943

Gene Fowler (1890–   ), *Goodnight, Sweet Prince: The Life and Times of John Barrymore,* 1944

Russel B. Nye (1913–   ), *George Bancroft: Brahmin Rebel,* 1944

Fawn (McKay) Brodie (1915–   ), *No Man Knows My History: The Life of Joseph Smith, The Mormon Prophet,* 1945

Stanley Vestal (1887–   ), *Jim Bridger: Mountain Man,* 1946

Alpheus T. Mason (1899–   ), *Brandeis: A Free Man's Life,* 1946

Morris Bishop (1893–   ), *Champlain: The Life of Fortitude,* 1948

Dumas Malone (1892–   ), *Jefferson and His Times* (in progress, 3 vols. published), 1948–

Ernest Samuels (1903–   ), *The Young Henry Adams,* 1948 (Followed in 1958 by *Henry Adams: The Middle Years.*)

Thomas Coulson (1886–   ), *Joseph Henry: His Life and Work,* 1950

Arthur Mizener (1907–   ), *The Far Side of Paradise: A Biography of F. Scott Fitzgerald,* 1951

David J. Mays (1896–   ), *Edmund Pendleton, 1721–1803,* 2 vols., 1952

Leon Edel (1907–   ), *Henry James* (in progress, 3 vols. published), 1953–

Wallace Stegner (1909–   ), *Beyond the Hundredth Meridian: John Wesley Powell and the Second Opening of the West,* 1954

Talbot Hamlin (1889–   ), *Benjamin Henry Latrobe,* 1955

Mark DeWolfe Howe (1906–   ), *Justice Oliver Wendell Holmes* (in progress; 2 vols. published), 1957–

Mark Schorer (1908–   ), *Sinclair Lewis: An American Life,* 1961

Newton Arvin (1900–1963), *Longfellow: His Life and Work,* 1963

Arnold Schwab (1922–   ), *James Gibbons Huneker: Critic of the Seven Arts,* 1963

50 · *Humor in the Twentieth Century*

Somewhat apart from the shocks of world conflict and intellectual battles over the nature of art, morals, and society, certain traditional forms of American writing went forward, absorbing only so much of the novel and the controversial as readers could take. Humor is not a literary genre but a mode of interpretation; nevertheless, in American literature the humorist is a sufficiently well-known type, skilled in light verse, in brief essay or comic story, or in whimsical or sardonic commentary upon human folly. After World War I, folk humor became the possession of the folklorist; and under the aegis of the immensely successful *New Yorker,* the twentieth-century American humorist has become increasingly urbane and "sophisticated." Undoubtedly the twenties set a fashion, yet the fashion for urbane humor is old (see list 8); and the humorist in recent decades has quietly yet sturdily asserted an intellectual independence of cult and fashion.

F. P. Adams (1881–1960), *The Conning Tower Book,* 1926

Fred Allen (1894–1956), *Treadmill to Oblivion,* 1954

Robert C. Benchley (1889–1945), *20,000 Leagues Under the Sea; or, David Copperfield,* 1928

Robert C. Benchley, *The Treasurer's Report,* 1930

Robert C. Benchley, *Inside Benchley,* 1942

A Benchley Round-up, edited by Nathaniel Benchley, 1962

Morris Bishop (1893–   ), *A Bowl of Bishop,* 1954

"Art" (Arthur) Buchwald (1925–   ), *How Much Is That in Dollars?* 1961

Clarence Day (1874–1935), *This Simian World,* 1920

Clarence Day, *Life with Father,* 1935

Clarence Day, *The Best of Clarence Day,* 1948

Peter De Vries (1910–   ), *The Mackerel Plaza,* 1958

Marion Hargrove (1919–   ), *See Here, Private Hargrove,* 1942

Samuel Hoffenstein (1890–1947), *Poems in Praise of Practically Nothing,* 1928

CONTINUING ELEMENTS

Jean Kerr (1923–   ), *Please Don't Eat the Daisies,* 1957

Ring Lardner (1885–1933), *The Ring Lardner Reader,* edited by Maxwell Geismar, 1963

Don Marquis (1878–1937), *Hermione and Her Little Group of Serious Thinkers,* 1916

Don Marquis, *archy and mehitabel,* 1927

Don Marquis, *The Best of Don Marquis,* 1946

David McCord (1897–   ), *Stirabout,* 1928

David McCord, *And What's More,* 1941

Phyllis McGinley (1905–   ), *Times Three: Selected Verse from Three Decades,* 1960

Ruth McKenney (1911–   ), *My Sister Eileen,* 1938

Ogden Nash (1902–   ), *Free Wheeling,* 1931

Ogden Nash, *The Bad Parent's Garden of Verse,* 1936

Ogden Nash, *Verses from 1929 On,* 1959

Dorothy Parker (See list 32.)

S. J. Perelman (1904–   ), *Perelman's Home Companion,* 1955

S. J. Perelman, *The Road to Miltown: or, Under the Spreading Atrophy,* 1957

Will Rogers (1879–1935), *The Autobiography of Will Rogers,* 1949 (Essentially a chronology of Rogers' utterances.)

"Leonard Q. Ross" (Leo C. Rosten, 1908–   ), *The Education of Hyman Kaplan,* 1937

Damon Runyon (1884–1946), *Guys and Dolls,* 1932

Damon Runyon, *The Best of Runyon,* 1938

Cornelia Otis Skinner (1901–   ), and Emily Kimbrough (1899–   ), *Our Hearts Were Young and Gay,* 1942

H. Allen Smith (1907–   ), *Low Man on a Totem Pole,* 1941

Frank Sullivan (1892–   ), *A Pearl in Every Oyster,* 1938

Frank Sullivan, *A Rock in Every Snowball,* 1946

James Thurber (1894–1961), with E. B. White (1899–   ), *Is Sex Necessary?* 1929

James Thurber, *My Life and Hard Times,* 1933

AMERICAN LITERATURE

James Thurber, *Let Your Mind Alone!* 1937
James Thurber, *The Thurber Carnival,* 1945
Ira Wallach (1913–   ), *Hopalong Freud,* 1951
E. B. White, *One Man's Meat,* 1942
E. B. White, *The Second Tree from the Corner,* 1953

CONTINUING ELEMENTS
51 · *Fantasy, Murder, Science, Escape*

In the literary histories the detective story and science fiction seem to begin and end with Edgar Allan Poe. Beginning in the late nineteenth century and increasingly in the twentieth century, however, science fiction and mystery stories have drawn larger and larger audiences. The "whodunits" furnish much of the material for paperbound books; and science fiction, whether "straight" science or fantasy, not only appears in the paperback library but is also the stock in trade of a number of magazines. In both categories there is much trash, an enormous amount of hack writing, and the overworking of stereotypes of plot, character, and motif. In the highly moral world of the detective story virtue always wins, if sometimes by outrageously mechanical means; nor is the world of science fiction less moral, inasmuch as, if distant planets or the distant future are now and then populous with supermen capable of crushing out the odious little race of men, evil nevertheless vanishes either by some trick of fantastic discovery or by virtue of the superior strength of goodness. Both branches of fiction are considered to be beneath the dignity of literary history— it is not clear why; yet both branches have their passionate *aficionados;* and the rules of the game are as scrupulously maintained between writer and public as are the rules of baseball.

A good background for understanding the cult of the detective story is Howard Haycraft, *Murder for Pleasure: The Life and Times of the Detective Story,* 1941. A good background for understanding science fiction is J. O. Bailey, *Pilgrims Through Space and Time,* 1947. A good background for understanding the use of supernatural elements in the fantasy story is Peter Penzoldt, *The Supernatural in Fiction,* 1952. However, the supernatural in Mr. Penzoldt's sense of the word is mostly absent from science fiction proper, though it may appear in science fantasy.

The following lists are (i) a list of detective stories of literary merit by American authors arranged in the order of publication to illustrate development; (ii) a list of science fiction *not* in chronological order but chosen because of its superior intellectual appeal.

THE DETECTIVE STORY

Anna Katharine Green (1846–1935), *The Leavenworth Case,*

AMERICAN LITERATURE

1878 (Listed here, despite its date, because it marks the resumption of the writing of detective fiction after Poe and because it stands at the headwaters of the contemporary American detective story.)

Jacques Futrelle (1875–1912), *The Thinking Machine*, 1907 (Reissued in 1918 as *The Problem of Cell 13*.)

Mary Roberts Rinehart (1876–1958), *The Circular Staircase*, 1908

Mary Roberts Rinehart, *The Man in Lower Ten*, 1909 (Written earlier and serialized, but not published in book form until the date given.)

Melville Davisson Post (1871–1930), *Uncle Abner: Master of Mysteries*, 1918

Earl Derr Biggers (1884–1933), *The House Without a Key*, 1925

"S. S. Van Dine" (Willard Huntington Wright, 1888–1939), *The Benson Murder Case*, 1926

Frances Noyes Hart (1890–1943), *The Bellamy Trial*, 1927

"Ellery Queen" (Frederic Dannay, 1905–   , and Manfred B. Lee, 1905–   ), *The Roman Hat Mystery*, 1929

Dashiell Hammett (1894–1961), *The Maltese Falcon*, 1930

John Dickson Carr (1906–   ), *Hag's Nook*, 1933

John Dickson Carr, *To Wake the Dead*, 1938

Erle Stanley Gardner(1889–   ), *The Case of the Sulky Girl*, 1933

Richard (1898–   ) and Frances (1896–1963) Lockridge, *Mr. and Mrs. North*, 1936

Richard and Frances Lockridge, *The Faceless Adversary*, 1956

Rex Stout (1886–   ), *Some Buried Caesar*, 1939

Rex Stout, *The Black Mountain*, 1954

Raymond Chandler (1888–1959), *Farewell, My Lovely*, 1940

Raymond Chandler, *The Long Goodbye*, 1954

Elizabeth Daly (1878–   ), *Evidence of Things Seen*, 1943

Mabel Seeley (1903–   ), *The Whistling Shadow*, 1954

Mignon Eberhart (1899–   ), *Jury of One*, 1960

"Ross MacDonald" (Kenneth Millar, 1915–   ), *The Ferguson Affair*, 1960

CONTINUING ELEMENTS

SCIENCE FICTION

Groff Conklin (1904–   ), ed., *The Best of Science Fiction,* 1946 (short stories)

Groff Conklin, ed., *The Treasury of Science Fiction,* 1948

Groff Conklin, ed., *The Big Book of Science Fiction,* 1950

H. L. Gold, ed., *Galaxy Reader of Science Fiction,* 1952

Damon Knight, ed., *A Century of Science Fiction,* 1962

Donald A. Wollheim, ed., *Flight into Space: Great Science Fiction Stories of Interplanetary Travel,* 1950

Isaac Asimov (1920–   ), *I, Robot,* 1950

Issac Asimov, *The Caves of Steel,* 1953

Edwin Balmer (1883–1959) and Philip Wylie (1902–   ), *When Worlds Collide,* 1932

Edwin Balmer and Philip Wylie, *After Worlds Collide,* 1934

Herbert Best (1894–   ), *The Twenty-Fifth Hour,* 1940

Alfred Bester (? –   ), *The Demolished Man,* 1953

Ray Bradbury (1920–   ), *The Martian Chronicles,* 1950

Ray Bradbury, *The Golden Apples of the Sun,* 1953

Algirdas Budrys (1931–   ), *Rogue Moon,* 1960

"Hal Clement" (Harry C. Stubbs, ? –   ), *Mission of Gravity,* 1954

Robert A. Heinlein (1907–   ), *Rocket Ship Galileo,* 1947

H. P. Lovecraft (1890–1937), *The Shadow Out of Time,* 1939

F. Wright Moxley (1889–   ), *Red Snow,* 1930

Frederik Pohl (1919?–   ), and Cyril Kornbluth (1923–1958), *The Space Merchants,* 1953

"Akkad Pseudoman" (Edwin Fitch Northrup, 1866–1940), *Zero to Eighty,* 1937

Clifford D. Simak (1904–   ), *The City,* 1952

Edward Elmer Smith (1890–   ), *The Skylark of Space,* 1946

A. E. van Vogt (1912–   ), *Slan,* 1946; reissued, 1951

Kurt Vonnegut, Jr. (1922–   ), *The Sirens of Titan,* 1961

Stanley Waterloo (1846–1913), *The Story of Ab,* 1897

Index of Authors

INDEX

INDEX

INDEX

INDEX

INDEX

INDEX

INDEX